**STEPHEN**

'Britain's renowned medium
has helped thousands of people
to contact their loved ones
through his nationwide tours'

*HELLO! magazine*

'Big powers in other-worldly communication
and healing'

*Irish News*

'Britain's brightest young medium.
Power seems to radiate from his fingertips.
These eyes can see beyond the grave'

*Daily Star*

'It's hard to be sceptical of the psychic world
when a stranger tells you precisely what you
were doing that morning, and even days before.
I was startled, almost shocked'

*Liverpool Echo*

'There is no doubting his sincerity
or his honesty'

*Girl About Town, London*

*'Without Love,*
  *we are nothing…'*


                *Stephen O'Brien*

**'VOICES FROM HEAVEN'**
**A VOICES BOOK**
ISBN: 0-9536620-4-7

PRINTING HISTORY:
Aquarian Press edition published 1991
HarperCollins edition reprinted in 1992
HarperCollins edition reprinted 1992 to 1997 (four times)
Voices Books New Revised Edition 2001

Typeset by *Voices*.

Reproduced, printed and bound
in Great Britain by Omnia Books Ltd.,
Glasgow, Scotland.

# Voices from Heaven
## Communion with Another World

**Visionary and Poet**
## Stephen O'Brien

*happy Birthday Nan - Love Tina xxx*

*Happy Birthday lots of love Lillie x*

### Voices
PO Box 8, Swansea, United Kingdom, SA1 1BL.

*For your Questing Spirit,*
*ever in Search of Itself…*

# Contents

## Part One
*A Servant of the Spirit*

## Part Two
*Journeys Into the Spirit World*

# Part One
## A Servant of the Spirit

*Death is an Illusion.*
*When a traveller passes hence,*
*we grieve and mourn our loss;*
*but those in the Realms of Light shout for joy,*
*for they have welcomed Home*
*a lost and wandering soul.*

Stephen O'Brien

# 1

# Voices in the Night

It was a dark and stormy winter's night. Black clouds covered the moon and trees lashed wildly in the gale, making ghostly shadows fly across the street. Lightning lit up the sky as we in the pathetic bus queue huddled together trying to dodge the rain that whistled through the holes in the shelter windows. How we cursed the vandals on that dark night.

I pulled up my collar, and icy water ran down my back just as I spied a drunken man standing at the corner of the road. Swaying on the edge of the pavement, he was teetering to and fro – quite unaware of the grave danger he was in: that corner had caused many horrific pedestrian deaths; drivers just couldn't see around the blind bend.

I gasped as a flash of headlights shot over the hill – the old man was going to walk out right in front of a speeding car. But just then, something strange happened. I stood transfixed, as a ghostly gleaming-white mist appeared behind him and quickly condensed into the radiant form of a middle-aged spirit woman. Her hair was strangely unruffled by the gale – not a drop of rain had wet it – and her flowing white spirit robes were bone-dry.

The car came hurtling down towards the old man when all at once the spirit stooped down, drew back her arm, and delivered a swift blow to the back of his knees. My heart jumped into my throat as he fell backwards like a collapsing house of cards and landed on the pavement with his legs in the gutter.

One second later, the reckless car swerved round the corner at over fifty miles per hour and missed his feet by half an inch – then it zoomed past the bus queue, splashing us with muddy water.

Brushing the rain from my eyelashes, I watched as the ghostly woman knelt down and kissed the old man's troubled brow; she smiled then vanished into the dark night, faded back into the spirit world from whence she came.

People rushed to help the old man but I knew they weren't aware of what had taken place 'behind the scenes'. I knew they hadn't seen his spirit-wife save him from a gruesome end, for they were not mediums, but I am.

I've had these psychic abilities from my earliest years; I was born with them, and visions of other worlds beyond death often came to me in the strangest ways, at the oddest moments, and usually without warning.

Yet each psychic experience taught me something useful about life and its meaning; and some of them impressed my mind so powerfully that they still haunt me today.

As a young child of even a few months old, I vividly recall being visited by people who were surrounded by a strange and glimmering light; and sometimes they startled me by reaching out their arms to tickle my stomach or chin. My visitors also spoke, of course, though I didn't understand them then. But there was never any need to worry because my spirit people were quite smiling and friendly folk, and they never did me any harm.

As an infant, I'd often wake at dawn in the hazy half-light and hear the angelic voices of a children's choir singing that wonderful old hymn:

> *All things bright and beautiful,*
> *All creatures great and small;*
> *All things wise and wonderful,*
> *The Lord God made them all...*

Their voices were marvellous, so real and crystal clear that I often joined in with the happy singing, thinking to myself, 'Oh, I must be late for school and they're singing in Assembly.' Then all at once I'd realise that I was still in bed – and my voices in the night immediately ceased, because my earthly thoughts had drawn me back to this dull grey world again. I'd jump up and quickly go to the window, but there was no one there, of course; and the school gates near our house were firmly locked.

Sometimes the voices were objective and clear, as if originating right outside myself, but more often they were 'voiceless' tones that came from within; yet they still surprised me with their clarity because they often came when least expected. One such voice gave me a clear 'warning' one night as I came walking home much too late: I was ambling along when quite suddenly it ordered me to, 'Cross the road and go home a different way!' I obeyed quickly; and glancing back as I turned the corner, I saw a group of trouble-making youths fighting one another as they ran along my previous path. It was a welcome escape, for which I remain grateful.

The spirit people were obviously watching over me, even at school.

I remember when I took an important Biology examination: sitting at the big desk among the other nervous candidates, fiddling with my pen and biting my lip, I dreaded the prospect of unanswerable questions. My face flushed red because I knew I hadn't studied adequately. But then – quite out of the blue – a clear voice said, 'Don't worry, you'll pass this test.' It was such a real sound that I turned round quickly to see where it had come from.

'Face the front, O'Brien! No cheating!' cried the headmaster.

When we came to start, my hand hovered above the paper, half-afraid to touch it, but when I flipped it over I was delighted: I knew all the answers to the set questions. And, of course, my inspirer was right: I passed the test with flying colours.

But perhaps the most mysterious voice I heard as a young child was the one that came at frequent intervals in a strange recurring dream. I began to worry, so I spoke to my compassionate mother about it.

'Sometimes I get frightened,' I said.

She looked into my eyes and smiled. 'Don't be silly,

Stephen, dreams won't harm you. Now, tell me what happens.'

I took a deep breath. 'It all starts with a pillar of golden light, set against a background of deep space and twinkling stars. There's no end to this golden column, which stretches from the Earth right up to Heaven, and there are hundreds of sad-looking people walking endlessly around it, in a mindless procession leading nowhere. Then...'

'Yes?' My mother leaned forward.

'Then a deep voice says to me, "This is the Circle of Life." And suddenly the people discover a gap in the pillar, and inside there's a broad golden stairway, ascending.

'They start to climb it quickly, and the voice says, "They are moving onwards and upwards, into the Light." '

There was a stunned pause as my mother's deep green eyes glanced from side to side; then she engaged them with mine, looking quite concerned.

'Stephen,' she said, 'for the moment, try to put it out of your mind, and it'll soon fade away.'

No doubt she was startled by my dream's deep symbolism, especially as I was so young.

Looking back now, I think the vision signified the monotonous round of daily life from which we suffer here on Earth (possibly through many incarnations, many circles around the pillar) until we realise there's an eternal ladder of progression in front of us. Once this realisation is made we can break the cycle and move onwards into Eternity.

Sometimes my strange dream came to me as a vision in my waking hours, and I believe this led my mother to realise that I was slightly 'different' from other children.

The power of spiritual healing first manifested in me when I was still in short trousers. Rather embarrassingly, I grew an unsightly wart on my right knee, and no one could remove it – not even the doctor. My mother, poor soul, was on the verge of rubbing raw bacon on it and then burying the bacon in the garden; and our superstitious old neighbour, Florrie, twinkled with glee: 'I'll get the gypsies to curse it off next time they come round selling pegs!'

In the end I shouted, 'I'll do it *myself*!' Gripping the tough skin tightly between my fingers and thumb, I issued a command. 'I order you to vanish!' I said. But when I opened my eyes and looked down, it was still there. Nevertheless, I kept my mind firmly fixed on its removal.

The next day, I was running through the park when out of the blue something made me glance down at my bare knees, just in time to see the ugly wart popping off my leg and onto some nearby gravel. I was utterly astonished. There wasn't even a scar left on my skin.

I think I've always had an aura of healing around me, for even when I was a child, many youngsters, some older than I, came to me for advice. 'You're calm,' they'd say, 'and we feel much better after talking to you.' Of course, I realise now that Older Minds on the Other Side had inspired me to give them the answers they needed.

But probably the most tangible evidence of the spirit people's presence around me came in a photograph that my mother took when I was eleven.

I was sitting on the back garden wall.

'Smile, Stephen.' *Click!* – and it was all over, until my twenty-second year when a medium in a Spiritualist Church gave me a message. The old woman pointed a bony finger directly at me and declared, 'Get the photo-album out, young man. There's a picture of you as a lad, sitting on a garden wall. What's more, there's a spirit visitor peering right over your left shoulder.'

I couldn't wait for the meeting to end. I dashed home, flew up the stairs, pulled out the album, and there – exactly as described – was the cheeky spirit face: a young man smiling for all he was worth. I was more than impressed.

I've never doubted the spirit people's closeness to my young life. As I recorded in *Visions of Another World*: when I was ten years old, phantom spirit-hands hammered on our front door at two o'clock in the morning. The echoing thuds sounded hollow and eerie but no one else in the family heard them or was woken by them, only me. It was a powerful message which, in later years, the spirit people described as a symbol of their link with me:

'Behold: we stood at the door and knocked. We were waiting for you, Stephen,' they said.

The invisible world was anxious that I should discover my latent psychic abilities and try to understand the strange thoughts that came to me, thoughts that were often beyond my years.

As a youngster I remember looking down the terrace where we lived, and thinking, 'All these houses are made of cardboard, and the people inside them are nothing but shadows.'

And I often used to say, 'I don't belong on Earth,' for that's exactly how I felt. Like a goldfish forever circling in a small round bowl, I frequently stared out at a distorted world and saw shapes that confounded me. It's taken me a long time to come to terms with living in a physical body 'locked' inside a material world.

Now, of course, I realise that the Earth is just a training-ground where souls may grow, a place into which souls incarnate to expand their minds and learn from their experiences. Even in my childhood some deeper part of me must have been aware of this, and that's why I sometimes felt so terribly alone. Now, with maturity on my side, I fully understand that I really don't belong on this planet: none of us do. My true home is in the spirit world, in the world of light from whence I came.

As a child, the dull adult world around me often failed to attract my attention, to get inside my dreamy head, or to understand why some of my utterances immediately silenced it.

Whenever grown-ups fretted and moaned over what seemed to me to be unimportant things, I'd often say, 'Why are you worrying? Worrying won't solve the problem, and it'll make you ill.' People glowered at me and stood open-mouthed, uncertain whether to scream or to take a well-aimed swing at my head. But more often than not they'd admonish me with, 'What do *you* know about it? Be quiet! You're only a kid.'

And of course, apart from my visions and voices, they were quite right: I was just another ordinary boy – but one who often felt ill-at-ease in a world he sometimes thought was filled with insensitive, cruel, and unkind people.

Looking back now, in many ways I was rather a lonely little boy, always standing apart from the crowd, always standing just a little outside of life. I loved my own company and would walk on the hills or by the rolling seas in absolute silence. I'd be astonished by the beauty of a flower, or I'd sit by a bubbling stream and think of the Mind that moves through all Creation.

It's not that I wasn't interested in other children, because I was; but sometimes I felt strangely mis-fitted among them; and such feelings led me to contemplate some of the Great Imponderables: Where have I come from? Why am I here? And where am I going?


## A Voice from the Void


A Voice From The Void
Am I,
A gathering mind
Forlorn.

A wandering soul
Am I,
From yestermorn.

Everywhere
Am I,
Yet nowhere
At all.

A timeless sentient cloud
Am I,
Omnipresent thought
As yet unborn.

A drifting spirit
Am I,
With no fixed home.

I'm
A wishing-star
In someone's mind,
A liquid dream
Of womankind...

...A blast of fusing light
I see,
Beckoning me...

...A folding darkness
Covers me,
And memory is gone...

A babe in the womb
Am I,
Plasmic blood and bone.

A cry in the night,
Am I...
A wrenching form,
And I am Born...

Somewhere now,
Am I...
Yet nowhere
At all...

But who would have thought in those far off days that 'little Stephen' would be known to millions through television appearances, radio and press features; or that he would take huge public meetings all over Britain, offering comfort, hope, knowledge, and evidence of a life after death to so many people? Who could have guessed that in my adult years I'd stand beside and mix with famous celebrities, 'household names', and eventually become a reluctant 'celebrity' myself?

If some old gypsy had gazed into her crystal ball and forecast all of these things then, no one else would have believed her. But I might have, for as maturity came I began to feel a deep call from within my own spirit – a call to serve. And before I was twenty-one I was already publicly representing the spirit world, fulfilling the prediction they'd made to me years earlier when they'd said, 'We're calling you to represent us to millions. Unto you is granted the Power of the Word.'

In child-like innocence I believed my inspirer without question; and, indeed, his prophecy has to come to pass.

When my first book, *Visions of Another World*, was published I was taken completely by surprise by the whirlwind of publicity it generated. They say ignorance is bliss, and in this case they're right. I thought all you had to do was write a book and wait for it to appear in the stores. I couldn't have been more wrong.

Publication day passes quietly for most writers, who can sit at home with their feet up, but not when an author tour's been arranged; and I soon found this out on a never-ending catch-a-bite-to-eat-if-you-can-manage-it whistle-stop tour of twenty major British cities. I was shooting all over the country like a jet that never stopped.

Rising at dawn, bleary-eyed and only half-awake, I'd shout up at the singing birds, 'It's all right for you, boys! You can go back to bed and get some shut-eye!' – but I'd be off on a continuous round of television, press, and radio interviews.

For such a quiet man as myself, life soon became a living nightmare. I was dashing in and out of taxis, newspaper offices, and television and radio stations like a thing demented. Half the time, I was so tired it's a living wonder that I found the right buildings.

Yet everywhere I went the reception was the same: switchboards jammed with callers. The only light relief came when I shared amusing snatches of conversation with celebrities and filmstars as they whizzed past me in strange corridors.

It's hardly surprising I felt exhausted after my public meetings because I gave my audiences every ounce of dedication and energy I possessed; and quite rightly so.

Thousands of people travelled hundreds of miles to reach some of the most prestigious venues in Britain simply to listen to the message of the spirit world, and they deserved the best I could give.

But I never dreamed just how *profoundly* my life-story would affect people: not just the media (who gobbled it up voraciously) but ordinary folk like you and me, who seemed deeply touched by it. Readers were moved by my mother's tragic passing from cancer at forty-nine, by her deep love for me, and by the remarkable way in which she broke the silence of death and returned from beyond the veil. They cried at the touching meeting between me and my spirit guide, a magnificent North American Indian who gave his tribal name as White Owl. They were enthralled by his deep spiritual love for me, and by his calling of my soul to serve all those who stand in need.

Reading my story, the public were all at once stirred and fascinated by my life, and they wrote to me in droves. I did feel sorry for the poor postman who had to climb three flights of steep concrete steps every day to deliver the mail. And I lost count of the times when my vision blurred behind a film of tears as I read those emotional letters. Out of all the people in the world, I was the only one who could help them, the public said.

What a frightening responsibility.

From deep inside their tragedies, people reached out and cried, 'Please, please help me to contact my loved ones again: help me to find my husband, my wife, my parents, my child. Although I know you're such a busy man, please don't desert me in my hour of need...' Or, 'My baby has is dead. My life is over, finished. I want to kill myself to be with him. But where is he now? Is he still alive? Who's taking care of him? Tell me, Stephen, will we ever be together again?'

I assured all my correspondents that one day there would be a glorious reunion in another world, and that there'd be plenty of opportunities to settle any misunderstandings or relieve any deep-seated guilt or regrets – for that is the Universal Law.

One young mother wrote to say that her six-year-old son had undergone major surgery because 'he'd been born with his heart back-to-front, and on the wrong side of his body. The surgeons operated, but his heart swelled to twice its normal size, so they had to leave his chest open for twenty-four hours. Then they sealed his little body, and we prayed so hard for his recovery. Thank God, he did become fit and well again. But afterwards he caught a series of infections, and my darling little boy died. Is there any news of him? Is there any message?'

I tried to alleviate this mother's tragic grief as best I could.

Strangely enough, she later stepped forward at one of my meetings in England, gave me a sincere embrace, and kissed me. She then said through the microphones to the seven hundred people present, 'You'll never know what you've done for me, Stephen O'Brien. Your letter contained evidence that no one else on Earth knew. You brought my boy back to me, and gave me so much comfort.' She hugged me again. 'May God bless you,' she said.

I thanked her, and immediately sent my gratitude to the spirit people.

Other writers also deeply touched my spirit, such as the young man in southern Britain who'd lost his father: they'd been up on scaffolding together, repairing the outside of the house, when the supports suddenly gave way and they plummeted to the ground. The young man landed on grass but his father fell onto concrete.

I shed tears as I read the poignant story: 'I cradled my Dad close to me, but there was nothing I could do. I just had to watch my wonderful father take his last breaths, while he died in my arms.'

I hope and pray that some of my words may have comforted this bereaved son.

But sometimes I was completely at a loss as to how to reply. One woman wrote to share her dark secret: her father had sexually abused her in childhood, but with his last breath he'd made her reaffirm her promise never to tell another living soul.

The pressures of her silence were too much to bear and she underwent a mental breakdown and was admitted to hospital. 'Can you help me? Is there any word from my father? Is he sorry now? Does he understand?'

Thankfully, I was able to relieve some of her anxiety by relaying her spirit father's 'plea for forgiveness', because he'd now realised his terrible mistakes and how much torment and anguish they had caused.

After this, the woman regained composure and her life brightened considerably.

One of my many spirit friends, sometimes my guide and teacher White Owl, is always nearby when I read my mail, and help is immediately dispatched.

But most correspondents don't realise that the aid they so desperately seek doesn't always come from me, as they request.

The power of thought is mighty, and there are many great souls in the next life who are capable of bringing relief to sufferers, their only motivating force being the power of unconditional love.

Here's what my spirit guide once said about the

role mediums play in the modern world:

> A servant of the spirit should educate and comfort, heal the sick, and uplift those who feel they stand in darkness.
>
> Go forward then, proclaiming from the mountain tops this timeless glittering message: Love is the strongest power the Universe. Love conquers all fear, and it is even stronger than death.
>
> True mediums for the spirit world are chosen. They are marked out by the light of compassion that shines through their works, brighter than the spirit of the sun.
>
> Our message is one of toleration and peace; and our task is to touch and awaken all sleeping materialistic souls to the eternal power of the spirit that is within them, and to the wonderful opportunities for growth and service that this affords.

To those people who think of spiritual mediums as 'fortune-tellers' my friend's words may come as a revelation; but to the many people who are already enlightened, his words confirm that mediums are trying to effect in the human race a moral, ethical, and spiritual change for the better.

So far, the adventure of my life has contained many fascinating experiences.

Glancing back, although my inspirers haven't led me along an easy path, I do feel great rewards have come through being richly blessed by the Love of the Spirit. I've even been privileged to experience time-slips, during which I've either visited the past or been granted powerful visions of the future.

Along with my spirit friends, I've met, and hopefully helped, thousands of people in both worlds.

Now I'd like to share what I've found with my fellow travellers, with anyone who will listen, and writing books is a good way of achieving this.

Speaking of writings, countless intriguing stories still pour through my letterbox: tales of sadness and joy, murder and suicide, blinding grief and ecstatic happiness – all proving that we're evolving through experience by playing out our parts in the great drama of life.

I'd like to thank all those who've written, and I hope my words brought you some inner peace.

But irrespective of how my replies are received, I was soon left in no doubt that news about my work was spreading across the world, for one letter with a foreign postmark arrived safely, even though it was only partly-addressed. It simply read:

> *To Stephen O'Brien,*
> *(medium)*
> *Britain.*

One day the telephone rang.

'Hello? Mr O'Brien?'

'Yes?'

'Would you please find time to help my aunt? She's in dire need of comfort, solace, and evidence of survival. Please, Mr O'Brien, promise you'll help her.'

'Of course. What's her name?'

'Mrs James.'

'Ask her to come round next Wednesday evening.'

# 2

# Between Two Worlds

The door knocked and Mrs Phyllis James entered, accompanied by her daughter. When I glanced at Mrs James, I saw a petite middle-aged woman in obvious distress; and psychically I felt my mind reeling under the crushing power of a blinding, inconsolable grief.

Of all the people I'd ever helped, I don't think I'd met anyone so unable to cope with the death of a loved one as Mrs James, which was why I'd agreed to see her.

With my psychic vision I gazed into the electro-magnetic fields of energy surrounding her – the aura – and saw recorded there an endless string of lonely nights, and a powerful wish to die and fall into the arms of someone she loved. She'd spent many hours crying and struggling to come to terms with some deep and tragic loss – and this battle was draining her of the will to live.

Mrs James was a woman caught between two worlds, and she certainly knew the pain of grief.

'Come on in, and we'll have a cup of tea first, shall we?' I said.

She and her daughter slowly began to relax when I explained how private consultations work.

'I can't guarantee anything,' I said. 'It's out of my hands. All we can do is wait and see what happens. No one can make anyone Over There communicate with us, and sometimes we don't get the people we'd like to hear from.

'I can't bring anybody back – only you can do that, because they love you. Some communicators try very hard to get a word through but I don't always hear them clearly, and sometimes not at all. It's very much an experiment, but it works better if we all relax and just wait to see what they can transmit.

'And remember, if they do come through I can't govern what they'll talk about. They bring their own thoughts, the things that *they* want to say, which may not necessarily be the things that we'd like to hear. But we can't demand anything of the people in the spirit world: they still have their own minds and they exercise their own free will.

'However, I won't bring any family skeletons out of the cupboard; and I'll vet the messages only if they start using "choice" language! They don't change upon dying, you see: they're the same people one second after death as they were one second before it; although as time moves forward people do progress and their characters alter. It's all up to your loved ones now; some find it easier to communicate than others – that's the way it goes.'

'I understand,' said Mrs James in a trembling voice, fearing that the one she wanted to hear from wouldn't get in touch on that bright evening.

'Just relax, Mum,' said her daughter reassuringly. 'Stephen will do his best.'

But conditions for contact were very good and we didn't have long to wait before I became aware of Mrs James's 'dead' husband. Not only was he present, but he also began to give his evidence in a rather surprising and clever way.

'I can see a man's hand here,' I relayed, 'holding what looks like a rug-making tool, and he tells me to say: "Thank you for recognising that I needed something to occupy my time. I felt so useless, there was no point in living, the way I was." '

These words made a great impact on his wife, who now perched on the edge of her seat and was eager to hear more.

From her husband I learned that he'd been brain-damaged and that she'd nursed him for four years when he hadn't any knowledge of his plight. There were many sad weeks, he said, 'when I couldn't recognise my wife or my children.' He knew that his family had found his illness so difficult to bear that they'd bought him rug-making kits, in the hope of filling his days with purpose and bringing some awareness back into his mind.

'And he gives me the name of "Brian" here. Does "Brian" mean anything to you?'

'That's his name,' his wife replied tearfully, barely able to speak; and her daughter clasped her arm and they squeezed each other's hands, as I went on:

'Well, he's telling you not to worry. "I'm alive and I was with you right up to the funeral, and for a few weeks afterwards," he says, "and after that I went across to the spirit world where they taught me how to guide you to a medium." '

His wife began to weep freely, but not with grief: these were tears of joy.

'Now Brian's holding up his passport,' I continued, which puzzled me, until Mrs James said:

'Yes, he died abroad while we were holidaying in France.'

Her husband then kept showing me pictures of what turned out to be his last moments on Earth. He'd been swimming, then as he walked up the beach towards his wife he suffered a sudden massive heart-attack, and he collapsed and died instantly. He clearly remembered all of this, and also that she 'had to go through an agonising week's wait before the French Authorities could release my body and fly me home.'

'I came home without him,' Mrs James cried. 'I loved him with all my heart, but I had to come home without him...' and she dabbed her eyes with a lace handkerchief.

Brian was acutely aware of the pain that his sudden death had caused his dear wife: he knew that for her it was just as if the light of her life had been extinguished; so, in an effort to stem her tears and bring her happier memories, he mentioned 'a special cigarette lighter, and a bedspread that she's given away.'

'Do you know anything about these?' I asked.

Her eyes shone. 'Oh yes, he never did like that old bedspread, and he used to take cigarette lighters to pieces, then he couldn't put them back together again!'

We smiled, because Brian had scored another hit. But not content with his success so far, he recalled that, 'Yesterday, you were totally alone, and you got out every single photograph of me that you possess, and you cried like a baby.'

'Yes, I did...'

'And you won't let anyone touch my things; none of the family's allowed to change the rooms around either.'

Mrs James agreed. In fact, her grief had been so deep that she'd created a kind of shrine, a place of remembrance for all of Brian's belongings, and no one was allowed to disturb it.

Her husband then went on to reveal a remarkable knowledge of her life and thoughts, and to offer her some excellent and sensible advice; but first he reported that, 'You prayed many nights for God to take you, so that you'd wake up in the morning in another world, next to me.'

'Yes, I did...' she said tearfully.

'But you can't come over to me before your time. Just remember the kind of love we've shared – it binds us together: it's the kind of love that never dies. So go on living and fighting – and don't give up.'

'I wish I could, but I don't think I can.'

'Yes you can. Live for the children, look after them for me,' he said to her.

Then he asked me to emphasise the sacredness of life, and to point out that committing suicide wouldn't solve any problems; so this I did.

'If you did cross over, your husband would have your company, yes, but then you'd be further away from your daughters and your grandchildren. And "dying" wouldn't remove your inability to cope with life – you'd take that with you into your new world, and you'd have to learn to alter your way of thinking Over There.'

Mrs James said she understood, but added with a heartfelt cry, 'Then Stephen, please tell him that I love him and miss him with all my soul. Tell him that not a night goes by without my thinking about him or crying myself to sleep over his death.'

'He knows all of these things,' I reassured her gently, 'and often catches your thoughts, so just speak to him and he'll hear you, Mrs James. The power of love will link you together, no matter how far apart you might sometimes feel.'

These words brought her great relief.

Although Brian's passing was sudden it wasn't unexpected, it seems, for incredibly he told us his spirit family had been waiting to receive him: with their special kind of vision they'd seen that his heart was weakening.

Still speaking of his transition Brian asked his wife to, 'Stop thinking of me as I was when I "died", with all the indignity.'

She fully understood these remarks, recollecting the traumatic events when the police and foreign officials had arrived on the beach where his body lay in public gaze. The painful formalities and fuss that followed, before the authorities would release his body, had caused her great anxiety.

But from his new world her husband was now sending 'all of my love to my three daughters,' and mentioning the personal difficulties one of them had been through.

Then I received the words, 'Sandra's baby was sickly.' For a moment this puzzled my sitters, but the mystery was soon solved. Sandra, one of his daughters, had lost a child, but her 'dead' father announced triumphantly, 'I've got the little baby with me, and it's a boy!' No sooner had this been said than Mrs James began sobbing uncontrollably. Floods of tears and consolation followed, until she felt able to explain: 'We always wanted a grandson, Stephen, but up to now all the children have been girls. The little baby's a boy... *a boy!*' she kept saying, overcome with happiness.

'And we've named him Julian,' declared Brian, 'so when you go to bed tonight, now you can also say: "And God bless Julian." '

It's impossible to judge the effect that such a simple message like this can have on those who've experienced tragedy.

Brian James was a very good communicator; and it's often the seemingly 'trivial' statements – like some of those which he relayed – that provide us with the best evidence of survival.

After all, what makes up our lives? If our loved ones spoke about Einstein's Theory of Relativity ordinary people wouldn't be interested.

The spirit people's messages are usually packed with comfort and hidden meaning, or intimate facts known only to the two people concerned – to the one sending the message, and to the one receiving it.

Mr James was a clever man who brought through plenty of seemingly 'inconsequential' details: he mentioned facts like 'the rug having to be picked up because she's always tripping over it'; and he referred to 'Porthcawl', the place where they'd spent a lovely caravan holiday when younger.

But with particular emphasis he spoke about 'the pair of shoes and a special suit' which he said were significant objects. I wondered why these were important until his wife explained:

'The undertaker offered to dress Brian in a suit, so I picked out his wedding suit, shirt and tie, and a pair of his best shoes. It's quite unusual to place shoes on those who are resting,' she pointed out, 'but the undertaker was very kind to us, and very understanding.'

Brian mentioned these items because he fully recognised their significance: they were important details to him and to her – and *only* to them, and to no one else.

Towards the end of the consultation he promised his family, 'I'll often visit you at home – so watch out for me!' And even though he knew his presence wouldn't always be registered he was determined his wife should 'see' him again.

He then revealed where he was living in the next world: 'It's a house in its own grounds,' he said, 'surrounded by country lanes, and it has a pink rambling-rose bush on the trellis-work over the door.'

'We grew that very same rose bush before,' said his astonished wife, smiling and nodding. 'That's wonderful.'

His final evidence was quite clever too. When he spoke about 'a ship' Mrs James's eyes filled with tears. 'Brian was making a tapestry of a ship before he died. We've had it framed and it's hanging in pride of place on the living-room wall,' she said.

After that quiet consultation, the woman who picked up her coat, and left with her daughter, was not the same dejected soul who'd entered my flat an hour earlier. She was now uplifted and happy, renewed and grateful.

Mrs James clasped my hands and squeezed them tightly. Both she and her daughter embraced me, and thanked me. 'You'll never know what you've done for me today, Stephen. I've fought so hard to carry on,' she said emotionally, 'and my strength was failing. But to know that Brian is with me, still caring for us all, means the world to us. Thank you. Thank you so much, Stephen.'

'Please, don't thank me,' I said, 'thank God, and Brian. After all, he did all the hard work – I only transmitted his words. He made the effort because he still loves you very much.'

'God bless you.'

She and her daughter smiled as they made their way to the door. 'God will be kind to you, Mrs James,' I said. 'The sun will shine again, you'll see.'

Then, much happier than when they'd arrived, my two visitors left – but not alone. Following close behind them was Brian James, a man from another world, someone whom the world once thought of as 'dead'. And I daresay he followed his family all the way home: unseen maybe, but walking beside them nevertheless.

## Do Not Forget Me

Do not forget me when I go,
For go I must, I cannot stay;
But do not forget my face, my love,
Nor my life, I pray.

Yet, if you should forget awhile
When I am gone – do not despair,
But keep your tears at bay,
For the silver love we shared
Will never fade away.

And one dawn soon,
Together we will stand
Upon some silent mountain, in some silent land,
And gaze into each other's eyes once more;
Then, hand in hand,
Along some distant shore,
We'll remember all the times that slipped our minds:

Our fond goodbyes;
The times we loved;
The time we met;

My love, we'll not forget.

*Stephen O'Brien*

# 3

# When A Child Dies

Picture a seven-year-old boy lying unconscious in a hospital bed, his eyes are tight-closed and he's unable to speak. He is dying of a rare form of liver cancer, and not even major surgery can save him.

At his bedside is the father he loves more than anything else in the world, yet his Dad can do nothing but watch, and pray: he is powerless to stop his young son's life ebbing away and moving out of sight, for ever.

Then the little boy dies...

What do you say to his Dad?

How do you comfort him?

Do you tell him to have faith, and that one day there may be a reunion in some far distant heaven, about which we nothing?

Will a blind faith replace his son's shining eyes, his fun-loving spirit, and his sparkling personality that made him so special? I think not.

Should you, then, maintain a cruel silence? Or – if you were able – would you throw back the gates of 'death' and offer him evidence of survival, offer him proof that his beloved child is still alive in another world?

If you were the bereaved parent, which of these options would you choose: a blind faith, or a certain knowledge?

William Allen was a fortunate man because the people in the spirit world delivered the knowledge he so desperately sought.

I had little to do with it: the Other Side organised the communication because they loved both him and his son. I was simply the channel that young Jamie used to contact his Dad, who'd suffered endless heartache.

When forty-year-old William lost his child his whole world seemed to fall to pieces. 'I prayed to die, myself,' he said. 'Little Jamie was such a happy lad – so full of life. When he died, a part of me died with him. Suddenly there was a big empty void inside me. My life was empty. You see, Jamie and I shared something very special.'

William started his search for evidence of his son's survival after reading an article about mediumship in a copy of the *Reader's Digest*, which thoroughly intrigued him. 'If Jamie was still alive somewhere, *anywhere*, then I wanted to know,' he stated with conviction. 'I wanted to find him again.'

On the evening when he received his spirit message, William was just another face in the crowd at my public meeting, listening to one of the thousands of messages I deliver each year. But strangely enough, I do remember the occasion because seven-year-old Jamie was such a lively communicator, full of fun and wicked grins. The vibrant youngster joined me on the platform in the middle of my demonstration.

Spirit children always come to my meetings and they often misbehave and pull at my coat or prod at my legs, or sometimes they sit at the side of the stage and play with their toys until it's their turn to communicate. They're not always well-mannered either! But there was nothing naughty about Jamie Allen. In fact, there was something rather special about him: he seemed strangely 'old' and 'wise', but he was brimming with vigour and a wealth of love, 'Just for my Dad.'

Mr Allen remembers the occasion far better than I do. So here, in this interview, he reveals the story of his son's illness, his remarkable bravery, and his sad untimely passing. He remembers, too, that memorable evening when Jamie drew back the silent curtain of death and proved his survival to the Dad he loves so much.

William's story deeply moved me: it's a poignant tribute to a wonderful child whose short but fruitful life was full of light and happiness, and love and laughter, until a fatal form of cancer struck him down in all the beauty of his youth.

As Shakespeare once penned, 'If you have tears, prepare to shed them now...'

### My son, Jamie.
### By William Allen:

Stephen, I wanted to say thank you for the help and understanding you have given me in messages from the next world from my mother and my son, Jamie, seven, who passed away in 1986. Jamie died of a very rare form of liver cancer, so rare that out of a million children maybe just one might be unfortunate to contract it.

I'd like to tell you about him, if I may.

For seven years he was really full of life, so active. He loved to run along the beach, laughing and shouting for all he was worth, feeling the wind blowing through his hair – and even in winter we had a terrible job to get a coat on him. He was such a wonderful son; and so loving, too.

If he hurt his head or leg he'd come running to me saying, 'Dad! Dad, will you kiss it better for me?' And when I did, he'd cuddle me up with his little arms wrapped tightly around my neck. We shared something very special, Jamie and I.

Then just before one Christmas he was very tired and went to bed at midday. I had to wake him at four o'clock, which wasn't like him at all. At first I put it down to getting over the Christmas excitement, but the following day there was no change in his condition so I called a doctor to examine him. It was then that we were all shocked to find his navel had swollen to the size of a clenched fist, and it was coloured black.

The doctor hadn't a clue what was wrong, but quickly admitted Jamie to hospital.

We were all very worried about him. Tests were started immediately: blood samples were taken and X-rays were done; then he was put on an intravenous drip to combat dehydration.

The consultant told us it was 'a burst appendix, with solid pus'. I said to him, warily, 'You must mean tumours?'

'No,' the doctor assured us, 'his temperature's fluctuating up and down, indicating pus infection.'

This meant that still further tests followed but none of them drew any solution. Suddenly I got frightened, more and more scared as each minute passed – cancer began to creep into my mind.

Jamie was then transferred to another hospital for a complete body-scan and the same tests all over again. It was then, for the first time, that my heart broke as I heard my son pitifully cry out to me, 'Daddy, please take me home! I want to go home... Please take me home, Daddy. Take me home!'

I couldn't speak for a moment, as I was shedding silent tears inside. No one will ever know just how much I cried for my young son. Gradually, after I calmed myself down, I spoke gently to him, saying, 'Jamie, you're the bravest little boy I know, and when you come home you'll be wearing a gold medallion on a blue ribbon, with some words written on it: *To Jamie, the bravest boy in the world, with love from Mam, Dad, and your little sister Emma.*

To see any child suffering is terrible, but when it's your own child you can't begin to imagine the agony and heartache you go through. It rips you apart inside, and shreds you to pieces.

We waited for the body-scan results: but still no answer was found. It was then that we were told Jamie had to go into the operating theatre to discover the problem. On that awful day his Mum and I both walked beside him, our hearts full of love. We held his little hands in ours, and were kissing him over and over again. Little did we know then that this was the last time our son would be able to speak to us, for within two hours he was rushed into Intensive Care, having vomited into his lungs under the anaesthetic.

My little boy never regained consciousness...

The surgeons discovered liver cancer, which had a good chance of being cured in some adults, but – as in Jamie's case – it had revealed itself far too late for successful treatment, and there was no hope.

I was summoned, alone, into an office where a consultant surgeon and two doctors gave me the news. It all happened so quickly.

'Your son is dying,' said the surgeon, as if it was just another everyday phrase. I was completely stunned. 'There's nothing we can do. He'll have to go back into theatre tomorrow.' Then he left, and the doctors didn't really know what to say. I was offered some tea, and then they too left me alone: it was all over in a matter of thirty seconds – so cold, so hard and unfeeling, as if they hadn't time to sympathise because there were other pressing tasks waiting.

I was totally numbed – and then I broke my heart and wept like a child, shivering with tears; I was going to lose my special little boy.

All the next day we kept talking to him as he lay sleeping, unconscious in his bed; and somehow, even though his eyes were shut fast, we both felt he could hear us, for as they took him to his operation something wonderful happened. His mother asked for a cuddle, and Jamie – with eyes tight closed – held up his arms for both of us. It was so touching; even a nurse nearby dabbed her eyes.

Once again we walked beside our boy, placing his two favourite cuddly toys next to him on the pillow. Then the orderlies gave us a few more precious moments alone with our brave, blond, blue-eyed wonderful son.

We embraced him, saying he'd be all right – and

our eyes followed his little body as they wheeled him out of sight behind the swing doors. There was nothing we could do now, except perhaps one thing.

Alone, I went to the hospital chapel and sat in the quiet silence... and I prayed. I prayed and prayed so hard that Jamie would be safe and well.

Then at 11.15 a.m. a nurse came out of the operating theatre to tell us that the surgeons had removed a large tumour from Jamie's liver. A flood of emotion filled my mind, and his mother and I hugged each other. Rather than seeing the black side of things, we felt it was good sign. 'He's going to live,' we cried; 'he's going to live!' After all the worrying and uncertainty, now there was a flicker of hope, and I went back again into the chapel and once more prayed gratefully, 'Lord God... Jesus... thank you for letting my son live. Thank you for giving him back to us. Thank you.'

But by 6.30 p.m. that night, Jamie was back in Intensive Care again: something went very wrong. Suddenly his tiny heart gave out, and they rushed him back to the theatre for emergency treatment and oxygen. After desperately struggling to keep alive, he barely survived the stress of that, but by some miracle he pulled through. And then came a terrible week of waiting; but still there was no change in his condition. They were monitoring him day and night.

Unwilling to give up, we kept speaking to him and playing cassette tapes, specially made for him by all his schoolmates, saying, 'Hurry up and get well, Jamie, and come home soon.' Every child recorded an encouraging personal message for my son, in the hope that the coma would break. But it didn't.

Through all these trials, and Jamie's brave fight for

life, the nursing staff were truly angels – especially one who had even cancelled a Spanish holiday to stay with him. 'If I went, I couldn't enjoy myself,' she said. 'I want to be here to see him get better. He's so handsome – he'll have all the girls chasing him one day, you'll see.'

I was very grateful for her kindness but, by now, time and hope were running out.

Jamie's response was slow, but much worse than this – they discovered he was in pain. His teeth were clenched tight and I used to try and prize them apart for him with my finger, fearful he'd bite his tongue, choke, or hurt himself – and I couldn't stand by and let that happen to him, not to my little boy.

I spent many restless, sleepless nights, haunted by my son's handsome face and by the terrible thought that he might never get better, and that I'd soon lose him for ever.

Towards the end, as our hope was gradually fading, we took the unusual step of arranging a christening service at his bedside. A vicar arrived, along with Jamie's grandpa and grandma, his mother, a good friend of mine, and that special nurse who'd come to love him over the weeks of his illness.

Everyone stood very quietly, stunned into silence, just thinking of the little boy in the bed: unconscious and helpless, but with the face of an angel. Silent tears fell from our eyes. I never thought I'd see a clergyman cry at a christening, but I did on that day. There was nothing more anyone could do. And I remember thinking, 'Oh God, why him? Why my Jamie…? Why?'

Shortly afterwards, at 7.2O p.m., his final moments arrived.

I sat and helplessly watched as my beautiful son's

life slipped silently away. I could see it happening, and as he was going I leaned over him with tears in my eyes and found myself saying, 'Jamie, don't fight anymore, just go to sleep, son... just go to sleep, Jamie...'

I tried to hold him close, but there were so many tubes and wires in the way, I couldn't... I couldn't hold my son; so I just sat quietly looking at him, crying and stroking his blond hair, and kissing his lips, knowing I'd never be able to do this to him again in this world: this would be the last time.

Then suddenly, his breathing paused; stopped... and it was finished...

Jamie had died, and in those moments my own life died with him.

But he looked so peaceful, so handsome and peaceful, and an overwhelming feeling of love filled me, mixed with sadness and a sense of the great pride I had for him, and still have for him. But now his young life was over.

But why? He had never harmed anybody, never hurt a soul. All he did was bring joy to everyone he met, and now he was gone, and I couldn't understand why. Why did God take Jamie from us? All I knew for certain was that I loved my wonderful son – the bravest little boy in the world.

Then, quite suddenly, a sickening feeling of absolute pure hatred for God thundered right through me: He'd taken my son away – and I quickly rose, ran out into the corridors and dashed back into the chapel and rushed up towards the altar. I stood defiantly and shouted out loud – I couldn't help myself. I spat towards the altar and violently shouted, *'Don't tell me there's a God!'*

And I swore at Him, and stormed away.

Then the slow, painful months of endless grief started, and never seemed to finish.

*

Time rolled onwards.

Then William Allen, who was a stranger to me, attended one of my public meetings.

Here's a letter from him:

I had no idea I would get a message that night. I just sat quietly amongst the people, waiting for the medium to start the meeting, wondering if there might be some news, some message or comfort from anyone belonging to me. The hall was packed yet during your clairvoyance, Stephen, suddenly you brought Jamie to me by name, with a great deal of love, and laughter too.

It was a wonderful moment. My son gave proof of his nearness, and spoke of his 'yellow plastic ducks and submarine'.

This was wonderful evidence because when I bathed Jamie he used to spend hours trying to sink his ducks with his submarine, dive-bombing them and soaking everyone and everything! These were special moments we shared together, full of happy laughter.

I was more than impressed.

As the messages came through I felt elated and deep emotions were stirred inside me. But it didn't finish there, Stephen, because you also said Jamie mentioned 'two little dogs in stripey jackets'. This was remarkably accurate, for when my son was desperately ill, while they wheeled him to the operating theatre for major surgery, my wife and I placed his two favourite toys beside him on the trolley pillow. These were Fluff and Scruff — *two woolly dogs dressed in stripey jackets.* I'll never forget the memories those words brought back.

Jamie was speaking to me through a perfect stranger, and I was uplifted and overjoyed. What's more, you gave his messages with such warmth, kindness and sympathy.

Then I remember that my mother, who'd also passed over, said she'd brought Jamie along to the meeting from the Other Side. She said she was taking care of him, and this brought me a great sense of peace. She told me, 'I know you've been through the mill for the last two years or so, but we're all proud of you, son.'

Stephen, you went on to describe Jamie's favourite Police Tricycle, his many hospital tests before falling into his coma, his passing, and how we'd both 'repair' his pedal-car by 'placing it on pretend home-made ramps': all meaningless things to anyone else who was listening, but to me they showed that my beautiful son was still alive. I was very comforted.

Jamie then said, 'Give my love to Emma.' This is his younger sister. And he asked you if you would, 'Tell my Dad I love him, as he thinks of me so much. I love my Dad.' I was very moved, and could feel my emotions rising. 'Don't cry for me, Daddy,' my son said, 'and think of the good times. Look up, Dad, not down. I love you.'

I can't begin to say what those words meant to me. Up until then I'd often thought my life was useless without my son. There were many times when I just couldn't come to terms with his loss, and I'd have been happy to die, myself – to join him. But messages like this gave me great hope and peace, and I feel very privileged to have received them.

My only wish now is that other parents who find themselves in my situation will be lucky enough to be helped like this. To anyone like me I would say: don't give up; if I can find the child I thought I'd lost, you can find yours too.

Some sceptical people might say these messages may be 'untrue'. I reply, '*Rubbish*!'

Those messages came from people I loved – and precise facts given through a stranger could only have come from them. There's no way anyone could have known those personal things. You even gave me my son's name.

I think I'm very fortunate because I've found Jamie again, through knowledge and love, and not just faith. And now I've come to accept that he's not really far away from us all. I know he's alive.

Other parents in my position should hear my story: perhaps it'll give them hope – and the knowledge that death is not the end.

Of course, I still have my good and bad days, because you never ever forget. But I wish I could tell them to keep on looking for their child if they've lost one.

I can only draw from my experiences and advise parents to visit good mediums and Spiritualist Churches; then perhaps they'll get the comfort I've found.

In those small places they might find the love and support of people who not only understand death, but who are also able to show it isn't the final crossing it's made out to be.

So, Stephen, thank you from the bottom of my heart for helping me in my great sadness to realise that my son's life is not over, not cruelly ended, but continuing in the next world.

Thank you for helping me to understand that he lives on and is being cared for in another life beyond death.

And God bless you in your work.

*William Allen*

# 4

# Through the Mists

Jamie's story touches me deeply because I didn't share such a loving and close relationship with my own father. I was a determined but loveable child, they say, who'd raise both his arms in the air and open and close his fists, which meant 'Pick me up and carry me', and that's why they nicknamed me 'Ever-Ready'.

But I can't ever recall my Dad cuddling me; I never sat on his knee, nor was I ever hoisted onto his shoulders; so it didn't take long for my young mind to assume that he just wasn't interested in me.

I was much closer to my mother, who was a kind and loving soul. But although she taught me the value of expressing and receiving love and kindness, it was my father's indifference to these qualities that taught me just how important it was for me to place them at the centre of my life.

Everything we've experienced has deepened our characters and enriched our minds.

The sensitive people we are today have evolved

from the trusting children that we once were.

Love is the greatest power in the universe, and sensitive people learn to appreciate the fullness of this power not only by receiving it, but also by experiencing its opposite force of hate, and all the negative effects that this brings in its train.

Looking back at my formative years I recognise now that my father's personality taught me some valuable lessons about human nature; but he emerges from my memories as such a sad man.

Dad never attended school plays and recitals that I was in, and never showed great interest in my schoolwork. I used to be so proud of the pictures I'd painted or the essays I'd written (I once won a nationwide competition, coming top in Britain) but Dad was unmoved and nowhere to be seen.

My mother, however, was as pleased as punch and was always ready to praise and encourage me. I recorded my loving relationship with her in my first book – and so to Dad.

He was a distant, cold, and undemonstrative man; and from my earliest years I felt he didn't love me. Perhaps I'm wrong, but two horrendous scenes still freeze my blood when I recall them today. It isn't easy for me to write about these events, but they do reveal why I now place such a high value on the quality of kindness. I was just a toddler when they happened, a curious child eager to learn about life and to have fun exploring anything new. That's why the huge mud pool at the bottom of our street attracted me so much.

'Kids will be kids' they say, and my friend Anthea and I had a great time on that sunny afternoon, sploshing the brown mud everywhere with our dried-out rhubarb sticks until, quite by accident, I fell in.

'Oh God, my Dad'll kill me!'

'Don't be *silly*,' rebuked the matronly Anthea, pointing her stick at me. 'Your mother wouldn't let him.' And she was quite right of course; my mother worshipped the ground I walked on.

'But my Mam's at work today,' I whimpered, desperately trying to scrape the mud off my bare arms. Then I ran all the way home to wash it off, but I had to get in without my father seeing me. I stopped in the doorway and crept silently past Dad, who was reading his newspaper. I tried my best to be invisible but suddenly he turned and bellowed out, 'Stephen! Come here!'

My knees trembled, for I feared my father's voice and knew the terror that can strike at a child's heart when it's truly afraid. Pathetically I slunk back into the living-room, where he stood waiting for me, hands on his hips, feet wide apart, and his stern face frowning hard.

Awkwardly, I tried to hide my muddy arms by twisting them behind my back; this was the second time I'd got them dirty and I feared the worst because I'd disobeyed my Dad. I felt so painfully frightened; all I could hear was the loud ticking of the mantel-clock and my thudding heart as it pounded against my chest and up into my throat. Although what came next happened quickly, I felt as if each tick of the clock dragged by in a hundred years.

'Show me those arms!' he commanded.

I obliged weakly, but smarted backwards when he caught hold of them in his strong hands.

His eyes flashed red with sudden anger. 'What did I tell you? I ordered you to keep away from that mud, and what have you done?'

I was too afraid to speak: excuses only fired his temper.

His gruff voice rose sharply. 'What did I tell you? I'll teach you to disobey me, once and for all!'

He seized me by the shoulders and dragged me off into the kitchen. In a frantic bid to escape I scuffed at the floor with my shoes, but he was too strong. Fear struck and I panicked. 'Please Dad, I'm sorry. I was only playing... Please, I won't do it again,' I pleaded, but his mind was firmly set on punishment.

He stripped me to the waist, grabbed a dry scrubbing-brush from the sink and scrubbed my back until it was sore. I shouted for him to stop but it seemed as if a flood of rage had possessed him. My muddy arms were left well alone – my back received the lesson until his authority had been well and truly stamped upon me.

'You'll do as you're told in future! When I say something, I mean it. I *demand* respect, and if I don't get it, I'll make you give it!'

While all this was happening, some distant part of my mind rejected him out-of-hand – I knew he didn't love me. How could he love me, having done such a terrible thing? Surely fathers shouldn't treat their sons like this?

There and then, I decided I didn't have a real Dad – not like the other boys had – as this was the only way I could survive without further emotional pain. It's better to live without a father, I reasoned, than to exist with one who didn't love me.

A child's mind is so pure and trusting, yet each day millions of adults cruelly scar their little ones with an unkind word, a hasty hand, or worst of all the sins: a blatant rejection of their innocent love. Children trust so completely; what a shattering and soul-destroying moment it is when their image of adults as caring people explodes in their faces.

I now realise, of course, that many adults who can't cope with their own personality disorders often vent this anger by punishing their children.

It's a vicious circle: children are treated with cruelty and they grow up with emotional problems; they become parents themselves, then they treat their offspring with the same cruelty from which they suffered in childhood.

Fortunately, this didn't happen to me when I grew up, because the light of my intelligence, and my peaceful nature, broke this circle.

The subconscious mind, where all our past experiences still 'live', is easily programmed when we're young; and it's easily frightened in adult-hood, which can cause all manner of anxieties for some people. But although we're creatures of habit, our thought-patterns *can* be broken, and they can also be re-programmed.

But what a twisted dark world many adults live in, which brings me to another painful memory lurking at the tip of my pen, one that could only have happened while my mother was out because my father would never have harmed me in front of her.

He and I were the only two at home, but he was

booked to play in a dart's match at a local pub and he couldn't take me, a lively toddler, with him. Our dear neighbour, Florrie, was out; so I couldn't be left there. What could he do?

He was in a dilemma, which he solved thus: he placed me on a high-backed chair and bound me to it, hand and foot, using several of my mother's nylon stockings; then he left for the pub.

I've no idea how long I tried to break my bonds: painful experiences are hard to recapture. I know only that I was frightened and alone, and that the whole house echoed to my cries. In the end I fell deathly silent; this was my mind's way of divorcing itself from a horrendous experience.

I can't remember who freed me: it was probably my brother, for if my mother had witnessed this cruelty the roof would have been sent into orbit. A protective curtain of forgetfulness blanks further details from my young mind.

Poor old Dad.

As I grew older, I realised that because he hadn't been raised in a loving family, he couldn't recreate that secure environment for his own children.

Not long ago, a woman who'd suffered similar abuse in her youth spoke to me about her father's cruelty. There was great bitterness in her voice when she declared that she could 'never heal the rift' that lay between them.

I took her hand, and looked into her eyes. 'You must learn to forgive him,' I said, 'as I have done.'

When Dad was in his early sixties and in hospital for an operation, I nipped out of work and got specially extended lunch hours to trek all the way to his bedside. Yet whenever I arrived he grumbled, 'Oh, not you *again*. Why are you coming here every day, boy? There's no need for that, I'm all right – don't fuss about.'

Dad always called me 'boy', even when I reached adulthood. It seemed he might never perceive me as anything but a child. Isn't it sad, the way some people get 'trapped' within their own thought-patterns?

On a lighter note, however, one of our more amusing clashes still makes me grin whenever I think of it; it wasn't funny at the time, of course, but now I can laugh at anything (and frequently do). I was about twenty, and after one of our shouting matches Dad pulled me to the ground by my hair then stomped off to the pub.

I left the house in tears, feeling I couldn't return that evening because he'd been so angry. At midnight I sat alone on a cold park bench, gazing at twinkling stars in a bitterly cold sky. Where could I go? Where would I sleep tonight?

In desperation I called on my mother's best friend who lived down the hill, our long-time neighbour, dear old Florrie. She was in her sixties then, was small, thin, and quite brown-skinned (pernicious anaemia and liver problems). Crouched over the metal sink in her kitchen, she was dyeing her short white hair jet-black. Her wrinkly bird-like face was covered with a million furrows, running with dye. Florrie was the proud possessor of only four green teeth – but I'd always loved her, for her heart was kind and she thought the world of me.

'I can't go home, Florrie. I wouldn't feel safe,' I said, plonking myself down on a rickety old chair.

'Shame on him!' she seethed through her tooth-gaps, while wrapping an old towel around her hair. 'But God never sleeps. There's One above us all!' she warned vehemently, jabbing a finger heavenwards. 'Stay here tonight in the spare bedroom, Stephen,' she said kindly, patting her locks dry. 'There aren't any sheets, but you can lie on the bed and I'll fetch some old coats or something to keep you warm.'

My voice was quite small. 'Thank you.'

Then, not realising her own wit, Florrie lamented, 'Oh, if your mother was alive today she'd turn in her grave.'

Now here's the funny part: I couldn't fall sleep in Florrie's spare bedroom because next-door she was snoring like a steam train at full pelt. As the air whistled through the gaps in her four green teeth, she wheezed and shook the silent night, and kept me awake for hours. Just when I thought she'd had a nightmare and frightened herself into silence, off she'd go again: wheeze, rattle, whistle, snore...

Finally at 3 a.m. I dressed, slipped quietly from her house, and walked 'home' – still able to hear her loud grunts from half way up the hill!

Dad was fast asleep; so on tip-toes I sneaked into my own bed, grateful and undiscovered.

When I later told Florrie that she snored like a pneumatic-drill she categorically denied it. '*Never*! Not me! *Never in your life*!' she declared, affronted, spraying saliva into the kitchen.

'It's all right for you,' I replied, 'you can't hear it because you're asleep. If you got those teeth pulled out we'd all have a bit of peace.' And we laughed together.

'You come down here any time you like, son,' she said, stirring her tea with a fork. 'And don't let your father bully you. Your mother was one of the best; she was a good friend to me. I'll never forget Mrs O'Brien. Never.' And I was grateful for the love she showed.

But I think Dad and I passed through our stickiest patch just after my mother's death; I was in my twenties, and we were both argumentative; and these were some of my darkest hours. Because I was unemployed at the time, I avoided daily confrontations on his days off by staying in bed until he left at midday for the pub. But he assumed I was 'a lazy good-for-nothing', which caused him to turn bright blue and rave like a madman:

'Get up, boy! If I've got to work, *everybody* works!'

Covering my head with the sheets I turned over and pretended not to hear; a difficult task because he had a voice like a foghorn – and my silence had got his goat; so next, he issued bans.

Although I contributed £16 a week for my 'keep', which in the mid-1970s was quite a sum, and I did my own washing and cooking, and bought my own food on top, Dad still wasn't satisfied. 'I want you up at seven in the morning to make my breakfast!' he commanded.

I'm afraid I wasn't impressed, or polite. I think I told him to 'Get lost!' – then I ran for the hills.

But I lived to regret it.

First he confiscated the small one-bar electric fire from my bedroom, where I then lived to keep out of his way. Next, he banned me from taking showers because 'it burned electricity' and it was 'too expensive' (a daily shower cost less than two pence).

Finally, the washing-machine was pronounced out-of-bounds:

'You're not wasting my money when you're not working!' was his usual gripe, which smacked of his own mother's meanness: she used to padlock the larder to prevent her unemployed sons eating 'unpaid-for' food.

But the final straw came when Dad shouted, 'If you're not in work by the end of the month, you're on the road – *homeless*. And I mean it: *you'll be out!*'

Devastated, I couldn't believe my ears. But he *did* mean it. His eyes were as hard as flint. 'You'll be chucked out!' he threatened, shaking a stocky fist in my face.

The days wore on and, at my wits' end, I trudged the town and pleaded with three council officials to help me, but they didn't give a damn – one of them couldn't even remember me from my first visit, two days previously. No one cared where I'd lay my head at the end of the month.

Finally, I visited a Spiritualist Church and sat in the front row, hoping to receive some other-world guidance. But I got none. During the stirring hymns I felt a tear trickle down my face, and thought of how I'd tried to help so many people, and that my reward for this work was to be homelessness.

I remembered then that it's only because of our darkest times that we learn how to plumb the depths of our souls, and to rise again, triumphant in the knowledge that we've developed our characters and grown from our experiences.

At such times, our spirit friends often stand by silently, and observe us: occasionally they might transmit a comforting thought or two; but mostly we're left alone to learn life's lessons. Ultimately, that's the kindest and wisest way.

My tears fell in vain in that little church, for despite heartache, sleepless nights, and days of walking the streets trying to find somewhere to live (all of which failed), at the very last minute Dad released his cruel threat of homelessness. But he withdrew it coldly, with a deathly silence. Not another word on the subject passed his lips: never again did he mention my expulsion – not even to say that he was 'Sorry'.

My spirit was deeply wounded.

Over the years, of course, as we grew older and wiser, Dad and I became closer and learned to understand each other much better when we lived apart, than ever we did when we lived together.

On her death-bed my mother had made him promise to 'Take care of Stephen'. And to be fair to Dad: my brother John once spoke to him when I was in financial difficulties and within a few days I received a substantial cheque to ease my pressures.

But in our earlier years Dad and I never saw eye-to-eye on anything. I still cringe when I think of that silly time when we crossed swords not long after my mother had died; it happened on the first anniversary of her passing.

'Go to the newspaper office, boy, and put in a memory-notice for your mother.'

'But Dad, what's the point?'

'It's tradition, boy,' he stated. 'People expect it of us, to show we haven't forgotten.'

Not one bit concerned about what people thought, I argued back, 'But *we* know we've not forgotten.'

'Do as you're told!' he bellowed; and, even though I was twenty-one, for the sake of peace and quietness I took his few shillings and sloped off to the newspaper office, armed with bright ideas which eventually got me into more hot water.

I stood at the big desk, completely ignored as usual, and thinking, 'I've gone invisible again,' (this always happens to me when I stand at a counter).

When I miraculously became tangible, two bored assistants looked up and confronted me: one was very big, the other was painfully small – but the strangest thing was that their voices matched their bodies. Miss Little twittered like a church mouse scampering over hot pipes, and Miss Large boomed like a foghorn over Swansea Bay.

Miss Large snatched up my notice and her plump eyes bowled disdainfully across the lines.

Then she summoned Miss Little who chattered her disapproval, after which they whispered in a huddle. Miss Large flumped back to the desk.

'We can't put this in!' she boomed.

'No, we can't,' squeaked Miss Little.

Then someone flung aside the swing doors, like the cowpokes do in saloons in cowboy films, and in strode Madame Pink, the Supervisor.

Dressed entirely in shades of pink – pink blouse, pink skirt, and pinky-brown hair set like a golf ball – she grasped the notice and muttered her way through the usual 'loved and sadly missed' bits. Then she waved the paper in my face and blurted out, 'Did *you* write this?'

'Yes. Is something wrong?'

'This part here: "Loving thoughts *to* you". Have you some vague connection to the Spiritualists?' she squeezed out through tight-pursed lips.

'Yes, I have,' I said firmly. 'What's the problem?' This must have thrown her, for she lowered her rigid hair (a miracle of modern technology, for not a strand of it moved) flung the note at Little and Large, and with a grimace ordered them to, 'Print it!'

Then she quickly glided out through the swing doors like the Duchess of Kent on a skateboard.

My father was far from pleased.

'Why did you put *that* in?' he grumped. 'Everyone at work's laughing at me. Now get it into your head: your mother's *dead*, boy. She's *gone*. How can you send thoughts to someone who's dead?'

'It's easy,' I said. 'You just do, and they'll receive them.'

But this was all too much for him, and his blood-pressure soared. 'That's the last time I'll ask you to do that!'

'Good!' I barked defiantly. 'I didn't want to do it anyway.'

Then he cursed under his breath and stormed out of the house; and I retired earlier than usual.

Snug in my bed, I decided to get out the old photo albums.

And there, in the orange glow of the streetlamps filtering through the lace curtains at the window, I flicked through dozens of snapshots of bygone days.

There were scores of happy memories: sultry summer afternoons, and crisp winter snow scenes; and each shot was filled with smiling faces. My mother was there, too, holding in her arms the two young grandchildren she'd worshipped. All our family's special moments were spread before me.

I couldn't help filling with emotion when I came across one of the last pictures taken of my mother, shortly after she'd had major cancer-surgery and just before she'd become too weak to stand. She was at my school's hundredth anniversary dinner, seated at a refreshment table among a crowd of smiling guests. Her face was thin and drawn, and her eyes were glazed over with deep sadness. She seemed far, far away from the happy celebrations going on all around her.

She had the look of someone who was facing death, and who knew it.

A cloud of sad memories enveloped me in the stillness. Then something unusual happened:

Behind me I sensed a presence. I glanced over my shoulder, fully expecting a voice to speak because I knew someone from the spirit world was watching me.

Then a gentle tapping sound came from the windowpane. I swung round, but there was no one there of course. Yet the tapping came again – this time from a different place and in a rhythm that betrayed an invisible intelligence at work.

Someone was trying communicate.

But who was it?

Intrigued, I spoke out loud the names of all our family members who'd passed over, but drew no response until I mentioned my mother, Beatrice.

The window tapped once in agreement.

I was pleased and fascinated.

I'd just been viewing images of her past, but now she was here, behind me. I could even smell the distinctive perfume she often wore.

I asked her a few questions.

'Are you happy, Mam?'

*One tap, for yes.*

'Were you looking at the album with me?'

*One tap for yes.*

'Did you hear me and Dad talking about you earlier?'

*One tap.*

'Are you annoyed with us?'

*Two taps, for no.*

'So you're still close to the family?'

*One tap for yes.*

And so this went on for over half an hour, during which time my mother confirmed a number of family 'secrets', far too personal to print here.

On occasions her soundless voice spoke to me through the mists and directed my line of thought. It was an inspired conversation filled with answers which had to be checked; and needless to say, they later proved to be correct.

My heart sank when the tapping grew fainter until I could barely hear it in the quietness of the night. Suddenly a flood of unanswered questions raced through my mind.

'Don't leave yet,' I said.

There was a short pause, then:

*One tap for yes.*

'Is your "power" weakening?'

*A gentle, faint tap.*

'Then before you go,' I whispered, 'just know I'm grateful that you came; and I'm proud to be your son.'

I sensed my mother's tears falling in the silence, just before:

*One tap came, for yes.*

She then inspired me to look in her well-thumbed autograph book, treasured by her when she was just sixteen: it was nestling amongst old sepia photographs, and when I opened it my eyes fell upon some writing on the inside cover, lines my mother had penned decades earlier when she was just a schoolgirl.

> *Beatrice Price is my name,*
> *Wales is my Nation.*
> *Tredegar is my dwelling-place,*
> *Christ is my salvation.*
> *When I'm dead and in my grave*
> *And all my bones are rotten,*
> *Open this book and think of me,*
> *To show I'm not forgotten.*

I smiled at the young girl's innocence and purity of heart.

In the dark bedroom I heard my mother's faint voice whisper through the mists, 'All my love to you, Stephen.'

I replied, 'And all my love to you, too, Mam.'

Then there was one further pause, and one more *faint tap* at the windowpane, and she was gone...

I settled down, snug and warm under the duvet,

wrapped in nostalgic thought, and gently drifted into the peaceful sleep of someone who feels secure in the knowledge that there's no such thing as extinction.

Love lasts for ever.

Love is eternal, and it is even stronger than death.

# 5

# A Gift of Peace

One morning the telephone rang and Ulster TV was on the line from Ireland.

'Will you come to Belfast and make a guest appearance and demonstrate your mediumship "live" on *The Gerry Kelly Show*?'

This is one of Ireland's top chat shows, and I must have been inspired because without thinking I said, 'I'm packing my bags.'

UTV said they'd book an all-expenses-paid jet flight direct from London's Heathrow airport, and that they'd reserve a luxurious suite for me in Belfast's Europa Hotel. Excellent facilities would be laid on: a courteous reception, delicious five-course meals, unlimited telephone calls, and even a trouser-pressing and laundering service – all so very far removed from my own penniless existence.

But on the day of the show I had a shock. In the hazy early-morning light the telephone rang, and it was my tour manager, Jeff Rees Jones, wanting to know if everything was all right. 'Of course it is,' I said, rubbing the sleep from my eyes. But I gasped because my alarm clock had stopped! I had less than twenty minutes to wash, dress, pack my bags, get a taxi, and speed to the railway station to connect with the only suitable flight to Belfast on that day.

'For Goodness' sake, Jeff!' I screeched down the receiver, jumping out of bed and hopping about, trying to struggle into my socks, 'Get me a taxi or I'll never make it!'

'Right!'

I slammed the receiver down, and adrenaline rushed through my veins as I dashed around my flat like a thing demented. I danced around the rooms, grabbing toiletries and clothes, and shoving things into bags right, left and centre.

I was out of breath by the time I flew into the cab and I'm sure the driver expected me to yell, 'Follow that car!'

When we reached the railway station I was redder than a beetroot. With perspiration pouring down my face I flung my luggage into the first carriage then boomeranged myself in behind it, just as the train chugged off towards London.

'What's the matter, love?' asked a frail old lady, perplexed by my distress.

'Oh, nothing; it's just man's trouble,' I wheezed, and she gave me a peculiar look.

It took me ages to get my breath back, but there was plenty of time to relax, especially on the coach trip from Reading station into Heathrow Airport.

I'd never realised just how big the airport is; it seemed like a sprawling city in its own right: there were towering new buildings, runways, lounges, restaurants and shops: it took forty minutes to reach the flight terminal.

I was even more surprised by the security checks and full body-searches, conducted under the Prevention of Terrorism Act.

A flint-faced official shepherded a group of us behind some security screens, where he searched through our luggage, bag by bag. My suitcase was opened and meticulously rifled; he even pushed his hands right down inside my spare shoes.

I must have a shifty-looking face because he seized my alarm clock and ordered me to, 'Turn the hands round one hour!'

But before I completed this task, meant to reveal hidden time-bombs, he'd snatched up my electric shaver and told me to, 'Switch it on!'

I obeyed, and noticed that several other security men were standing high above us on a raised gantry, scrutinising every twitch of our eyes as these orders were given, looking for tell-tale signs of guilt. It was all most unpleasant, and I couldn't help wondering how embarrassing these checks might be for shy passengers. In my mind's eye I could see a plump woman, flushing crimson red as her vast winter bloomers were hoisted aloft with the cry, 'This one's clean, Joe: she can go!'

After a predictable passenger-groaning delay we trooped into the jet; and I must admit to an inward prayer asking God to spare us an explosion over the sea, and reminding Him that I didn't want to visit Mexico, thank you. Well, you hear such strange stories on the news about hijackers and terrorists.

Soon the powerful jet engines burst into piercing

screams and suddenly I was thrust back against my seat as we sped along the runway, then we lifted from the ground like a giant rigid swan with its head towards the sun. But as we rose gracefully towards heaven, I left my stomach on the tarmac; and when we juddered and shook through pockets of air turbulence I felt as if I'd floated right out of my seat.

One second I could feel the plane underneath me, and the next instant it had gone. My insides fluttered and my breakfast nearly made a guest appearance. I'd experienced this weightlessness before: on roller-coasters at fairgrounds, just when I was about to drop hundreds of feet, screaming to my death.

Suddenly my ears popped and clicked, quietened down, then popped again as we climbed to 37,000 feet.

But the smooth Irish accents of the air-hostesses eased our tensions, along with the fragrant aroma of real Irish coffee when it was served.

Outside the window everything looked so small and insignificant in the distance, lit by the yellow sun. But the vista was breathtaking as we sailed up through silver clouds and into a brilliant electric-blue sky. I peered out over the wing and marvelled at the green fields receding as we rose through the morning mists.

Then my eyes beheld an incredibly beautiful sight: in the crisp bright air, way out to the horizon, I could see nothing but hundreds of miles of undulating white cotton-wool clouds, carpeting the vast heavens beneath us.

They looked so solid and tangible, I felt as if I could

step outside and walk on their glimmering fleeces. But logic reminded me that beneath them there was nothing but miles of open space, leading down to Davey Jones's Locker: the Irish Sea.

But the most unnerving part of the flight was undoubtedly that dreadful tannoy announcement which crackled out menacingly:

'If there's a Mr Jackson aboard, would he please make himself known?'

All the passengers were mute.

They blinked but they didn't move; and I thought, 'Oh my God, he's got a bomb… We're all going to die – we'll be blown to smithereens.'

But of course, we were quite safe: Mr Jackson was a diabetic with special food requirements.

The crossing was soon over and we made our descent through deep grey cloudbanks into Belfast International Airport, the whole jet shuddering as its great wings resisted the 120 miles per hour head-wind.

For minutes I went completely deaf. All my catarrh shot down into my ears and jammed there, whistling away merrily. Passengers glared across at me, wondering why my fingers had disappeared into my head. I just smiled inanely and placed my hands back onto my lap.

After making my way through Customs as quickly as possible, where my bags were again examined and X-rayed, I was met by a chauffeur from the television station. He carried a card with *Stephen O'Brien – The Kelly Show* scrawled across it, and we were soon speeding towards the city and the swish Europa Hotel.

I was completely unprepared for the devastating sights that lay ahead of us on that short journey. It started with a huge green Army helicopter keeping us under surveillance: it hovered above the car as if we were threatening Ireland's national security, and followed us through plush green countryside for a few miles, and then on into the troubled city of Belfast.

As we did a round-trip through the trouble-spots I sat stunned and silent, my hand over my mouth in disbelief. I was horrified to see so many burnt-out businesses, blackened and charred shells that were destroyed because their owners 'had failed to pay up their protection money'.

Shops had been smashed and looted, and sharp barbed-wire lay on top of buildings and traffic lights as if to defy further terrorist attacks. Some of the streets were cordoned off by huge guarded gates which brought to mind gruesome scenes from George Orwell's *1984*.

Worse still, I sensed there was no deep feeling of trust in the city's atmosphere. But more shocking sights followed. British soldiers swaggered down the streets, carrying automatic rifles that were primed and ready to fire.

Silently they moved through crowds of shoppers, their narrowed eyes taking in every street-corner whisper, every unusual movement, and each child's progress along the road.

It sickened me to witness these instruments of war paraded in public; and I was left in no doubt that, if necessary, their bullets would be fired. The whole scene left a warped and twisted impression in my mind, which is hard to remove – even now.

And there was such a dreadful feeling of enmity between the soldiers and the civilians. Eventually breaking the silence, I remarked to my driver, 'It's all so sad. Why can't people live together in peace, despite their differences?'

'One of our staff was killed on this street last year,' he replied. 'He didn't stand a chance. The police were shooting at terrorists and caught him in the crossfire. His female passenger escaped, but she went into a mental hospital because she'd seen a man's skull blown apart in front of her eyes.'

I was stunned by the thought.

I just couldn't imagine the torment she must have gone through after witnessing such a wicked and senseless act. 'What on earth has happened to charity?' I finally said.

Then we drove up the Falls Road, and down the Shankill Road – two of the hottest gang-warfare streets in Belfast. The psychic feelings there were terrible: oppressive and heavy, and a trembling fear hung thickly in the atmosphere. Just seeing so many burnt-out shops made my mouth go dry. 'Young kids killed rival gang leaders here recently by dropping concrete slabs onto their heads from thirty feet up,' lamented my driver; and I groaned with him in the spirit, unable to understand the cruel minds that could do such a thing to another being.

The thought of all the dreadful carnage often reported on television, and the loss of so many innocent lives, sickened me. But then I'm a peace-maker, and always have been.

'I could tell you some awful things about the

"animals" that live around here,' he continued, 'for that's what they are: they don't deserve to be called human beings.'

And he did recount several horrific acts that he'd witnessed, unspeakable cruelties, far too upsetting or macabre to reproduce here: I wouldn't want them published, fearing they'd give innocent minds night-mares, or wicked minds ideas.

As I gazed at the passing streets, deep sadness numbed my brain and I realised that this world still has a long, long way to go before The Kingdom of Heaven is enthroned upon it, as preached by the One whom many religious groups claim as their Leader, especially in Ireland.

As the streets flickered past the windows, my mind began to wander and I couldn't help thinking that today's hateful terrorists are creating such a sad world for tomorrow's Irish children. By filling the psychic atmosphere with anger and suspicion, terror and vengeance, and a blatant disregard for the sanctity of life, unkind people are destroying all hope of peace for future generations.

Hatred and aggression radiate such coarse and powerfully negative psychic vibrations that even the souls of foetuses in pregnant women can be affected by them. And if men and women live in constant fear, their children will grow up fearful.

What kind of society does the human race want tomorrow's people to inherit?

Peace will remain only an idea until each man makes it happen in his life by changing his way of thinking and behaving.

The reign of Peace starts right here, right now,

within each one of us, and not within someone else. Parents cannot give to their children the treasured gift of peace, unless it already exists in their own hearts.

The car bumped over a pot-hole and brought my awareness back to the driver.

'Is it as dangerous here as we're told on television?' I asked.

'That depends on where you go. Let me put it like this: don't walk the streets at night on your own.'

'Don't worry,' I said. 'I won't.'

Presently we arrived at the impressive Europa Hotel, where I was treated like visiting royalty.

'Let me carry your bags, Mr O'Brien.'

'I'll hold the door for you, sir.'

'If there's anything you need just ring and we'll send someone up immediately.'

'Please, don't fuss,' I said, 'I've just left a council flat with a huge pile of dirty dishes in the sink.'

Things lightened up after that: the 'Mr O'Briens' ceased, but the star treatment went on. In the end, my clean shirt and trousers were whisked away by an attractive chambermaid – I wasn't in them at the time – and were returned an hour later, spick-and-span with needle-sharp seams pressed into them. 'Can't have you looking like a rag-doll on *Kelly* tonight, can we?' she laughed.

'No,' I said, 'I suppose we can't.'

Everyone at the hotel was terribly posh: they'd all dressed for dinner, and I hoped I didn't look too much out of place, sporting my black jacket and trousers, white shirt and red tie. (The whole outfit cost no more than £25, bought or donated from friends and colleagues.)

But I must have passed muster, because the head-waiter who escorted me to a reserved table commented on 'how smart' Sir looked.

Dinner could have been a lavish affair but, being a vegan, I settled for an avocado salad. 'The chef will make it *specially* for you, sir.'

I felt embarrassed. 'Oh no, please don't put him to any trouble –'

'Nonsense! You shall have an avocado salad with sliced mangoes and passion fruits, fresh greens and a special dressing,' and out he flounced with a triumphant swish of his coat.

In one corner of the restaurant a pianist and a small ensemble were ensconced near plush green palms, and during my meal I was asked if I had any special requests.

'Why yes,' I said, 'do they know *Memory* from the musical *Cats*?'

'Indeed. I am certain they *do*, sir,' and off he went again, in a flurry of crumbs as he whisked away the bread-basket. *Memory* was played while I ate like a king, but I felt pangs of guilt as the sumptuous food was served and I was plied with more delicacies from the sweet trolley. Such extravagance always makes me think of the millions of starving children around the world; and when I saw the bill my heart sank at the amount. It seemed odd not having to pay.

'Courtesy of Ulster Television,' the smiling waiter said; but he must have seen the look on my face.

'Don't worry, sir, they will settle *everything*.'

I skulked out of the restaurant, and trotted off to

freshen-up for my television appearance.

When I reached the studios in another hired car most of the *Kelly* guests had already arrived.

I was ushered past a lively queuing audience into a green-room to share some orange juice with the unusually-named Australian actor, Yahoo Serious (!) there to promote his hit movie *Young Einstein*. He was thoroughly fascinated by my work.

'You're amazing, Stephen!' he said. 'Enough to blow my mind!' But by the look of his mop of wild red hair, something else had already done that.

I also chatted with the British actor Gorden Kaye, best-known for playing 'René', an amorous French wartime cafe-owner in the BBC TV comedy series '*Allo 'Allo*. Gorden was pleasant and witty, and he held a firm belief in 'things unexplained'. When he spoke, I half-expected to hear that famous mock-French accent, but instead his voice was quite cultured:

'I was once given such a devastatingly-accurate prediction by a clairvoyant, Stephen, that it quite unnerved me,' he said.

He and another guest, the actress Madge Hindle, were charming people. For many years Madge had played 'Rene Roberts' in Britain's longest-running soap opera, Granada TV's *Coronation Street*. On the *Kelly* set she revealed that she'd been brought up in a Spiritualist home. The audience gawped. 'I bet that surprised you all, didn't it?' she said.

And, of course, it had.

In the make-up room, Gerry Kelly, the show's cheery host, asked me why a Welshman was named 'O'Brien'.

'My great-grandmother was Elizabeth O'Brien, and in the late 1800s she came across from County Wexford in Southern Ireland and took a job as a domestic in Swansea, South Wales.

'She was penniless, but fell madly in love with a publican called Billy-the-Boy, and she birthed an illegitimate child: my grandfather, William. But she gave him to the people she lodged with, Ned and Liza Quirk, because she was dying of TB. Her only possession in the world was a small writing-bureau which she'd brought over to Wales, and she gave it to the couple who raised her baby.'

Gerry wanted to know, 'What happened to her?'

'Elizabeth died in Swansea's Union Workhouse, at twenty-six, and was buried in an unmarked pauper's grave. But I found Ned and Liza's resting-place and planted forget-me-nots on it, to say "thank you" for taking care of my grandad. But when I visited the grave again, the flowers hadn't bloomed.'

Gerry said sympathetically, 'It's a pity we don't have time for that on-air,' then he rose and dusted some make-up powder off his jacket. 'Well, we'd better make our way.'

Down on the studio floor a technician wired me for sound and neatly tucked a radio-pack into my jacket pocket: the wires and aerial were stuffed down my shirt-front into my trousers, but I felt rather silly, for after all that fuss I wanted to visit the bathroom. They shuffled me towards the right the corridor.

'Oh, but wait a minute,' I said, 'I'm wired for sound. You'll hear everything. Can you switch me off, please?'

'Sorry, but you're plugged in now, Stephen,' smiled

the cheery technician. 'Don't worry, we've heard it all before!'

So off I skulked, wondering how to disconnect my microphone. Pull out the trailing wire aerial, I thought: that should do it. But as I bent forward in the cubicle the whole radio-pack lurched out of my pocket and I made a slippery grab at it but missed – and the electronics crashed to the floor with a resounding *bang*! I did feel stupid, and prayed no one in the control room had heard what I'd said. But at least the microphone was silenced, and I appreciated the privacy.

Later, I returned to the technician, shame-faced, proffering the ruins like Oliver holding out his begging bowl, asking for more.

I was given a new pack only seconds before Gerry startled me by announcing, 'Ladies and gentlemen, would you please welcome the UK's top mystical figure, Stephen O'Brien.' And they did.

After a bright and lengthy interview about life after death, during which I answered a live telephone caller, Gerry asked me, 'Is there anything fraudulent about what you do?'

'No,' I replied, 'nothing.'

'Well Stephen, you'll have a chance to prove yourself with our studio audience.' Then he warned them, 'Now you all know what Stephen's going to do; so if there's anyone who wants to leave, please go now.'

Not a soul moved.

What on Earth did they think would happen?

My mediumship is a natural ability which had never frightened anyone before; but Ireland is such a deeply orthodox country that I understood why he delivered the caution.

Immediately on cue, I began to tune-in, pressing my hand to my forehead, deep in concentration:

'Please claim the connection if you understand it,' I said to he crowd, 'or the whole link vanishes.'

The people were fraught with tension.

Then I felt a presence and heard a faint voice. 'Step forward, son,' I said to the apprehensive spirit lad trying to make contact.

'I have a young man here, he's about sixteen or seventeen, and he passed over very quickly and tragically to the spirit world. I feel he was thrown: catapulted over a bike.'

A nervous young lady in the front row raised her hand, her eyes were wide with astonishment.

The audience sat in absolute silence: they hadn't a clue what to expect next; but I felt sure the young woman was the correct recipient, so I continued with: 'Someone's been lighting candles for him, and praying for him in a Catholic Church.'

'Yes.'

'And I get the name of Tom,' I said.

The woman's eyebrows raised in surprise, and her face lit up as she glanced at her friend sitting next to her.

By now the feisty spirit lad was excited and eager to talk. As well as conveying his love to his family, he mentioned he had a link to somewhere called 'Anderson's Town', and that his mother should be told he was still alive, and that she wasn't to cry for him anymore.

Privately he expressed his gratitude, but publicly

he sent so much love to his relatives that my heart went out to them, and to the woman who was startled by his link, yet overjoyed to accept it.

And while he spoke he kept impressing me with the strange sensation of being 'catapulted' into the Beyond, as if he'd been 'thrown' over the handle-bars of his bike.

I then received a few details the woman couldn't immediately place, so I advised her to question his family about them.

The whole connection was quite difficult to main-tain, not only because of the tension in the studio but also because of the boy's emotions.

Nevertheless, I thought he'd been successful; and he seemed pleased, even though his recipient was crying.

The audience applauded as I left the set, and Gerry Kelly approached the girl and asked, 'Have you ever met that guy, ever before in your life?'

'No,' she said, nervously.

'And was all that he said true?'

'Yes.'

Someone nearby gave a little gasp.

It turned out that my communicator was none other than her young brother who'd been killed seven years previously: he'd been blown up while on his motorbike. Thoughtful Gerry presented a large bouquet of flowers to the attractive woman, who'd been moved, and more than a little shaken, by the link.

Audiences at my meetings know exactly what to expect, but when this lady attended the *Kelly* show, she hadn't a clue she would receive a message from another world; so her reaction was quite understandable.

In the green-room afterwards, people clustered around me, firing questions and showing deep interest in what I'd done.

At the end of the evening when I said goodbye to Gorden Kaye, all at once I had an overwhelming psychic feeling of impending danger – a powerful 'impact' of 'something' came crashing down onto me. I didn't want to worry the actor so I simply said:

'Drive safely, Gorden. Mind how you go, won't you?'

(Months later, he suffered a freak accident in London while driving his car: abnormally-high winds ripped away billboards and sent splintered wood smashing through the windscreen, and into his head. He was rushed to Intensive Care and placed on the critical list; but many people prayed for him and he recovered.)

As I left the Ulster Television studios, a flustered receptionist jokingly shook his fist at me:

'I've been on this damn phone for the last forty minutes because of you!' he said. 'The switchboard's been jammed with calls from all over Ireland. You'd better give your tour dates to the researchers.' And with that, another set of flashing lights hurled him into activity as I slipped out into the cold night, smiling.

Next morning in the hotel restaurant, a stunning young waitress, who'd recognised me, conducted several delightful conversations. She was quite amusing: she kept passing my table, clearing things away, then disappearing into the kitchens; then popping back to sweep up invisible crumbs from the floor, whispering things like, 'So they *do* have bodies Over There then, and memories too?'

She was delighted that they did.

But I soon discovered a more serious side to her nature: her sixteen-year-old boyfriend had been shot and killed in a sectarian murder, and she desperately needed to know if he'd survived his horrific death.

'Of course he has,' I assured her, 'it doesn't matter how we pass over, there's life for everyone beyond this world. 'Neither does it matter what religion we hold, because we all belong to God.'

She was pleased, and deeply thankful that the 'Father in Heaven', in whom she fervently believed, shows kindness and mercy to all of His Children, irrespective of their creed.

'I'd kiss you if I could,' she grinned, pretending to clatter some plates about, 'but I'm on duty.' So we passed that by, and instead both laughed at that morning's *Irish News*, which had featured both me and the film star Julie Andrews.

'Oow, look!' she chuckled, 'they've given you a much larger photograph and more coverage! But if you don't mind my saying so, that mug-shot doesn't do you justice – you're much nicer-looking in the flesh!' Then against all the rules she pecked my cheek and even threw me a regal wave as I left in my taxi.

At the airport I was spotted by other passengers who stared at me as if I'd just stepped out of a UFO.

Silently, I crept away to collect my overnight bag. However, the embarrassing red-carpet treatment continued at the Customs desk.

'Oh, *you* can pass along with no bother, sir,' said the beaming official, without so much as inspecting my cases. 'Saw you on *Kelly* last night – great show!'

He smiled and tipped his hat as I passed through the barriers, wishing I were invisible, while other travellers swivelled on their heels for a final open-mouthed gawp.

Into the jet I went, humming the tune of *Danny Boy* to myself, and for most of the sunny flight back home I relived the last two days.

The televised link had certainly stirred the media in Ireland, and telephone lines around the country had buzzed with discussions and debates about the existence of an eternal life.

Because of one simple spirit message, a family's grief was helped to heal, a nation's thoughts were provoked, and inquisitive people now questioned more closely their religious beliefs.

(Indeed, the week after my appearance I learned that the *Kelly* show invited my recipient back on to discuss her experience, and Ireland buzzed again because she confirmed more of the details her deceased brother had relayed. Hundreds of viewers then wrote to me through my publisher's office, eager to know more about the afterworld.)

I answered all the letters and hoped that my comments pointed the many enquirers into a more spiritual direction.

But for me, the most important part of the trip occurred on the morning I left, when I plucked a single pink rose and knelt on Irish soil.

The sun was misty and the earth was damp.

I looked into the quiet sky and pondered on the thought that the majority of Irish people are good and kind, and that they carry with them the hope of better times for tomorrow's Irish children.

Planting the flower in the green grass, I closed my eyes and whispered within my mind:

> *Great Spirit, hear my prayer.*
> *As this perfect flower dies,*
> *So may its beauty touch the Earth;*
> *And in the touching,*
> *May Peace be born,*
> *And then flourish,*
> *Within this troubled land.*

# 6

# Marilyn Monroe,
# Sir Laurence Olivier,
# and Earl Mountbatten

Four friends and I gathered in the dark room for a
special séance the Other Side had asked us to hold.

Quite by chance (?) one of my usual psychic circle
had suddenly announced over his Sunday lunch, 'I
feel inspired that we should sit for the spirit people
tonight.'

Everyone agreed and we arranged for the séance
to be taped, each of us feeling that some hidden
reason for the request might be revealed.

And so the plan was set.

But at eight o'clock when I entered the dimly-lit
room, instead of feeling excited I felt rather sleepy.
My spirit guide was near; so I allowed his warm
relaxation to overtake me and free my mind, and I
lost touch with my surroundings; then White Owl's
strong voice, much deeper than my own, spoke
among us:

## *White Owl:*

Be still, and we can come near. Our world is very close to yours: it interpenetrates the Earth.

We know your thoughts and aspirations, and your innermost desires.

We bring you greetings from a world of eternal light that is blending with your lives, and is intricately woven into the very fabric of your being.

We bring good news for your world: where two or three are gathered in the name of Love, there shall we be in the midst. Through this power of your love we manifest in your plane of thought. Our untiring concern for the people of Earth brings us close to its grey, dark, and often selfish sphere of life.

*Long pause.*

There will be great tribulation, great trials and also bloodshed in the years to come – in the East of your world, as people strive for freedom of expression. We are watching with interest.

Every birth comes through the pains of labour.

*Pause.*

Man has polluted his planet so much: now he begins to pay the price with many flash-floods, hurricanes, and disturbing weather-patterns right across the Earth. He has poisoned and neglected the Great Mother. Her waters are polluted, her atmosphere is full of harmful rays and gases. She must be cleansed and respected by those who dwell upon her.

And until this time she will react adversely against man's foolishness, to his detriment.

*Long pause, as if gathering strength or power.*

Now we wish to bring forward from my side of life a man whose name is not unknown to you. He, like many millions of souls before him, has discovered what Jesus spoke of as 'The Kingdom of Heaven'. He is a man of deep sensitivity with great heart and unbounding kindness. He is a man used to the public gaze, and his message, we think, is of vital importance to mankind.

Please be patient while he endeavours to speak, for what will happen is that *my* mind and *his* mind, and *my medium's* mind, these three will blend in order to transmit. He will not be able to reproduce his voice exactly as it was known when among you, but his thoughts will be expressed clearly.

*White Owl now addresses the writers present:*

You may rest your hands and switch off the tape-machine until his blending is complete, at which time we can start again.

*After a long pause a faint voice speaks.*
*It is Sir Laurence Olivier, who died near London on 11ᵗʰ July 1989:*

...Very hard... very hard... to... difficult, difficult to speak... clearly... very hard...

I was glad to die; not that I didn't love my people, because I did.

*The voice continues slowly, haltingly, right the way through.*

I'm not... I'm not inside this body... I'm close by it, trying to use it like a typewriter – it's very hard work. I never thought I'd do it, but I've done it... I never thought I'd speak, but I'm speaking. You'll never guess who I am.

I want my wife to know that I've survived.

I made a promise once to her that if life continued beyond the cold grave, I'd be back to say so; *and I'm back*. My wife is Joan...

*Pause.*

(*In jocular mood*)... 'A horse, a horse; a kingdom for a horse.' (sic)

My speech is difficult...

I was a grand old man...

I can't blend my mind sufficiently to hold the communication, but if I could just say: of all the roles I played, of all the parts I undertook, this is the greatest role of all. When I died I made the most spectacular entrance of my whole career. I entered an eternal world and fell into the arms of my former wife, my dear, dear Vivien.

She's beautiful; she's taking care of me. And I want Joan to know that I will meet her when God calls her name to join me here. I want Joan to know I'm near, and I love her very much. I'm not dead, I'm alive; and I'm finished with make-believe, and I've just begun to live.

Vivien is taking care of me. She's so kind. She didn't mean to die, it wasn't suicide – it was a mistake.

Tell Joan – Joan Plowright, my darling wife – there's nothing to fear: there's light, not darkness. She'll understand.

I slipped away so quietly. I'm so happy where I am. My love to the children...

Don't move away. Tell her not to move away. How we would sit on the lawns and watch the sun go down! I know now that Vivien sat with us...

Oh, and tell her not to worry about the finances, it'll be all right; it'll be cleared soon. She means more to me than anyone else alive.

I've been very busy speaking...

*His voice trails away, almost to an inaudible whisper:*

Farewell...(?)

*A long pause followed, then White Owl's voice spoke again.*

**White Owl:**

I'm afraid he cannot hold his contact. He is crying for those he loves. He speaks of a reunion between many friends, many people on our Side of Life. There has been a great party.

He wants his friends to know his love is with them, and that he thanks them for the great honours and love they have bestowed upon him. There are no titles in our world, but he stands beside friends who were known in your world through their service to millions. Their names will be familiar to you. He has mentioned Vivien Leigh, he has spoken with Tyrone Power, he has met Marilyn Monroe.

He is saying that his wife, whom he dearly loves, is grieving still. She sorely misses his presence; she kisses his photograph by her bedside, and he wants her to know that her feelings and sensations of his presence are true.

'I want to pass through to you,' he says, 'the greatest news, the biggest Universal Contract I've ever signed, and the name of the picture is *Sir Laurence Lives*, not as a ghost but as a complete man.'

He says, 'My legs are strong, my body is young again, my wrinkles have forsaken me. My time is endless.

'There five major biographies accepted and in the writing now concerning me. Be kind to me. Tread softly, for you tread upon my dreams.'

Silence followed. The séance was over.

But Sir Laurence sent us all off to the Library to find out more about Vivien Leigh's passing. We discovered that she'd died of tuberculosis, but that there'd been some doubt about her intentions. One of her closest colleagues had said of her, 'She didn't try to get well.' Another report told of Vivien speaking through a medium and saying that she was very upset because she didn't want people to think she'd committed suicide.

But without doubt, many who were close to her reported that she'd consistently failed to take her medication, and that she'd continued 'smoking, drinking, and entertaining, instead of resting'.

It was all very intriguing, but unless Sir Laurence returns to explain himself further we may never know exactly what he meant.

An older circle member thought she remembered reading a gutter-press report about Vivien Leigh's 'suicide'. If that's correct then Sir Laurence's statements do make sense.

Not long after that message arrived, another startling link came from someone whom Sir Laurence had mentioned: the late screen goddess Marilyn Monroe. I assume that on the Other Side they must have talked about my work and that Marilyn then saw the chance to communicate her sensible but controversial thoughts to our world. However they planned it, it came as a complete surprise.

And yet, some friends told me afterwards that she and Sir Laurence had starred in a film called *The Prince and the Showgirl*, which was something I hadn't known.

Marilyn's presence drew near to me on a train, of all places. Her voice broke into my consciousness in an idle moment but I recognised it immediately: yet it sounded strangely metallic, as if it had been recorded on the crackling sound-track of an old movie, which – thinking back – makes complete sense now. But she displayed a radiant spiritual quality in her words and feelings.

I scrabbled in my pockets for a pen, then wrote down exactly what I heard.

Marilyn – or should I call her 'Norma Jean', for that's how she referred to herself during the link (her real name was Norma Jean Baker) – delivered some tough, uncompromising criticism to everyone who is currently making money out of her celebrity status. She was, and still is, very conscious of the publicity generated by her exquisite features, form, and timeless sensual presence, all of which appear on multifarious items world-wide: printed on tee-shirts, record sleeves, billboards, and millions of posters and picture postcards.

Marilyn, who was only thirty-six when she died, was very unhappy about the way she's been treated since her 'mysterious' death in Los Angeles on 5th August 1962, officially from 'an overdose of barbiturates'. But the screen idol has different ideas about her passing.

**Marilyn Monroe:**

This is Norma Jean – Marilyn – here. It's been such a long time since I had the chance to send a message to Earth. I guess people still remember me so much. I keep getting many thoughts and, well, almost star-worship wishes from people down there I never even met.

I suppose you're wondering why I'm getting in touch? Well, I've got something to say. I want to set a few things straight about me and my life. So many people and writers paint me as tragic. Well I wasn't. How can they know these things? The answer is, they can't. They know what makes a good story though, and far too many of them used me for that.

So many lies have been told about me... so many. Well I'm gonna tell a few truths now. First, I was a happy person – a little lonely on times, perhaps, but then how else can a person feel when everybody in the world wants a little piece of them? I never had a moment's peace from the media. They hounded me to death. Oh, and that's another sore point – my death.

It's been kinda veiled in mystery for a few years, hasn't it?

*She chuckles.*

Well, I don't much care now about it. It's gone; and it's the best thing that ever happened to me. This place is so much better than life was in America. But I wish people would stop saying I committed suicide, 'cos I did no such thing. I didn't take my own life, and that's all I'm prepared to say – nothing more. That's all over now.

Second, I'm kinda glad, very happy that my pictures still give people a great deal of pleasure. That's why I did them. I really tried hard to be a good actress – a darned good one; not just another name and another glamorous face flickering on the silver screen. And, if it's OK for me to say it, I think I made my point. *The Misfits* and *Bus-Stop* were my two greatest roles, and they give me a sense of deep pride and accomplishment when I think of them now.

There's something I want to ask of you. I want to say something to the media. I want my memory to generate money for children – kids down the block with no shoes on their feet, and others in the hot countries who don't have any hope, any food, or any love from anyone.

It kinda grieves me that a lotta money is made out of my face and name, and, though some of it does go to good causes, not all of it does – and I want it to. I know what it is to be unloved, without anyone to care for you; and if any money's being made, then it should go where I want it to. After all, it's my face, my figure, and my pictures that get the stuff in.

I wanted to say that. Tell everyone you can, and get it done. Can you do that for me?

*Mentally, I said 'Yes.'*

Good for us.

Oh, and there's just one more thing I'd like to say. I've found out a good deal since I came over here, and the best message I can give to everyone there on Earth is this: be kind to each other. There isn't enough of that about. Be kind, and look after the hungry, the poor, the needy, the lonely and the grieving.

My life here is just great. I'm having a wonderful time, but I won't be far away from you, Stephen. I'll come and talk with you again.

Hold a good thought for me.

Marilyn blew two kisses, and she left.

I've fulfilled my promise to Marilyn by publishing her words in this book, and by sending the message to her American Management Agency, who didn't offer the courtesy of a reply.

Her comments about knowing what it feels like to be unloved and uncared-for intrigued me, but research revealed that her mother had suffered from mental illness, and that Norma Jean had been raised in a series of orphanages and foster homes.

I remember another controversial message that came through to me, but this time from Earl Mountbatten of Burma, and it was meant for Prince Philip.

Lord Louis was assassinated in a terrorist bomb attack on his boat while holidaying in Donegal Bay, off Mullaghmore, in County Sligo, Ireland, on 27th August 1979.

Mountbatten communicated before the funeral of

Emperor Hirohito of Japan, who died in Tokyo on 7th January 1989. Prince Philip was to represent Britain at his funeral – but Mountbatten tried to persuade him to stay away.

In the Second World War many servicemen were cruelly tortured or killed by the Japanese during captivity, and most survivors held the Emperor directly responsible for their suffering. They could neither forgive nor forget his 'war crimes and atrocities'. From the world of spirit Mountbatten shared these intense feelings, and he wanted his views known.

As with all the messages that I've received from renowned personalities, I'm ever loath to publish; but in this case I think the thousands of disgruntled British servicemen have a right to hear Mountbatten's thoughts.

In his communication, Lord Louis indicates that he tried to send messages to Prince Charles, to warn the British Monarchy about the implications of royal representation.

His statements contain unquestionable evidence that he was indeed closely in touch with the grass-root feelings of former British soldiers, most of whom were then senior citizens, because in protest against Prince Philip's intended presence at the funeral, hundreds of war veterans marched in the streets all over the land.

One pensioner made headlines by undertaking a hunger-strike to the death – an action which drew a personal plea from Her Majesty Queen Elizabeth II asking him to end his protest.

He complied, but grudgingly.

As instructed, I sent the Earl's communication to Buckingham Palace in London.

*Earl Mountbatten:*

My dear Philip,

As the family is aware, I am still conscious of the dealings and daily business of 'the business', and feel duty-bound to use any means at my disposal to reach you presently with my thoughts on a matter of international importance. I know your mind well, and it is strong and self-governed as mine is, but on this issue I cannot remain silent and have taken this opportunity to once again make my thoughts heard.

On the grave issue of the funeral of the Emperor Hirohito, I must say that I can fully appreciate the concern in the family as to its status in the public mind, yet I have tried my very best to communicate to Charles that for one of our family to attend this man's funeral would not be in the interests of the monarchy.

While it is good and right and proper for us to be represented, I feel honour-bound to state – after much soul-searching – that I would not have gone, and would have preferred some lesser official to take my place.

International relations are, of course, of vital importance to the nation and its image, but I would have had before me all the horrific faces of the tortured and maimed that were given a dreadful termination to their earthly lives under this man's iron rule.

My love for you all is evident in my almost daily presence around you, but forgive me for my outspokenness on this issue; yet, do please, I beg you, think once more.

It is never too late to send a substitute. I always maintained that, and still do now.

I have been anxious to communicate many things to you all but have resisted the urge many times, believing that I should firmly stay in my place, in my world, but having suffered through the hands of terrorists myself I cannot condone the support of similar acts.

I cannot write too personally here, because it is my full intention, without any malice aforethought, to make known my plea; for the sake of those who died; for the sake of the grieving families hurt by any British Representation at Hirohito's last journey; for the sake of standing up for one's viewpoint so that one's honour can be maintained, even from my world.

I have indeed spoken with Hirohito himself, and he still will not renounce his cruelty, believing – as he always did – that it was done to preserve a great and noble family-line's status. Perhaps his viewpoint will change, Philip. Time alters one's mind so frequently, don't you agree?

I will end by thanking the man through whom I am able to communicate, and sending my dearest love and fondest best wishes to everyone 'at home'.

Your friend and adviser,
*Louis.*


However, Prince Philip did attend the funeral, but I think the public and the media agreed with Earl Mountbatten that he might have acted more wisely if he'd stayed away, for the rumblings amongst old soldiers continued for months afterwards. One ex-prisoner of war said in the press: 'I don't think we'll ever forgive him.'

Incidentally, a journalist, who expressed great interest in the style and delivery of Earl Mountbatten's message, later raised an interesting point concerning this link. The reporter believed the message to be genuine, but pointed out that in his letter Lord Louis had committed a grammatical error by 'splitting an infinitive'. When using the verb *to make,* he had 'split' it by placing words between its two parts.

Mountbatten had declared: 'I... have taken this opportunity *to once again make* my thoughts heard', when he ought to have said, 'I... have taken this opportunity *to make* my thoughts heard *once again.*'

An interesting point, but not a very scientific one in these times when good English seems more and more to coalesce into a colloquial form.

Since the 1960s, millions of people have been 'splitting' their infinitives after hearing the famed Captain James T. Kirk of the *Star Trek* television starship *Enterprise* announce to the world that he was '*to boldly go* where no man has gone before', instead of telling us that he was '*to go boldly* where no man has gone before.'

I think we can allow Lord Louis his freedom of expression.

Feature articles about my mediumship have been published in different languages in countries around the world, and media attention brought so many interviews that I can barely recall them all. But the one I gave to Britain's popular tabloid newspaper, the *Daily Star*, sticks in my mind.

After completing two days filming in London for television programmes in a paranormal series, I was invited to attend the station's private screenings, given to the press.

Ever ill-at-ease amongst the media, I gritted my teeth and attended out of courtesy.

After sitting through the shows, groaning, (it's terrible to watch yourself on TV) I met a charming *Daily Star* reporter called Liz Phillips. Petite and attractive, with a sparkly personality, dark-haired Liz viewed the programmes with interest and afterwards invited me to lunch in a French restaurant near the studios.

She was inquisitive, and scribbled away furiously in her notebook while guzzling down oysters. Two hours later, we shook hands and parted company on a windswept London road. 'I'll telephone you in Wales,' she smiled.

Her call soon arrived.

'Stephen, the editor's giving you a double-page spread with photographs, but can I attend one of your psychic circles?'

'But I haven't done them for ages, Liz. I'm forever busy touring, these days.'

'Well, could you find the time for us?'

Grudgingly, I surrendered. 'All right,' I said, then telephoned a friend, Clare, who ran a happy guesthouse. 'I'm on the beg again, Clare,' I confessed, and she kindly agreed to hold the circle in her spacious lounge. 'I'm not bothered how you assemble the group,' I said. 'In fact, the less I know about it, the better.'

'Leave everything to me, Stephen.' And I did – which was just as well because on the day of the meeting a *Star* photographer, who'd travelled from London to take pictures for the feature, kept me quite busy.

We met at Swansea's Grand Theatre, which he hired on the spot. But then came the worst part. 'I want a smoke-machine,' he ordered, as if he were asking for a bag of sweets, 'and the full use of the stage and auditorium. Send the bill to London.'

The administrator obliged, but made him promise not to mention the theatre, 'Or we'll be inundated with calls asking about Stephen's next appearance.'

Within minutes, he asked me to emerge out of smoky grey clouds, with my hands raised as if I'd just stepped out of a UFO. And, naïve fool that I was, I did it.

But never again.

After all that trouble and expense this picture wasn't published, thank God. But he was used to that. 'Oh, that's nothing,' he said after the shoot, 'last year I spent three days in a village called Christmas, hired half the population in fancy-dress costumes, and did shots of the entire *Twelve Days of Christmas*– even down to the lords-a-leaping and the maids-a-milking. We really went over the top. In the end it cost us £2,000 but we never used a frame of it – come to that, we didn't even run the story.'

Needless to say, this did nothing to alleviate my misgivings about the media and its methods.

Circle day arrived and I met Liz, the reporter, at the railway station. With her she'd brought from London a smiling mystery guest called Rose, a vivacious blonde woman with a vibrant personality.

When we arrived at Clare's guesthouse, we met the six circle members and the séance got underway.

It was successful from the start and the first link came from a crotchety old woman to a sitter called Susan.

'Yes, I looked after her,' she said.

'Well, she thanks you for your patience because she wasn't the easiest of people.'

'You're absolutely right!'

Then the old spirit lady pointed across to another woman, Carol, sitting at the opposite end of the room.

'She knows you, too,' I said, 'and asks if you can remember when the oven exploded?'

Recognition was instantaneous. 'Oh my Gawd! Yes I do!' laughed Carol in her thick Lancashire accent. 'That woman was cared for by Susan, then I took over. So you see, she *does* know the two of us. And one night the stove overheated and caught fire!' Everyone laughed. 'And you're quite right: she were a right old misery sometimes!' chuckled Carol wryly. 'But we all loved her for it.'

'Well, she's remembering you with smiles.'

And then I got a link for Rose, the attractive mystery guest from London. Her grandmother, who said she 'knew her when she was tiny', spoke about 'a special shawl' she used to wear, and I described its pattern. Rose nodded in acceptance.

Her grandma then delivered a warning about legal documents. 'You're about to sign a partnership agreement,' she told her, 'which makes you and a gentleman liable for each other's debts in Law, if the new business venture fails.'

Rose's mouth dropped open. 'Yes,' she replied, her eyes widening in perfect understanding; then she craned her neck forward, eager for more news.

'Well your grandmother's giving you some advice: "Think twice! It's a big step, and he might not be the right man for the deal," she says.'

Rose was visibly impressed.

Liz scribbled everything down, while I continued:

'I can say two things about your grandmother's passing: it was sudden and peaceful.'

The young stranger wholeheartedly agreed.

'That's spot on! She died of a heart-attack in her sleep.'

I added, 'she says Tom met her, and they walked off together into the light.'

'That's my grandfather!' said Rose, touched by the news.

Liz pronounced the whole séance as 'remarkable' and 'amazing', and within a few days millions of *Star* readers saw in their newspapers (if I might say so) an enchanting a picture of my eyes, with the caption written underneath them: *These Eyes Can See Beyond the Grave.*

There was also a two-page centre-spread feature with pictures, which had been headlined *The Star puts Britain's Brightest Young Medium to the Test:*

Clairvoyant Stephen O'Brien is the man who has taken the crown from queen of the psychics, the late Doris Stokes.

Stephen is different from most people you are ever likely to meet.

Power seems to radiate from his fingertips.

And when he speaks in his soft Welsh accent his followers hang on his every word.

I saw an amazing example of his ability when I went along to a quiet terrace house in his home town of Swansea.

It was the most ordinary of settings, but it was one of the most extraordinary afternoons I have ever spent. The atmosphere was one of a cosy tea-party until Stephen closed his eyes and muttered, almost to himself, 'Let's see what's here. I'll take what comes.'

An elderly woman appeared to him, who he felt was Rose's grandmother. He passed on messages about sorting out her jewellery-box and that she must sort out her life too.

Stephen mentioned a legal agreement Rose was due to sign, and pinpointed the cause and manner of her granny's death. He accurately described her clothes and appearance.

'Everything you said was spot-on,' Rose told him when he finished.

Thousands of people pack out halls to hear him speak, many others travel hundreds of miles to visit him and he receives sacks of mail every week from strangers begging him to help them...

This article drew a tremendous response from the public: letters poured in from all parts of Britain and from the continent too; and they kept on arriving for four months afterwards. People wrote from places like South Africa saying, 'I've been sent this cutting from the *Star*. Can you help me?'

On the day it was published I was invited to Sky Television in London to do an eight-minute live chat on a show called *The Frank Bough Interview* – but the producers hadn't realised I lived in Wales and that I couldn't possibly get there in time.

Frankly, (no pun intended) I was quite relieved. All I wanted to do was to relax and take things easy.

But as my old grandmother used to say: 'There's no peace for the wicked.'

# 7

# 'Dear Stephen...'

As my public profile heightens day by day, my postbag increases. Each week sacks of letters arrive and I answer them all personally. They make such fascinating reading that I thought I'd share a few of them with you.

To start, here's an edited selection of some cheery tonic letters that brightened up my day; and some of these correspondents reveal just what it meant to them to receive evidence of their loved ones' survival.

Dear Stephen,

I must write to relay my gratitude for the message I received from you at Seaham Harbour (England). You began by asking for someone in the back row who could recall the names 'Mr and Mrs Williams', but it didn't click.

No one took this, and you said, 'I'll try for more information to pinpoint the recipient later on.'

You then gave several messages to various people, all accepted; some through tears of relief, others with happiness.

You showed such compassion in your attitude, and a great understanding of, and a natural rapport with, the people.

Then suddenly you said, 'Mr and Mrs Williams are back again and they're insisting the message is for the lady right at the back of the hall. They've brought Ethel with them.' I raised my hand, and you told me, 'Ethel worked with you many years ago in a fish-and-chip shop.' This was very true, but what startled me more was when you said, 'Ethel tells me Mr and Mrs Williams were your employers – they owned the shop.'

I then remembered them, and was astonished.

Ethel advised that I needed medical attention – true, for I had suffered sleepless nights and was physically run-down. You even mentioned the exact names of several streets all around the place where my mother and father used to live.

Then you explained, 'A lady called "Mers" is contacting you. This is her nickname.' 'Mers' was my father's nickname for my beloved mother who'd passed away twenty years earlier. I was so thrilled, I had to write.

Travelling home that night I felt much happier knowing that my family were watching over me and knew my needs. I slept a lot easier too, better than I'd done for months.

Thank you once again, Stephen, for the caring and compassion you showed everyone on that evening. I do wish you every success for your future in this work, and good health – so you can continue with your calling.

Yours truly,
Mrs B., Tyne and Wear.

Dear Stephen,

I must tell you how wonderful your book *Visions of Another World* is. I bought it when I came to see you in Bristol.

It took me ages to read it, the main reason being you wrote each chapter with so much emotion that I was crying near enough continuously all the way through.

I must say that your poem *The Voiceless Ones* was written in such a way that on the same day I read it I became a vegetarian and I haven't touched anything from animals since. Every time I read that poem I cry too!

I must add I don't often cry at all. It takes a lot to even produce one tear, let alone bucketfuls. Bristol was the first time I'd ever attended a Spiritualist gathering. You were truly amazing and I am proud to have seen you 'in action'. I can't wait to see you again, nor can my family and friends.

I have also seen you on TV, and you defended mediumship well.

Please take care and be happy,

Love,

A. R., Bristol.


P.S. Have enclosed a stamped addressed envelope to save you both money and time.


Dear Secretary,

*Psychic News* in London printed what could have been a very nice photo of Stephen in their May Issue, but it was all black and dark in my copy.

Hopefully you'll send me that photo of Stephen as I am a grandmother, and find I feel so peaceful and comforted whenever I see his picture in my *Psychic*

*News*. I would dearly love a proper photo; I'd love it to be signed by him, too, but I don't want to be a worry.

I've enclosed 40 pence for same if possible.

Yours sincerely,

Mrs L. F., Berkshire.

Dear Mr O'Brien,

My wife died of cancer at 62 and I felt so dreadful I must admit I didn't want to carry on living. I lost everything; we'd been married for 43 years and were very devoted to each other. When she died I felt so devastated, that's why I decided to come to your meeting, hoping to get some proof that she survived death somewhere.

I'll never forget the moment you brought a message from her – the proof you gave was so wonderful, I was elated. You told me things from my wife that only we two knew of; plus my daughter, you said, was with her. My wife had miscarried years before, and you reported that the little one had grown up in the spirit world. And when you said they were both so happy together, it made me feel overjoyed, and impressed – for I'd never even met you.

I am now totally convinced of their survival, and I know that when my time comes, my wife, my child and I will live in eternity, which means everything to me.

Now, when I look upon death, I have no fear at all. The message changed my life.

Your meeting was excellent, Stephen, and you struck me as a very likeable person.

I wish more people could have the help that I've been privileged to receive, and I just can't ever

thank you enough for everything.
Yours faithfully,
Mr R. P., Brecon.

Dear Mr O'Brien,
I have read and re-read your book *Visions of Another World*, and I know that I will continue to read it for many more times. It has given me so much hope, confirmation, so many things.

Perhaps you could let me have a list of your public meetings?

Once again, thank you for sharing your feelings and beliefs, and please write another book before too long.
Yours sincerely,
Mrs I. C., Leeds.

Dear Stephen,
I just had to write to you to tell you how much I enjoyed your book. I've never written to an author before, praising them, but I had to.

Your book had me laughing in places and also wiping my eyes.

Enclosed are some poems for you, in the hope of helping you whenever you're down.

## Tomorrow is Another Day

Today tears may have been shed
The pain so deep
While hearts have bled

Today everything may not have gone as planned
Not milk and honey
But instead a place of mud and sand

Today you may feel the darkness will never end
It isn't easy
Being alone without a friend

Today the hill may well have been steep
Knees scraped badly
But don't sit and weep

After dusk there is tomorrow
No more storms
Only a beautiful rainbow

Jan Castle, Hetton-le-Hole, England.

Dear Stephen,

I'm writing to say the message I received from you at your meeting last night was brilliant. I was totally amazed.

I should have been going on holiday that day, but strongly felt the urge to cancel and, instead, go along to see you. When I arrived, the hall was packed with hundreds of people, but I was just happy and contented to sit and listen, yet was astounded when you said out loud, 'Someone has postponed a holiday date to come along to this meeting.'

Of course, the message was for me!

You told me how I'd sat quietly and decided to cancel, then brought me superb evidence from my darling daughter, who died as a baby, mentioning the final arrangements we made for her, even telling me 'she was buried in a special vault at the hospital, with all the other babies,' which was absolutely correct. You also gave me her correct name and a perfect description.

Then love came through from my grandad, after

you rightly said he'd committed suicide, suffering from cancer.

Grandad showed how close he was to us all by talking about 'car tyres needing attention'.

My son's car was stopped by the police *that very night*, but luckily they overlooked them!

It was all so remarkable, I really can't put into words what it meant to receive it. And it most certainly made my holiday the happiest ever! I can't believe how fortunate I was.

God Bless and take care,

Love,

Mrs C. J., Wales.

Now here are some letters containing fascinating spiritual experiences, chosen from sackloads of examples, which prove that we're all psychic. Each one of us has the ability to see, hear, and sense the people in the next world through the extrasensory powers of the mind.

The term 'Psychic' stems from the Greek word 'Psyche', which roughly means 'Soul'. Therefore, psychic powers are soul powers. We all have a soul, and we're all psychic to greater or lesser degrees.

The world of spirit is nearer than hands and feet.

Dear Stephen,

I was reading an article about you in the daily newspaper. I'm an unmarried mother with a little boy called S., aged six.

When he was four he had a terribly ulcerated mouth and he was really suffering, so I gave him a *Rinstead Pastille*, and he was sat there sucking it when suddenly he looked at a chair next to him (which was empty) and a puzzled look came over his face. And he said, 'What?' And then he took the pastille out of his mouth and said, 'Nana, children's not supposed to have them.' And my mother asked him, 'Who's told you that?' And he said, 'Andrew.'

And his Nana said, 'Well where's Andrew?'

And S. pointed to the empty chair.

When I asked the doctor if I should give him *Rinstead Pastilles*, he said, 'No.'

I'm a Roman Catholic and I'm reading your book and it's really interesting. If you write any more I will surely buy them.

Good luck and God Bless. Thank you for being so patient in reading my long long letter.

Yours sincerely,
Miss S. D., Lancashire.

Dear Stephen,

A few years back I had an abortion. It was my choice. I was four months pregnant at the time and the sex of my child is not known. Anyway, moving on, I sometimes see a little boy in my bed, aged about three, holding out his arms to me with a smile (one in a million), but as I try to get closer he seems to fade out like a light.

This child even brings me flowers. Could this be the little boy I aborted?

Please could you reply to my letter,

Yours in need,
T. L., London.

*Answer: Yes: your family in the spirit world brings your boy to visit you because you're his mother, and he loves you. Both stillborn and aborted children continue to develop and grow up to maturity on the Other Side. The next time he pays you visit, why not speak to him?*

Whenever you feel like sitting down and moaning about your life, perhaps you should read through a few of the following letters; then, like me, you'll realise just how fortunate you are.

We should count our blessings more often.

There are always people worse off than we are, as these heart-breaking stories prove.

Dear Mr O'Brien,

I would like to know if my husband's spirit is at rest. My daughter's boyfriend murdered him three years ago.

Not a day goes past that I don't think about it, worrying in case he's not at peace.

My husband was only 41, and the man who did the murder got just four years.

After 18 months he's free, and trying to come back into our lives again, for access to his two children.

I know my husband would be livid at the cheek of him, and frustrated that he can do nothing to prevent him. I would dearly like to know how he is.

Hoping to hear from you soon.

Have enclosed a stamped addressed envelope,

Mrs –

(full name and address supplied)

Dear Stephen,

I listened with interest to your broadcast on BBC radio today, and I must say, listening to you filled me with a sense of well-being.

I have a severely mentally-handicapped daughter, who is 34 years old. When her time comes, will she be normal in the next life? She was brain-damaged at birth, and is so very important to me.

Yours faithfully,

Mrs M. F., Liverpool.

*Answer: Yes: she'll be fine. When the physical body dies, the mind and spirit express themselves clearly through the spirit body, in which no handicap exists.*

Dear Stephen,

My 18 year-old brother X. got stabbed to death, just around the corner from where we live, as he stood talking to some friends.

My Mum and the rest of the family are terribly upset, as my brother was stabbed straight through the 5th and 6th ribs into the heart, and he died straightaway.

And now my Mum is blaming herself, and no matter what people say she still says it's her fault, and we're all scared in case we lose her as well.

I have told my Mum that X. will always be with us and that he's safe, but she won't listen. All she keeps thinking about is him dying in pain, without any of us being there with him.

Could you get in touch with our X. and tell him that we all miss and love him so very much, and reassure my Mum if he did or did not die in pain, as she's going through so much pain herself thinking about it.

All my thanks,

(name and address supplied)

*Answer: I gave this correspondent a confidential reply, which included my saying that of course her brother was now safe and well on the Other Side of life. We all inherit eternal life when our days on this planet are over.*

Dear Stephen,

I am 16 and still at school. I was reading about you and hoping you could contact my Dad, as he was killed in a car crash. But with me being only seven when I lost him, I can't remember much about him. I'm just getting over leukaemia, which I developed at ten. At first it was pretty rough, but I'm nearly through it now and I believe and hope that my Dad was with me all the way, just as Mam was.

Please tell my Dad I love him and not a day goes by without me thinking about him, tell him Mam also feels the same.

Ask him to say hello to Nana X. and Nana Y., and to my Grandad: tell him I miss him also.

It doesn't matter too much about those little messages, as I send up my prayers each night. But please just tell my Dad I love him and want to know how he is. *PLEASE*, if my Dad is contacted, please write back to me and tell me what he said.

God rest your soul, Dad. I'll love you always, and so will Mam.

    Love you, (Christian name)
    XX
    Thank you very much
    Stephen O'Brien.
    Yours faithfully,
    (name and address supplied)

*Answer: If you send your thoughts out to your loved-ones, they will certainly receive them: it's rather like sending them a letter, or a tape-recorded message.*

*You don't need to use a medium to tell your loved ones*

*how you feel: just talk to them.*

Dear Mr O'Brien,

Three years ago my boyfriend died in X. Prison, by hanging himself. The following Friday I had my baby girl. I still cry most nights. I can't understand why it happened. I'm now living with my mother, as I am uneasy staying by myself.

Even though my boyfriend's spirit is in Mum's house, she's talking about moving. I don't want to, I don't want to leave him.

Mum's seen him three times, in different clothes, and my sister has seen him once.

They say he looks as though he's still alive but with a shimmering glow around him. I've heard him calling my name. Could you please help me to understand?

(name and address supplied)
Northern England.

*Answer: your boyfriend will be with the people that he loves; the location of the house doesn't matter.*

*Whenever our spirit friends visit us they 'home-in' on our personalities, on the frequency of our minds, by using the power of thought. They'll find us no matter where we are.*

And Now For Something Completely Different!

Dear Mr O'Brien,

Over the years, various astrologers have forecast 'sums of money coming my way'; 'you will have a windfall' and so on! Had all this money arrived I'd have been worth Billions, and wouldn't have lived long enough to enjoy the spending-spree.

The result of these predictions: no windfalls, and all I did was pay out again and again.

The next forecasts were that I would get a well-deserved promotion and a large increase in salary; that was ten years ago! What happened? I was hit by a three-hundred-weight lawnmower, was laid up for six months *and* lost the job as a gardener!!

Another forecast was that I would win large sums at Bingo, and on the horses, none of which happened. Then I was told of 'a fabulous job offer' coming my way, this never happened *at all*. Finally, after a number of years of being unemployed, we had to sell the house we lived in, and get a council flat.

A great come-down, is it not? After all these forecasts, it seems something's bringing me bad luck, but I don't know what it is. That's about it then, and the best of luck in your work,

Yours sincerely,
Mr M. E., Oxford.


*Answer: well, that's life! I'm not a fortune-teller, but good luck!*


Dear Stephen,

I cannot possibly go on living, I'm at my wit's end.

You see, I've lost eight pieces of jewellery. Can you tell me where they are?

Sincerely,
Mrs X.
(name and address supplied)

P.S. I've also lost my husband, do you think he knows where they are?
(!)

(no date or introduction)

Reading your rubbish in the local paper you and your Doris (Stokes) are a load of old conns there is lots of your kind jumping on the bandwagon the only spirits you get intouch with are in bottles if you are what you say you are ask your spirits to tell you how to find this lost baby, and you and your Doris tell us who will win the Derby and FA Cup also tell us what you charge you must be laughing all the way to the bank, like your Mystic Meg and TAROT, my mother was conned for £40 by one of your sort, you look a couple of conns I shall look for a reply in the paper, by the way the one who conned my mother what used the same paper as you told my mother that my farther and her would have long and happy life three week my farther was killed, both OAPs and easy minded people fall for your patter, stars and spirits are lot of rubbish all this rubbish you wrote you have only you to believe any body can write that, you asked your spirits to give me the Derby winner and I will give you half

Mrs S., Norwich.

*Answer: I was unable to reply because no address was supplied, which is a pity because I wanted to help this lady.*

*(If you wish to write to Stephen O'Brien, please be thoughtful enough to enclose a stamped self-addressed envelope with your letter, without which he regrets he cannot reply.*

*Stephen also welcomes stamps and other donations,*

which help him to answer his many correspondents around the world.

Because he receives vast quantities of mail, please keep your letter brief and to the point, and be patient when waiting for your reply. Thank you.

For a contact address: please see page 384.)

# 8

# Bouquets and Brickbats

*'Fame ain't easy'*
*Stephen O'Brien*

Fame, of course, is a two-edged sword that not only 'knights' but also 'cuts'. I'm not at all flattered by the attention I've received, and don't cope well with being in the limelight. I'd often like to fade away from public gaze because there's a heavy price to pay when the world comes knocking on your door.

Some people thrive on public adulation and seem to 'come alive' in its presence – but I'm not one of these.

Sometimes the public pressures can be intolerable, and all that keeps me going is the thought that millions of people might benefit by hearing the Truths of the Spirit.

I think *New Zealand Woman's Weekly* summed up my feelings when they quoted me saying:

I live almost as a recluse, in a small place of my own. I prefer the quiet stillness of the mountains and hills of Wales to parties and pubs. The first love of my life is silence, and I enjoy going for days without talking to people – except to my spirit friends.

Because I think differently from many people I've had some nasty brickbats thrown at me – but there have also been some lovely bouquets.

For instance, I've met interesting people I'd never have known if I'd remained in the shadows; people such as a professional composer who presented me with a specially-recorded music tape in London.

'I was so moved by your book, Stephen,' he wrote, 'particularly the part where you met your spirit guide, White Owl, that I sat down and composed this music for you both.'

I was deeply touched; and with the music tape came an inspired poem:

### The Meeting

*Borne on the Wind, he came;*
*That same Wind which had*
*Carried a Host of Winged*
*Messengers throughout Eternity.*

*He came to meet his Earth Brother.*
*By the cool waters, he stood.*
*The Light in His eyes, and the*
*Warmth of His Smile*
*Said simply – 'I Love You.'*

When I realised that people were being so deeply affected by my work, and that they wanted to hear more about it, I tried to disseminate my teachings more widely. Some people wrote to say they lived so far away from cities and towns – in the outback of Australia, for example – that they'd be grateful to listen to my spiritual thoughts on tape. To meet these needs I recorded several cassettes, feeling that this was a constructive way to put my notoriety to good use!

In later years, of course, the Internet turned the Earth into a global village: and now, in an instant, the world comes into your living-room.

But notoriety has its down-side, too, and my work has attracted some unwanted attention. I've had my fair share of dramatic moments.

One stinging brickbat was hurled at me in a meeting in Wales, and I regret to report that it hit me right in the eye. Just hours before the event, young religious fundamentalists telephoned the theatre and demanded that my appearance be cancelled. But the manager replied, 'As long as people pay their rates in this town, they have a right to use its amenities.' So the meeting proceeded and the hall filled to capacity: five hundred people were seated, and another hundred-and-fifty were turned away at the door.

Backstage, I felt very uneasy and paced back and forth, twiddling my thumbs, unable to get a spirit link. This was so unlike me: I'm usually quite calm and composed. At that time, of course, I had no idea there were seventy-five protestors outside the building, singing and chanting, and shouting abuse at the public who were queuing to get in.

Eventually, the police arrived and the trouble-makers were removed.

After receiving an enthusiastic welcome I began

the meeting, but I was only six minutes into my opening talk when three young women in the front row suddenly stood up, marched towards the stage, and started screaming at me.

They shouted: 'Renounce the devil!' and 'Save your soul now!' Then one of them stepped forward and spat into my face. The crowd was so appalled that quite spontaneously they retaliated by yelling at the women, ordering them to: '*Stop peddling your religion!*' and '*Get out!*' and '*Shut up and go home!*'

Other choice phrases were also offered, some too coarse to be repeated here; and then five hundred audience members stamped their feet and clapped, and chanted loudly like a mad forest tribe:

'*Out! Out! Out! Out!*'

Stewards rushed in through the exits and immediately dragged off the demonstrators to hoots of derision and fist-waving from the angry public. But even as they left, one of the protestors bellowed to the people in the gallery: '*Repent! Repent! Repent!*'

These ill-mannered Christian Fundamentalists were lucky to escape unharmed. They so infuriated the audience that if they'd stayed I'm certain there would have been a free-for-all fight. That sort of behaviour is expected in a gangster movie, but not at one of my appearances. But such has been the fate of any narrow-minded bigots who've tried to disrupt my meetings over the years. Protestors beware! The crowd is on *my* side, not on yours.

However, for each unpleasant memory, I can recall dozens of amusing ones to balance it; and one of these happened when a caretaker telephoned from the Southampton Guildhall in southern England:

'Do you want the tower clock silenced during your performance?'

I was confused. 'What on Earth do you mean?'

'Well, you see, on the stroke of every hour the clock-bells ring out, deep and loud.'

'Ring out what?'

'That lovely old hymn "*Oh God our Help in Ages Past*"!' I was highly amused, but didn't think it would help the demonstration, so we paid the man a few pounds to silence it!

Southampton provided further merriment, too, when I provoked a major incident by losing my black briefcase: panic swept through me because everything of value was in it. Then a brainstorm prompted me to ring the restaurant where I'd had my tea. Their staff were laughing uncontrollably.

'We've just had the Bomb-squad in here! We were petrified to death!' they said; then more wearily, 'You'd better come and collect it before it goes off.'

And I can recall another funny occasion, but this time involving a sceptic at BBC Radio Nottingham.

From the moment I entered their building the transmitter signals went haywire.

'Stephen O'Brien, this is *your* fault!' the sceptical interviewer admonished. 'It's your psychic powers!'

'I'm sorry,' I replied, quite innocently, but went on to explain that this kind of electronic chaos had followed in my wake before:

'I was recently photographed for a magazine, but my house was standing in the background, which made me unhappy because this was an infringement of my privacy – so the camera-shutter refused to work.'

I then explained, 'But when *I* tested it and took a few shots of the female reporter, standing on the same spot, the shutter worked perfectly!

'She tried it again, but couldn't capture my image; so I suggested visiting a nearby park, away from my house, and she got a whole of reel of shots, which later appeared in countries around the world.'

As soon as I left the radio station its transmitters returned to normal.

(Could this have been a message for my sceptical interviewer?)

Speaking of unusual happenings, I remember one very comical event:

After one of my meetings my manager, Jeff, burst into my dressing-room wreathed in smiles, wiping tears of laughter from his eyes: 'Something really funny's just happened to me out there. I was sitting next to a thin white-haired old man who'd hobbled into the hall on two sticks,' he said, grinning. 'He looked about a hundred-and-fifty years old.

'Anyway, about half-way through the first half he mumbled something to me but I couldn't understand a word he said, so I just smiled back.

'Later on when he muttered at me again, I still couldn't hear him so I just grinned.

'Then after you'd been on-stage for over an hour, giving out your messages from the "dead", in the interval I *could* hear him properly and he leaned across and asked me in a serious, flat voice: "*When is the wrestling coming on?*" '

Jeff and I burst into hysterics.

When he eventually recovered his breath, he said he'd told the old man, 'Oh, there's no wrestling in here tonight,' then he hobbled away again on his sticks!

I commented, 'Sometimes it *feels* like a wrestling-match when I'm out there trying to place my connections!' – which brings to mind a horrendous episode that occurred in Glasgow City Hall.

I shall never forget it as long as I live. It's a stunning experience involving audience members who screamed out foul-mouthed language, which included the 'f' word.

Just before the meeting started, uproar broke out in the auditorium when several Glasgow 'ladies' accused a group of people of 'stealing' their seats in the front stalls. The group refuted this, and refused to budge – then pandemonium broke out.

Tempers blew, voices raised, fists were clenched, and arms began waving menacingly – and suddenly the air was filled with four-letter words, which included every expletive you can think of.

Other incensed crowd members 'booed' at the 'fishwives' to stop, but in vain – the 'ladies' behaved more like football hooligans than seekers awaiting spiritual contact.

And all this time I was standing high up out of sight behind curtains, some thirty feet above the stage, peeking out at the affray, but powerless to stop it. As the screaming reached its peak a kilted official ran on to the stage and screeched through the micro-phone: '*Sit down, all of you – and shut up!*'

This further enraged the women who bellowed out their contempt about his '*bloody silly rules!*' – while I stood stunned, gasping to myself, 'I don't believe this is happening: it's a nightmare.'

I had to force myself to remain calm when the official blurted out to a particularly raucous fishwife: 'If there's a message for you, you'll get it no matter where you're sitting, *you stupid woman*!'

Then she jabbed a finger at him and viciously screeched:

'*I'll* give *you* the f*****g message, sonny!'

There was immediate silence.

Everyone froze in their seats.

(Her threat turned out to be Glaswegian slang for '*I'll slit your throat*.' But I think it was the 'f' word that shocked the crowd most.)

Suddenly the hall manager seized a microphone and declared: '*Please*! Please be quiet and behave yourselves! People don't want to hear you shouting filth at each other – they've come to see Stephen O'Brien!' The crowd instantly burst into applause: they cheered wildly, and whistled.

On the threat of being removed, the troublemakers grudgingly plonked themselves onto hardbacked chairs which had been quickly-found.

I was announced immediately, and as I entered I received a tumultuous greeting. The place went wild, but as soon as I stepped to the microphone... absolute silence descended on the people. You could have heard a pin drop in the auditorium.

It was the weirdest sensation.

Quietly I said, 'One second after you've died, you will find yourself alive again.'

An unearthly calm swept through those hundreds of minds, stilling them completely; and from then on, they sat almost entranced, and hung upon my every word.

And the spirit people didn't let me down: their messages flowed as if nothing had happened, and their links were quite clear and detailed. I started with two communicators who gave me their full names as 'William and Mary Airdrie', and they turned out to be an aunt and uncle of someone in the crowd.

After this, the meeting flowed perfectly and was hailed as a roaring success.

Looking back now, of course, I can only see the funny side of it (a priceless gift I've always had), especially as those nasty people were eventually seated *in front* of the first rows, and all night long the microphone wires kept catching in their hand-bags and stockings.

Furthermore, none of them received a message. (There is a God!)

Sitting in the gallery at that meeting was the respected veteran Spiritualist medium, Albert Best, who later invited our party back to his home for supper. 'Stephen,' he said, 'I've done these big meetings for decades, but I don't think I've *ever* seen such disgraceful behaviour in an audience. Yet I must tell you: *I* couldn't have worked after that fuss tonight, but you handled it beautifully. If you can use your gifts in conditions like that, you can work anywhere in the world.' Then he went on to give me some helpful advice on how to improve my mediumship, for which I was grateful.

That Glasgow fiasco brings to mind yet another 'peculiar' event, which took place a little further down the coast in Northern England at the Tyne Tees Television studios. It was one of the oddest programmes that I did.

After the usual interview in front of an audience, which contained the inevitable sceptics, I can only describe what followed as a thirty-minute free-for-all get-your-voice-heard shouting-match.

Everyone interrupted everyone else, and no one – not even the other studio guests – had a chance to answer any points.

I remained calm, of course, and never allowed my dignity to slip; but I later told the producer, 'You might as well have plonked a huge plate of sticky-cakes on the studio floor, then shouted 'Go!' and let everyone have a bun-fight!'

If the television people had simply allowed me to work with the audience, as they'd originally asked, I might have been fortunate enough to deliver a meaningful message – as I did at the prestigious Royal Liverpool Philharmonic Hall.

It was an especially touching link that fell to a woman in the crowd, and my communicator was a man who'd died in a British tragedy.

The Hillsborough Football Stadium in Sheffield, England, was the scene of a horrendous disaster on 15th April 1989, in which ninety-six people, young and old alike, were crushed against high crowd barriers and were suffocated to death.

It was England's most horrific football accident, and the world was stunned when footage of it was televised across the globe.

My spirit victim located his wife's workmate and relayed a poignant message, which included his name and details of his last precious moments on Earth. Filled with sorrow, he remembered that, 'The pressure of the crowd crushed the life out of me and two girls, one at either side of me. We three must have died at the same time because when we climbed up over the barriers together, by standing on people's shoulders, and ran onto the pitch and pulled at the bodies gasping against the fences, suddenly our hands passed right through them. We were completely helpless – everyone was.'

I then heard him take a deep breath, as if he were sobbing at the memory of that appalling scene. He went on to convey his deep love to his grieving wife, saying that 'she couldn't come to tonight's meeting,' then he mentioned his family.

'He says he has three children,' I relayed.

'No, only two,' was the reply.

'Oh, please forgive me,' I emphasised, 'but he's quite adamant that he has three, and not two.'

The woman gasped out loud, 'Yes! They adopted a son. There *were* three children!'

Needless to say, his message of love and survival brought tremendous comfort to his grieving wife when she later heard it.

I owe my spirit friends such a lot.

But I think one of the most touching 'bouquets' the spirit world have given to the public in recent years – in the way of messages – was the link they relayed from a spirit youngster, who had been disabled, to his Carer seated in a crowd. It was an emotional message from a young lad who'd been crippled all of his Earth-life.

'I was starved of oxygen as I was born,' he told me, and he said he'd suffered great physical handicaps because as a spastic child he couldn't speak or stand.

When his link came through, his exuberant joy and enthusiasm touched everyone's heart. After giving his name, I stated, 'This young lad's Carer is here. Now he's bringing through a strong memory of "a Sunshine Coach". "I belonged to PHAB," he says, "The Physically Handicapped and Able-Bodied Society." '

A young woman immediately stepped forward to accept his contact, and his joy was instantaneous.

'I'm free!' he shouted to me. 'Tell her I'm free; *I'm free*! I can move my arms and legs. I can speak. I can stand up tall on strong feet, on my own! I've got a wonderful body now with no pain; and my tongue is loosed, and I'm free!'

We were all deeply moved.

Then he rattled off the correct names of some of his friends and of his social worker 'Jayne', after which he said to his beloved Carer, 'Thank you so much for taking the time to look after me. I now realise that by coming into the world I learned patience and self-control. My condition taught me to master my mental and physical difficulties. My illness also taught many others, who knew me, how to love.

'And I do thank God for those lessons, and for you too – for your concern and loving care. But I'm so happy now, because my new body gives me so much freedom. God bless you! *I'm free*!'

I was told later that in the audience on that night there was another young man, who was seated in a wheelchair and was suffering in a similar way, listening avidly to that message while holding his mother's hand. As this joyous link came through, the boy's Mum leaned across and wiped freely-flowing tears from her son's eyes. He found great comfort in the knowledge that one day he, too, will be free to move and speak; and I thank God that my words brought him a deeper sense of peace and a greater purpose to his days.

My spirit guide who, over the years, has helped countless communicators to relay their messages, does a tremendous amount of behind-the-scenes work; yet his praises remain largely unsung.

However, despite all his good works he hasn't escaped some unkind brickbats aimed at him by a few cynics in our world.

Certain sceptics have doubted his existence, but he's proved his reality to so many people, on so many occasions, that the cynics' arguments don't hold water.

Here is White Owl speaking about his critics:

Sceptics want to prove either that I do not exist, or that I am a fragment of my medium's imagination. But if I were to give my true name, birthplace and time, plus other 'relevant' information that could be proved one hundred per cent correct, they would only accuse my medium of researching the facts.

Those who wish to believe, will do so – the others must be left to themselves.

I am not concerned with personalities. What is important is my message – nothing else matters.

The mission I have undertaken has once again brought me into close association with the Earth, where I am trying to teach eternal spirit truths, to touch souls, and to open man's understanding to the Greater Realities of the Spirit that lie within him, and to the endless opportunities for growth and service that these afford.

These truths will be remembered long after I am forgotten.

He's quite right, of course.

And in his defence I'd like to add that many other accounts he's transmitted, concerning his short time on Earth, touch a pure note of authenticity. At the tender age of twenty-one he was murdered by a jealous brave from his Native American Indian tribe, as he recorded in *Visions of Another World*. It was a tomahawk blow to the base of his skull that took him over into the next life, leaving his soul-companion, his woman Running Deer, to return to his tribe and break the news of his murder.

But here's what he tells us about the 'burial' of his body:

From a clearing through the tall pine trees, I watched the celebrations for seven days and nights over my mortal body.

My people commended my spirit to the Great Heavens, as I stood beside my beloved woman, Running Deer.

So brave was she that not one teardrop fell from her eyes; but she was hurt beyond repair; her grief was stronger than the bright sunlight that blinds a desert-wanderer's eyes. Her deep and lasting love for me will always be branded in my mind.

On the dawn of the eighth day, I witnessed my useless body being carried high up into the Singing Mountains by torchlight procession, near my tribal home. Many valley braves and their squaws paid homage to my last climb; and there upon a verdant hill my body was placed upon a tall pyre of forest-wood, mighty and strong.

And a young brave said, 'Here we lay you to rest, true friend of the weak and the lonely. May the Great Spirit receive your soul into the Hunting Grounds of our fore-fathers with gladness.

'May the moon shine bright upon you in the Land Beyond Sunset. For as long as the rivers flow and the Great Snows fall, we shall not forget the courage and warmth of our friend and leader, White Owl, the Wise and Brave.'

Then the women wept and rent their tunics, and threw dust into their faces, and departed with heavy hearts down into the valley of my people.

For many months my body lay wrapped in the soft blanket specially woven for it by Running Deer, who climbed alone each day to sit and pray next to me, pleading with the Great Spirit, hoping that my soul would be allowed to wait for her Beyond the Land of Dreams.

'As I raise my hands to the skies,' she said, 'may my prayers follow until they are carried on the Great North Wind and heard by my Beloved One. Come back to me, my friend. Do not leave me comfortless. I am young and strong now, but I do not have you to warm my days. Do not let me age without your warmth. Come for me, White Owl – carry me across the Divide.'

My tears could not be contained. I was so near and yet so far away from her. I tried to show her my radiant new form, but her tears wrapped a grey cloud of blinding grief around her psychic vision, and I remained unsensed.

So I whispered into her mind, 'I will always love

you, my little one... always...' but the water from my eyes did not even wet the brown earth.

Over the seasons, the spirits of the air and water, and the birds, claimed my corpse as their own. The birds grew fat upon my flesh, and thereby carried part of me way up into the Great Spirit's Domain.

Every full moon, when the squaws sat around the watch-fires. and sang their songs of thankfulness, I appeared to my woman in dreams and visions; and only in this way was her sadness dried and her faith bolstered.

Then a few years later, some young braves travelled to my resting-place, and from my bones they made ornate necklaces and tools for use in the encampments below.

Nothing is ever wasted in the Redman's world.

His story shows us that death, when rightly viewed and properly understood, is not a morbid subject at all; and believe it or not, one of the funniest things I ever witnessed happened several years ago at a crematorium, of all places!

Before the cortège and the mourners arrived, my dear friend Kitty Jones, a bright-eyed and mature woman of considerably ample proportions, was investigating the pulpit button, which she was to press during the service to make the coffin to go down.

She'd climbed the four tiny pulpit steps and was just coming *down* when her driver, a heavy man with a walking-stick and a gammy leg, came hobbling *up* the stairs to poke his nose into Kitty's business.

He shouldn't have been there at all, and then it happened:

They suddenly collided – his walking-stick shot out between Kitty's legs and they instantly lost their balance, swayed, then clasped each other like dying lovers as they twirled ungraciously on the stairwell and crashed to the ground in a twisted heap of tangled arms and legs.

I dropped to my knees, weak with laughter, helpless with my sides aching, especially as they tried to be so polite and graceful about it. Normally they'd have filled the air with blue threats, but instead they exclaimed silly things like:

'Good gracious me!' and

'Oh my leg!' and

'Dear, dear, dear!' as they scrabbled and writhed in embarrassment!

There were limbs *everywhere*: I couldn't tell where one lot finished and another lot began!

I managed to unscramble them, only seconds before the doors opened and the solemn mourners arrived.

'Kitty,' I said later, wiping tears from my eyes, 'you're the only two people ever to have been laid out at the Crem' and got away with it!'

But little did I think then that I'd be back in that very same chapel to take the funeral service of Kitty's mother, who died not long after this event.

Although Maggie was ninety when she passed over, she'd been such a full-of-life, wonderful character. Despite her great age and infirmities, she'd always joked and was cheerful to the end.

At her home on the funeral day, Kitty asked me gently, 'Would you like to spend a few moments alone with Mum in the other room, Stephen?'

'Yes, I'd like that very much,' I said.

I entered the drawing-room and stood quietly by Maggie's coffin. Gently, I rested my fingertips on the closed lid and sent out kind thoughts to her.

'God bless you, Maggie,' I said, then added wryly, 'They won't know what's hit them Over There now *you've* arrived!'

Then I sensed her presence close by. She still had her wonderful sense of humour and was chuckling with me.

'Maggie,' I said, 'if you had the opportunity today, what would you like say to everyone?'

And back came her voice as clear as a bell: 'I'm grateful for the love of my family and good friends.'

I took her poignant words to the service with me and faithfully conveyed them to the mourners, and what wonderful, comforting thoughts they were.

If only all of the people on the planet, especially those who fear death, could have heard them, what a happier world this would be to live in.

### Reaper, Will I Dream?

Death Approaches...
Tell me, Reaper, will I dream?

> *In pictures
> and in thoughts*

Tell me, Reaper will I die?

> *Not in essence
> but in form*

Through misted haze the spirits come,
each face etched with deepfelt care;
and across their gaze
'Death Approaches'
is clearly written there

Tell me, Reaper, is it Time?

*There is no time,*
*there is no break*
*there is no sleep,*
*there is no death*

Then calls the grave?

*None can wait*
*and all must cross*

But will I feel a desperate pain?

*Only in the loss of bones*
*only in the world of sense*
*only when alone*

*And the Brilliant Lights*
*are those who've come*
*to take you Home*

And tell me, Reaper, will I dream?

*All Life is such —*
*dream it there, or dream it here*
*it matters not*

Then may I choose?

> *The choice is made*
> *the moment's spent –*
> *you came to me*
> *not longsince –*
> *The Veil is rent...*

But I'm alive: I feel no death

> *There is none*
> *only Light...*
> *Welcome to the Higher Life*

# 9

# Healing your
# Body, Mind, and Spirit

I've always believed in keeping fit – not only in body, but also in mind and spirit. We're not bodies with minds attached, as some people think; we're minds registering through temporary physical shells.

Man's physical body is a self-creation, a vehicle of expression formed by his thoughts; and it's merely a reflection of his true essence, which is his spirit.

Your body is the Temple of your Spirit; if you keep it healthy, fit and strong, you'll remain on Earth and gain invaluable lessons in soul-growth, which is one of the main reasons why you incarnated.

Two truisms govern and balance our physical and mental states of health:

> *we are what we eat*, and
> *we are what we think.*

In recent years the huge sales-boom in health foods shows that humanity is finally getting the message that naturally-grown and wholesome foods provide more nutritious value than the frozen or processed varieties. More and more meat purveyors are suffering powerful body-blows to their blood-red industries as increasing numbers of people world-wide demand cleaner food.

The harmful 'toxins' found in murdered animals serve only to unbalance the delicate harmony of man's psychic structures, and certainly don't contribute to good spiritual and physical health.

The body serves to express man's thoughts in a physical world mainly through movement, which is why exercise is vital to health – and everyone needs it. Brisk walking can work wonders. Even severely disabled people can try to do as much gentle exercise as possible.

Deep breathing is also a must for good health: we can't live without air! The hidden energy-giving psychic and physical properties contained in air, 'fuel' our lives and fortify our bodies, minds and spirits.

Considering that maintaining good health is our personal responsibility, I'm amazed by the number of people who delegate this task to over-worked doctors. Even though I believe (and often recommend) that healers and doctors should work hand in hand, there's no getting away from it: ultimately your health is your own responsibility.

There's a lot we can do to help ourselves.

For instance, because of my lifestyle – no smoking or drinking, and a healthy vegan diet – I'm usually fighting-fit. In fact, I recently popped into a city centre tent and was tested for fitness on bicycle machines and heart monitors, as part of an inner-city health promotion. The astonished nurse said I was the fittest person she'd examined; but alongside me there was a much younger man puffing and panting away, exhausted after two minutes exercise. 'Well, I smoke and drink, you see,' he gasped. But he didn't need to tell us that!

The human body is a living miracle, and it must always be treated with respect.

All the body's cells are motivated by Mind, and they respond to the power of thought.

Your body can heal itself, as it proves when a cut is sealed or a fractured bone is mended. But if you transmit purposeful thoughts to any dis-eased parts these will speed up the healing process.

Cancer patients have tried Creative Visualisation and frequently worked 'miracles' on themselves: some sufferers visualised their malignant tissues being reduced, killed, or 'flushed away' out of their systems, and achieved remarkable results.

*You are your own spiritual healer.*

The Spirit of God, your Creator, vibrates within your soul; indeed, this same Divine Spark of life and consciousness forever links you to the Cosmic Mind, and you can tap into Its energies: *your* spirit can attune itself to *God's* Spirit.

You can also channel this God-Power to others who are suffering.

Remember that spiritual healing flows as follows: it comes *from* Spirit, *through* spirit, *to* spirit; *from* God, *through* you, and *into* others.

Once the patient's spirit body has received a power-boost it transfers this cosmic energy to the physical body, and the ailment is treated.

Of course, many spiritual healers are helped by

highly-trained spirit guides or spirit 'controls', who direct these psychic energy-processes from the Other Side of life.

Because I lead a hectic lifestyle, I often crash into bed in the early hours, and sense the presence of spirit healers gathering around my bed; my mother is often among them, acting as a 'nurse' to me.

When I questioned my guide about this, he revealed how people in the next world administer healing to their charges on Earth:

Your mother is a good soul who re-energises your spirit. She achieves this by attending specially-prepared places in my world where energies have been generated, gathered and stored.

These batteries of psychic energy are extra healing sources from which many healing guides can obtain their power.

She concentrates on absorbing the rays by a disciplined act of will. When enough (energy) has been imbibed within her aura, thus charged, she makes her way to Earth by the power of thought.

On arriving, she waits until you are gently resting. Then, along with others similarly self-charged, she directs her thoughts towards you.

Her great love enables the rays to flow into your auric fields of electro-magnetic energy.

Rather like a sponge, your auras drink in, and hold, her emanations.

Just as lightning jumps from one highly-charged cloud to another of lower-charge, so do these rays transfer, but more gently. Gradually you then feel renewed and refreshed.

And you don't need faith to make spiritual healing work: many have received help without knowing it, and have fully recovered. Even animals and babies respond successfully to the power.

*But faith certainly helps.*

'According to your faith be it unto you': if you *believe* it'll work, you allow the invigorating rays to freely enter your spirit; optimism will also kick-start your own inner healing powers, and speed up your recovery.

Healing energies will always help you; they will never harm you.

Speaking of the power: on a much lighter note, I recall an amusing incident when an elderly patient was receiving 'the-laying-on-of-hands' in a healing group. She was so concerned about the energies that she whispered to the healer, 'Pssst... I've got me curlers in under me 'eadscarf – will the 'ealing still work?' The poor soul thought that the power would 'perm' her hair instead of healing her!

These days I do a great deal of Prayer Healing – often called Absent or Distant Healing – in which the energies are sent to people via the etheric world. Patients often live continents away from me, but their location doesn't matter.

*Love knows no bounds.*

*God is everywhere, and distance doesn't matter.*

I've offered help in this way for several years now because I receive so many world-wide requests.

Many positive results have been reported, but some patients' relatives considered a few treatments to be unsuccessful because their loved ones passed over – yet the spirit people and I never view 'death' as a 'failure'. My inspirers always maintain that death occurs only when the time is right, and that no amount of healing can prevent a person from making the transition. However, spiritual healing *can* help to ease a traveller's passing, alleviate his pain, and endow his transition with more dignity.

*The ultimate purpose of spiritual healing is to touch the souls of people, and awaken them to their true spiritual natures. The healing experience provides them with a unique opportunity to discover who and what they really are, where they've come from, and where they will go after 'death'.*

Let's turn our attention now to another aspect of well-being: mental health; and this can best be maintained when your mind is filled with positive, calm thoughts. Harmful negative forces, which lurk behind agitated emotions, create mental whirlpools of energy which will disquiet the mind and will eventually cause disease in the body; for the body is but a reflection of your mind.

Your body is nothing more than Mind made manifest: it is 'materialised' thought, and that's why it's so important to hold a good self-image, because it helps you to create health.

Selfishness, greed, avarice, egotism, bitterness and grudging attitudes of mind: all these energies 'cripple' mental harmony, and pave the way for disease to take root. Without doubt, violence, anger and raging tempers are some of the biggest causes of ill-health. Even jealousy has a detrimental effect upon the whole person.

When working with emotionally-ill people, I often use my psychic vision and have perceived that 'unbalanced' personalities radiate into their auras dark colours and agitated energy-waves; whereas serene people are surrounded by gently undulating energy–fields, which denote a state of good health.

To attain a high degree of mental health we must obtain peace of mind; we must develop characters that are based on an outward-flowing concern for others, and not on an inward self-interest alone.

A 'middle-of-the-road', 'moderation in all things' attitude helps to create inner harmony; but harsh, aggressive and reactionary emotions always repel good health; and they aren't found in spiritually developed people because perfect love not only casts out fear, it also obliterates disease.

If you need healing there's a great deal you can do to help yourself: if you feel 'drained', 'tired' or 'under the weather', why not try the following exercises.

When you're alone, lie down on rich green grass and mentally 'draw upon' the powerful energies in the ground beneath you.

Mentally 'picture' or 'visualise' the vast battery of hidden psychic power as a bright-red revitalising light, rising and filling your inner psychic being, your soul, with renewed vigour.

Breathe deeply while you do this exercise for about ten minutes.

Or perhaps you love trees, as I do?

Trees are living souls, psychic beings who radiate powerful spiritual energy-fields into the ether, and you can absorb them.

Stand against a pleasant tree: close your eyes and breathe deeply while you visualise the energies in the tree radiating outwards, then enfolding you in their embrace.

These are psychic exercises, of course, and you require some awareness to sense the upsurge of power flooding into your spirit. But even if you're unable to sense these vibrations, you'll still benefit from them.

The spirits of trees are particularly willing to offer help; but please remember they're living entities who appreciate being asked for their co-operation first.

(There's a more detailed self-healing exercise later in this chapter.)

These days, I'm increasingly concerned about the health of our Great Mother, the Earth, because she's also a living entity and man is daily abusing her.

Imagine you can view the planet from a distance: she would be a glowing light, filled with sentient life and surrounded by vibrant energies.

Seen from space – something I've witnessed when astral travelling – the Earth appears to sensitive observers as a vast panorama of teeming consciousness: even her rocks, dust, and air are pulsing with life-force.

Mother Earth is a Living Being, and it's time we recognised her as such. She's a part of us, and we are a part of her: our bodies sprang from her womb, and back to her they will eventually return, where they'll slowly break down into the elements from which they came.

Her rocks are our bones; her rivers are our blood-streams; her fertile soil is our flesh.

Our bodies belong to our Mother, the Earth, and our spirits belong to our Father, The Great Spirit;

and this isn't a new concept.

Many centuries ago these teachings were lived out by a religious brotherhood called the Essenes, who were active around Palestine in the time of Jesus. As one of their sect The Nazarene wore their emblem: the white robe of the *Therapeutae*, which translates roughly from the Greek as 'Physicians' or 'Healers'.

Jesus learned many of the gentle healing arts from these peacemakers who loved the silence and tried to live a pure life.

The Essenes understood the necessity of clean living, and of balancing both the physical and the mental energies, and of tending with diligent hands and loving hearts their Great Mother, the Earth.

Here's my spirit mentor again, who is himself a healer:

If we look to Nature everything is held in a state of constant change, yet perfect balance; but once man interferes with Nature's equilibrium – disaster results.

Man is the greatest slayer of life-forms: he threatens to make the Great Whales extinct, chops down vast atmosphere-regulating forest-lands, and continually pollutes rivers and seas with dangerous toxic chemicals.

Untold harm is daily tilled into the Earth's soil: life-threatening sprays and fumes are dispersed far and wide into her atmosphere, which is now thinning out and enlarging the gap in her protective ozone layer.

This will result in harmful rays penetrating man's skin, and will cause all manner of problems and virulent diseases.

Harmful poisons in the Earth are absorbed by

plants which are eaten by animals, and unwise individuals who still consume meat welcome these toxins into their bloodstreams. Even compassionate vegetarians and vegans cannot completely escape these frightening side-effects. It therefore comes as no surprise that humankind suffers with widespread 'incurable' diseases, cancers, and generally poor health.

Man is now literally reaping what he has sown: no more, no less.

But the future doesn't have to be bleak: if we just changed our habit-patterns and *thought* about what we're doing when we purchase chemical solvents and household cleaners – which could destroy marine life, and subsequently us, when we dispose of them – we'd leave those poisons on the supermarket shelf and choose environment-friendly products. At least then we'd be helping our planet's slow recovery towards health, and harmony.

Meanwhile, the body of the Great Mother is daily damaged by nuclear waste materials: sealed in concrete blocks and metal drums, they're buried in secrecy, deep in caverns under the sea.

But the planet is an entity who is still evolving, and her activity will one day burst open these radio-active time-bombs, which will release life-killing poisons into her veins, and there'll be no escaping the harmful radiation.

How unthinking and careless can man be?

He is decimating the very source of his physical health and well-being; and for this he will pay a heavy price, because in damaging the planet he will eventually hurt himself.

The Great Mother will be recognised as a *living being* only if we educate the ignorant by raising our voices and shining out the examples of our thoughtful lives. We must protect our wildlife, our beautiful countryside, our rain forests, our clear-bright seas, and all the wondrous pageant and diversity of the natural world.

But if we *don't* take urgent action to cleanse the planet of the poisons that we've given to her, future generations could suffer from some horrific diseases and unspeakable miseries.

Now here's that exercise for self-healing I promised you earlier. I've formulated it to meet the requests of many readers around the world.

### A Simple Exercise for Self-Healing

Sit quietly for ten or fifteen minutes each day and think of being healed, or think of God; or visualise colourful flowers and trees, rolling countryside, or a candle-flame. Or picture any restful pleasant scene that will calm your troubled thoughts.

Eventually you'll achieve a peaceful, quiet state of mind, which generates a pleasant feeling of 'building castles in the air' – then healing energies will reach you more easily.

Embraced by deep tranquillity, you will place yourself in a receptive condition and will be able to more easily absorb the Cosmic Healing Powers that surround everything you can see, and everything that you can't see.

Remember: there's an endless well of Life-Giving Energy all around you and within you, and you can tap into it at will.

Visualise this Universal Energy either as a Cloud of Power or as a Brilliant Light, and breathe it in as if it were air, knowing that it will fill you with its healing rays.

It's a Golden Light that soothes, refreshes, and reinvigorates your spirit, mind, and body.

If you're not good at visualising and feel you need a more substantial focal-point, then select a photograph of me in this book and look into my eyes, and draw upon the invisible Power in that way, allowing its brilliance to warmly enfold you.

Or you could use a photograph of a loved one, for the God-Power resides in every soul.

Then, while you draw upon the light, tell yourself that you will never despair, that you'll always keep a bright and positive, cheerful attitude.

Speak the words out loud if necessary, or think them to yourself, whichever is the more positive method for you.

Instruct yourself to always *expect* improvements, to await them eagerly, and never to place limits on what the Healing Power can achieve: the lame have walked, the blind have seen, and down the centuries countless people have been greatly helped.

Realise that God will bless you in His own way, in the way that He and His Angels consider best for your soul and spirit.

Know that quietly, day by day, His Ambassadors will send you thoughts and inspiration; and they'll help you to find your inner peace.

*Peace is the key to health: peace of body, peace of mind, and peace of spirit.* Whenever your mind is at ease, your body will reflect this peace and calmness, and all dis-ease may be removed.

Remember: this ability to 'draw upon the healing light' needs no religious creeds or dogma to activate it. It requires no special intermediaries.

It's between you and your God: it's a personal and unique relationship, and it will bring you the help you need.

And according to your faith be it unto you.


## Morning-Light

Rising in a timeless lake of dreams
To conscious power,
Eyelids flicker and inwardly glean
The final fragments of a passing world.

He breathes again on Mother Earth
As nightlight fades, eager to be dawn,
And moving to the window, he feasts
Upon the coming of the morn.

Tactile trees, black-horizoned, still unmoved
As their tranquilled breeze desists and dies,
Know something wonderful is immanent.
And before his marvelled gaze,
Magic lanterns stream across the skies:
Gleaming, dying;
Starlight rods reaching out to God.

A distant skylark, spirit-moved, opens its throat
And brightlight sings,
While violet moves away for blue;
And the naked Watcher slips the latch, unseen,
And softly treads the dankerous earth,
Drawn by resplendent hue.

With outstretched arms and face to the sky,
In nakedness, he's
Washed in mystic energies on the height;
Alive again, reborn again,
To feel again and know again the Power of the Light
That wakes and breathes and touches him
And heals world-aching sight.

Purple to green, to orange to gold,
Till yellow daylight ignites his soul
And whitens the tranquil sky;
Imbibing and reviving,
Till every portion feels and knows
From whence it came,
And why.

  *'No man can paint*
  *Nor picture hold*
  *Its incandescent sigh...'*

Watcher, stand bare-breasted,
Beating At-One with the Greatest Heart, and rejoice
Lest you forget that from out of this
Came every lustrous shining part.

Feel the wind embrace your pristine soul, and
Bathe in glorious floodlit gleams;
Let body thrill with penetrating wonder:
Let loins and arms be totally engrossed
By the Cleansing Touch of the Highermost.

Pounding joysounds infuse with mighty awe
As the Watcher sparkles and glows divine;
Dazzling threads of visible Godlight, thrill
To him and through him and from him again.

It caresses trees and parklands; birds and houses;
Fixing dusky shapes apart;
Tickling awake longsleeping grasses that stretch up
To touch a Universal Heart.

Naked,
I behold the naked light,
Fashioned by Mind Omnipotent:

Naked,
I behold the fading of the dying night,
Composing magic strains fresh-lent –

For I am the Watcher,
And my soul from pure Omnipotence was sent.

Rise then, O sun, in beauteous sight –
But touch me not no other living thing –
These Watcher's tears are not for sorrow shed,
But for the magnificence of Morning-Light:

And naked they will stand and drink with me
A myriad glistening rainbow rays; at this,
The birth of another sunbless'd day.

# 10

# The Dark Night of the Soul

Have you ever been in a crowded room yet felt so utterly alone that you seemed to be surrounded by clouds of impenetrable darkness?

Have you ever sunk into such a deep valley of tragedy that you felt you'd never again rise up to see the sunlight?

Perhaps you've experienced such a profound state of grief that you felt it would never end?

Or maybe you've felt unloved and unwanted, or even unworthy of happiness?

The dark night of the soul takes many forms, and when its desolation and uncertainty strike at your heart, or at your mind and spirit, the subsequent period of soul-searching can last for weeks or months – and in some cases, even for years.

Is it possible to rise above these soul-numbing experiences? And what do the ancient, wise minds in Eternity say about our struggles?

Well, in learning about other people's trials and how they overcame them, we can often be spurred on to conquer our own difficulties.

I can well remember one of my own 'dark nights of the soul', and how I fought to resolve it.

It all started in August 1985 when I moved from Wales to England, but not before my friends had given me a big Welsh send-off. Days before my departure my colleagues at the Swansea Psychic Centre held a presentation ceremony for me: I'd established the Centre, served it for two and a half years as its Vice-President, and had also trained many new mediums there.

After a service of Psychometry – where psychics sense from everyday objects accurate details about their owners – the audience applauded when I was handed a large wrapped gift.

'Now come along, Stephen,' said the Secretary, 'you've just been teaching us Psychometry. Now show us how it's done! What's in that parcel?'

Without hesitation I replied, 'A copper plaque of the *Desiderata* writings.'

'Oh my goodness, *he's got it!*' she yelled; and everyone laughed.

After tearful goodbyes, I sallied forth from South Wales to live in the North-east of England, exactly as my spirit guide had predicted, an amazing *ten months* before the move took place. Accompanied by my meagre possessions, I was locked inside the back of a hired truck – spluttering and coughing from the exhaust-fumes on a seemingly endless ten-hour journey – until four hundred miles later it screeched to a halt, and my friends helped me to unload my stuff, then drove away shouting: 'Be happy, Stephen! *Be happy!*'

I had no idea then that a great deal of my life up north would prove to be anything but joyous.

Although my moving away to the county of Tyne and Wear had been predicted by my inspirers, they hadn't revealed that I'd be living in the poorest area of Gateshead town, where many soul-crushing hardships waited to pounce on me.

My council flat was a peculiar place that was built on three split-levels, joined by four flights of wooden stairs – twenty-eight steps in all – and I didn't have a brass farthing to carpet them. I was unemployed and penniless, and groaned when my English friends declared that I should 'Make ends meet'.

'Listen,' I said, 'I can't even *find* the ends to join them together!' I did try to make my flat feel more homely, but failed dismally: it never did become a home; it was just a place to live in, situated in the worst estate I'd ever seen in my life.

Nothing but trouble lay ahead of me there.

On most evenings the disgusting smell of burning paraffin oozed up through the floorboards into my rooms from the flat beneath mine, and was sometimes accompanied by other noxious aromas, too awful to describe.

On occasions the fumes were stifling: I didn't know what they were cooking downstairs, but I knew I'd never eat it!

Armed with some masking-tape, I crouched down on my hands and knees and tried to seal the gaps around the floor, but in vain. As fast as I blocked out one smell, another took its place. The stench was foul; and, like Marley's ghost, it wouldn't go away.

As time wore on, I discovered that I was trapped in

a rabbit-warren of filth: the shared and covered walkways became increasingly smelly, dirty, and daubed with unrepeatable graffiti; they were filled with litter, rotting garbage, and the stench of stale urine. Those corridors came to symbolise the minds of my neighbours, who cared for no one; neither for themselves nor for their children – and certainly not for their pets.

The tenants' lives were riddled with debt, crime, ignorance, and a marked disrespect for the dignity of life. Their children were plentiful and abusive, and many families lived in squalor.

When governments say there were no poor people living in Britain in the 1980s, I cringe at the shameful lie. I lived near youngsters who had no shoes on their feet: they had dirty faces, neglected bodies, and twisted thoughts, which were all sad reflections of their physical and spiritual poverty.

Each day, besides the human waste that was sometimes plastered on the walls, I never knew what I might find on the stone stairways that linked our blocks of flats in a concrete maze.

A few of the older teenagers behaved like wild animals, ripping down and burning garden fences for 'fun' and for 'something to do'.

Every door along my walkway was kept firmly locked. Empty flats were boarded up, bolted, and sealed with padlocks and six-inch nails, to ward off arson and vandalism, which were rife.

Robbers looted any empty properties, wrenching out electrical sockets, doors and windows, and disconnecting copper boilers, which they sold on the black-market.

It was a frightened community, living in fear of itself.

The actual dwellings themselves – their design, spaciousness, and panoramic windows providing breath-taking views of Newcastle-upon-Tyne – were great places in which to live. The flats weren't the problem: the tenants were. If you'd moved the Queen out of Buckingham Palace then moved in my neighbours, they'd have wrecked it in less than a week.

I was often unable to sleep at night, listening to fights outside my door. People would reel about blind drunk, maybe smash a few windows, swear like troopers, then punch each other until blood was drawn and left where it fell. I often cringed under the duvet when people screamed, but my doors remained tight-locked. As far as I was concerned, they deserved one another.

One night a couple were fighting beneath me and I heard a thunderous *bang* then the smashing of glass: he'd pushed her into a plate-glass door.

'Stephen,' I groaned, 'what on earth are you doing here?'

But I suspected this was yet another time of spiritual growth, another period of hardship meant to test the mettle of my character and spirit; and one night my invisible friends confirmed this in a startling way.

I was just on the verge of falling asleep when in the corner of the bedroom an eerie psychic light appeared. At first it looked like a vaporous white mist, but then it brightened, and hovering within it there was a shadowy spirit form, about six feet tall.

The man didn't show himself clearly; nevertheless, I quietened my mind and listened.

Then out of the light came a deep tremulous voice that said:

'We are aware of your difficulties, but you must be strong. You must overcome your fears; and you must be patient, and persevere.'

The light shimmered, and the visitor delivered a glimmer of insight. 'You are here in England to represent our world, and to work for it. You are to touch the souls of people seeking spiritual light and knowledge. Your work will move their minds and make them think more deeply. Serve us well, my friend. We will not desert you.'

Then the white light vanished, taking the form and the voice with it.

It was all very well for the spirit people to sound so confident, of course, but it was I who had to live there; and one night I was shocked when a drunken man tried to break down my front door. He hammered and kicked on it and threatened to kill me with a knife if I didn't let him in. I dashed to the phone (not a luxury but a necessity) and within minutes two breathless police officers arrived. But by then the man had made his escape.

The police were frowning hard. 'Take it from us, you're too good to live here: move.'

'But I've nowhere else to go. I'm from Wales – from four hundred miles away. Besides, I've no money.'

'Take our advice and *move*. Didn't you see the fire next-door? Someone tried to burn those people out. Nobody decent lives here; it's full of tax-dodgers, debtors, and all sorts. They run here to get away from troublemakers, but the troublemakers come to get them.'

A shiver ran down my spine.

'Are many incidents reported from here?'

'Hundreds each year: burglaries, fires, grievous-bodily-harm offences, malicious woundings, abuse and slander–'

'There's no need to go on,' I interrupted, rubbing my forehead in dismay.

'Take a fool's advice, Mr O'Brien, and get out – *and the sooner the better*.' Then they left.

In the early hours of that morning I considered their words, but decided that because soul-growth is born out of facing difficult challenges, and not out of running away from them, I decided to stay and complete my spiritual work.

My mind was made up but this didn't stop me praying to be given the house of my dreams. I wanted to live somewhere silent: somewhere far away from the noisy cities – in the country, maybe, in a small cottage nestling in a green valley, where birds fly in the fields and country breezes rustle the leaves of giant trees.

How wonderful it would be to wake up to the glorious sights and sounds of God's land; to listen to the bees humming and the birds singing, and to smell the scent of summer flowers wafting through my open windows.

I've always needed to walk alone in the silent hills, to be alone with my thoughts, to be alone with God.

In the country, peace and stillness would refresh my spirit, revivify my body, and re-energise my mind. I'd feel perfectly at peace watching the red sun setting beyond the fields of a little cottage of my own. But this was nothing but a dream; and unless by a miracle some kind soul bequeathed me this sanctuary, I couldn't see how I'd ever get it.

Poverty is a bitter pill to swallow.

Something else I couldn't swallow was the toughened strain of northern germs – or perhaps I *did* swallow them because within a week of arriving in Gateshead I was laid flat-out by the worst virus I'd ever experienced. My chest felt as if an iron band had been welded round it, and I wheezed away long into the night. Shivering hot and cold, with my vision blurring and delirium blanking my mind, I felt too weak to move; and the dark bedroom swam before me.

I've always fought off illnesses – and have often worked in public despite them – but a man knows when he's beaten. Like a limp lettuce leaf I hung over the bed weeping like a child with no one to care for it. How I cursed those northern bugs; and how sorry I felt for myself.

Although my Other World friends did draw close to give me spiritual healing, they didn't mention my personal difficulties again, so: with conviction I determined to end my illness by using the psychic power of positive thought, and I commanded my body's immune system to get to work immediately and rid me of the virus; which, of course, it did.

Nevertheless, it took days for me to fully recover.

Then I couldn't wait to explore the big city across the river, and what I found there cheered me up no end. Newcastle was a lovely place, a curiously old and yet young city, full of ancient and modern architecture.

My breath was taken clean away by the buzzing city activities: agile clowns and acrobats tumbled about on the quayside of the River Tyne, and skilful street musicians and a one-man band filled the sharp air with lively sound. Circling high above the heads of the bustling crowds were thousands of squealing black starlings, who swooped down into the city and landed on high buildings, where they huddled together warmly to fight off the biting cold winds.

And every day, in all kinds of weather, a ragged old bird-woman came into the city to feed the hungry pigeons that cooed around her like grateful children. What kind eyes she had.

Although still weakened by my illness, I explored a massive under-cover shopping mall: thousands of heads swayed and bobbed in front of my eyes, and I became so flustered by the jostling strangers that I nearly fainted.

When normality returned I got on the 'Metro', a network of fast electric trains linking together most of the North-east, and as it shot through under-ground stations then whizzed out into blinding daylight across the huge steel bridge over the Tyne, I felt quite dizzy. When I got home I went straight to bed.

On a cheerier note, through the huge windows in my flat, I had a panoramic vista of Newcastle City: buildings stretched as far as the eye could see, twinkling in a hazy blue light, and the magnificent River Tyne snaked between them, glinting in the cold August air. It dawned on me then that there were many new places out there to explore, and fascinating new people to meet.

I reasoned that at least my adventurous move 'up north' might give me the chance to make a new life in a new land.

One of my first challenges was to try to decipher the local dialect, known as 'Geordie'. It's English, but it's spoken with a peculiar accent.

People would say: '*Whyaye man, weerya gan noo?*'

Roughly translated, this meant: 'Well yes, man, where're you going now?'

I really loved the Geordie accent. One day I stood at a bus-stop for over ten minutes sympathetically nodding my head while an elderly woman prattled on endlessly about something or other, at the end of which I broke the awesome silence with: 'I'm sorry, but I didn't understand a word you said.'

Nevertheless, I'd really enjoyed listening to her say it! And another funny habit the Northerner's had was to show surprise or disbelief by punctuating their speech with an outburst of '*Eeee!*', delivered loudly and accompanied by a simian grimace with the jaw stuck out. It's their equivalent of, '*Well, I never did!*' I loved it, and was soon scuttling around delivering my '*Eeees!*' right, left and centre – even in places where they weren't needed.

The months tumbled onward, then the North's atrocious weather arrived, and it became so cold I thought I'd perish of hypothermia. While twisting winds whipped and whirled outside the flats, my now-famous cat, Sooty, and I curled up in a warm blanket in front of our one-bar electric fire.

'*Eeee*, never mind,' I said, as she stared up at my

blue nose, 'At least we've got our love to keep us warm.' And I ruffled her head-dress.

When crisp frosts glistened on bleak moonless nights, the relentless wind howled through the naked trees, and through our loose window-frames. With icy legs and freezing feet, I cursed the old saying, 'And the North Wind doth blow, and we shall have snow,' as the chilly air froze my breath – and I was *in*doors.

Outside, people rushed like lemmings into warm shops, or snorted steam like dragons as they clicked along hard stone pavements. Furious wind-speeds often dropped the daytime temperature to below zero.

Through my window one night, I watched a large windswept polythene sheet wrap itself around a lamp-post down in the blustery road; flapping wildly in the gale, it made a frightening noise that startled an elderly woman nearby. Suddenly it loosed itself, flew across the road and encircled her legs, pinning them together. She kicked and pulled at the ghostly parasite, but it wouldn't budge. The more she picked at its skin, the tighter its tentacles clung until she fell in its embrace. A mighty wind then whipped off her headscarf and blew it way up into the night sky, over the trees and out of sight, as she freed herself and scurried off after it in the darkness.

Tin cans bounced noisily down the streets and clanked past black trees, long-since stripped bare of every leaf. The birds had deserted the skies and were shivering inside their cold roosts; some were sheltering in the hedges that lurched violently back and forth as the wind screamed through their sturdy branches. 'No wonder the Romans banished people to Northern Britain,' I said to Sooty, 'this weather's the worst punishment there is.'

On some nights, gale-force winds dropped the temperature to six below zero, and when it rained – it *meant* it.

'You must persevere,' my invisible friends kept reminding me; and so I did.

But shopping was a regular fiasco which saw me struggling against the gales, bent forty-five degrees into the wind, battling forwards with two carrier bags catching the full blasts and billowing out behind me like parachutes.

All the way 'home' I'd be blown wildly around the roads; and if it rained I'd struggle uphill against what felt like freezing-cold ice-bullets piercing my face.

A clinging dampness seeped through even the thickest of clothes; but my only outer-coat was a blue plastic anorak, thinned by years of wear and tear. Even Sooty's fur felt clammy.

On bright sunny days we'd get what I called 'arctic sunshine': a brilliant blue sky with a blazing sun, but freezing winds that gnawed at your bones like shark's teeth. Always glad to get in out of the wind, I'd flop exhausted into an armchair and sit and listen to the banshees screaming and howling around the flats.

I'd been warned that the North would be cold right throughout the seasons, but I believed it only when I experienced it...

When the news broke that Stephen O'Brien had arrived 'fresh' from the South, offers of work began pouring in, which fulfilled another of my spirit friends' predictions when they'd said: 'You will support many charitable organisations through the ticket-sales of your northern meetings.'

They were right, and I was soon booked to take services and larger public meetings, as well as giving lectures on the paranormal and conducting mediumship training-seminars.

Suddenly I was very busy: my time was filled with enterprise and I became one of England's Northern Lights!

I was also invited to lead two private psychic circles in different towns, which I did; and their members eventually formed my close group of friends. There was always plenty of spiritual work to be done, for in any part of the world there are always people who need help.

Strangely enough, despite all the hardships and depressing conditions I lived through, my psychic powers weren't adversely affected. In fact, they became stronger. One day in a café I stood before a jukebox and looked at the record selection on offer, and simply *thought* I'd choose *The Crystals* singing an old pop classic. While I fumbled in my pockets, trying to find a coin, the machine suddenly clicked, whirred, then absolutely amazed me by playing my chosen record – *twice*!

'How's that for psychic power!' my astonished friends laughed, clapping me on the back as I popped the money into a collection-box for blind children.

Another display of physical power occurred in one of my public meetings. I'd been speaking about the Nazarene and his work when suddenly a weighty black leather-bound book came waddling down the lectern towards me.

'We've got a walking Bible here!' I announced, as people leaned forward in their seats to see it.

And later when I told a woman that she'd visited a fortune-teller, which she verified, but that tonight she would 'get the *truth* in here', an almighty *rap* cracked on a nearby mirror. Everyone in the front row ducked, thinking someone had thrown a coin at me; but of course, it was the spirit people's doing.

'Someone Over There *agrees* with me,' I declared, looking down at the crouching figures. 'It's all right, you can sit up now,' I said, to which someone from the back row shouted out: 'That always happens when you're here, Stephen!'

Such physical phenomena made me feel closer to the Other Side, but at another meeting I nearly *joined* them when I touched a faulty microphone and received a searing electric shock. I crumpled over and let out a yell, and the audience gasped.

The pain shot up my left arm, but I recovered quickly enough to wittily remark, 'The messages should be much clearer tonight, ladies and gentlemen, after that power-boost!'

But I was lucky. I could have 'died' and ended up *giving* spirit messages instead of *receiving* them!

The months rolled by, and the work poured in and I was kept forever busy, introducing many strangers to the great truth of an everlasting life.

Now it was approaching Christmastime, and this would be my first December living far away from home. Festive sights and sounds filled the air, and Newcastle city came alive with thousands of bright swaying Christmas lanterns. Crowds of smiling shoppers gathered around the famous animated figures in Fenwick's Department Store windows: that year scenes from *Pinocchio* were enacted by life-size mechanical puppets, accompanied by taped songs. There was even a huge whale in one of the windows. The sparkling Blue Fairy waved her magic wand and enchanted all the children and adults who crowded around the spectacle – until another street attraction caught their eyes: the Dancing Waters. Huge brightly-lit waterspouts and fountains dazzled they eye and 'danced' to festive music. As the water spurted twenty feet into the air in colourful sprays of silver, blue and gold, the magnificent thirty-foot long display made every passer-by stop and stare, and children cried out gleefully, '*Eeee*, look Mam! It's magic!'

Yet, despite these marvellous sights striking my senses, something else began to strike at my heart, and tighten my throat.

Homesickness.

At first, I couldn't believe that it was happening to me, the self-sufficient being, but a raw emptiness began to upset my thoughts and emotions. At these times, my new friends were often busy and I found little pleasure in solitude.

Some nights, I felt as if I wanted to run back to my homeland, back home to Wales, as fast as I could. But I had no money, and no house there.

It was then that I learned another spiritual lesson: in order to feel secure, sometimes a man needs to feel that he belongs somewhere; he needs to feel close to his beginnings, near to his roots; he needs to know that he has a special place here on the Earth.

At least, this man did, at that time.

The only way I could forget my troubles was to walk out in the crisp, empty Sunday night streets, where I'd pass silent terraced houses. Every door was locked and bolted against the bitter Christmas winds. Strangers walked past me swiftly with their heads covered and held down, and their shoes clicking by uncaringly.

How I longed to find some open door on those lonesome nights; how I ached to see smiling familiar faces beckoning me in friendship to sit by a blazing coal fire. I had plenty of friends in Wales, a lifetime's worth; but none in this place: not here; not now, not tonight.

The shadowy tight-packed houses formed long corridors of silence; the unwelcoming streets were endless; the park gates were padlocked, and not a living soul was in sight.

At such times, I'd sit anywhere: in cafés, outside chip-shops, in places where people gathered so that I could hear their muffled conversations.

Then, feeling cold and lonely, homeward I'd go. But sometimes I just couldn't face it: the dirt and grime, the selfish tenants and filthy surroundings – and on such nights I'd go anywhere but 'home'; and I'd be off on some spontaneous journey or other, a mystery tour. I didn't care where I went, as long as I didn't go back to my flat.

One wet evening I ended up miles away down in South Shields, a small coastal town with a ferryboat dock. Silently, I boarded the damp quayside ferry waiting by the banks of the Tyne. It was a purpleskyed night and the boat was empty of passengers. Despondently, I climbed the iron stairs and stood on the upper deck, my whitened fingers clutching at a rusty guardrail.

The ferry chugged its way out onto the chilly black waters; and I was feeling homesick and miserable. Christmas was coming, and sadness swept through me.

Here and there some squawking seagulls dived for bread-scraps bobbing on the dark, undulating river. As *The Shieldsman* ferry powered its way to the opposite dock, I no longer felt the numbing cold on my face because I was pondering on the great imponderables: why, where, and how – just as I'd done when I was a child in my homeland.

Somewhere, the foghorn of a distant ship split the night, and a dog barked in the hidden streets far off: they were lonesome, hollow sounds that stirred a loneliness deep within me.

A single seagull floated into view on the rippling black water, his wings folded, his head tucked well down on his chest; and I knew that he was just like me, facing the purple sunset and the brisk night breeze on his own.

His body broke the sky's twinkling reflection in the river and I couldn't help thinking, 'We're two of a kind, you and me; both alone – only, you belong here, but I'm four hundred miles away from home...'

I then had another spiritual realisation:

I knew that I'd 'die' in the North-east – but not physically. The older experienced man who would eventually leave this place wouldn't be the younger naïve man who'd arrived here from Wales.

Although I felt as if a soul-darkness was upon me, I realised that these experiences were spiritually challenging me, and helping my character to grow.

I was passing now through an inner twilight land, through a place of deep uncertainty: this was a restless black journey through the caverns of the soul, where the spirit is tested and assailed by doubts, temptations, and unkind influences.

I knew I wasn't the first visionary to suffer these kinds of torments; nevertheless – exasperated by my situation – I wanted to fling away the mantle of service, throw aside my spiritual work, and reject my pathway. I wanted to lose my sense of purpose.

And, taking advantage of my perturbed state, deceitful spirit voices gathered around me and tried to encourage my downfall.

Through these difficult times, my faith and loyalty to the Spirit of Love were tempted and tested.

I was out in a spiritual wilderness.

Face to face with my life, my work, my future, and my past, I struggled to fully understand them all... and I had to do this entirely on my own.

The dark night of the soul was indeed upon me.

It was in this spirit of thoughtfulness and longing that on the following evening I walked with two close friends, Sheila and Graeme, to a weather-beaten church for a Christmas Eve midnight carol concert. The gentle breeze turned cold and the first frail snowflakes of winter suddenly began to fall, pirouetting, dancing on the air, and carpeting the gloomy streets.

'It seems we'll have a white Christmas after all,' said kindly Sheila, brushing the crystals from her long black hair.

'I wonder if it's snowing in Wales,' I murmured, deep in nostalgic thought, as we made our way through the glistening streets and took our places at the back of the cold church. Most of the seats were already taken, for the service was underway.

The grand swell of organ music richly filled the ancient building with spine-tingling sound. Then the people stood tall and opened their hearts and sang their praises to the Prince of Peace.

And as the congregation and the choir harmonised the beautiful strains of *Silent Night, Holy Night: All is calm, All is bright*, a wall of tears filled my eyes in remembrance of a life and a land long-distant, a place that seemed so far out of reach now.

Christmases of long ago gently floated before my mind's eye, happy memories of when I was a boy and my mother was alive and full of festive smiles. I could see my dearest friends in Wales, and I cried silently for the many kindnesses they'd shown me down the years.

My song was for them.

My heart pounded loudly in that pensive hour, on that snowy, freezing night; and I longed to go home again.

As the beautiful music surged and my thoughts ran free, I made no effort to wipe away the tears on my cheek.

Yet, from that Greater World Beyond there came only silence…

There was no call of my name; no sweet sound of comfort from the family I loved; no touch of a vanished hand upon my shoulder; and no heavenly presence stood nearby.

I could hear only my own thought-voice, recalling what the spirit people had told me long ago. 'Life is a learning process, and conflict will always be a part of it,' they had said. 'But each man must face his challenges alone. He must rise above them himself; and in the rising, he will develop soul qualities that will help him to become a more compassionate spiritual being.'

Alone in this throng of singing people, my spirit wandered through a vale of sadness, haunted by precious memories.

Solitary in my longing for distant loved-ones, I wept gently, on this, my first Northern Christmas so far away from home.

# 11

# 'Suffer the Little Children...'

The power of prayer is an invisible but potent energy, and many times in my life it has intervened and changed the course of other people's lives, and always for the better.

I can remember one vivid instance quite clearly.

It happened every morning at 6 a.m.

*Thump*! *Thump*! *Thump*! *Thump*! – kicking and knocking on the walls and floors of the flat above mine. Every morning I'd be rudely woken at six on the dot, half-dazed and grumping for sleep. But I never got it because the noises just got louder and worse.

*Thump*! *Thump*! *Thump*! *Thump*! *Thump*!

Leaning out of bed in a semi-conscious state, I'd pound on the hollow walls – then the dreadful noise would stop. 'Ahh, peace...' I'd sigh, turning over and covering my grateful ears with the sheets.

But it would start again: knocking and banging, and kicking, and the rattling of bed-supports.

*Thump*! *Thump*! *Thump*! *Thump*!

One morning, my patience finally cracked and I shouted furiously, 'For God's sake, be *quiet*! Give me a break! *Let's have some peace and quiet!*'

An almost shocked, stunned pause followed, then blissful silence reigned.

But the awful noises started up again.

Nursing a banging headache to match the din, I buried my sleepy head under the pillows while the infernal racket clattered on and on; and the same fiasco repeated itself for hours each morning, for weeks on end.

Finally, I decided there was nothing for it but to seek out the culprit and deliver him a piece of my mind. But, predictably, none of my tight-lipped neighbours admitted to causing these disturbances.

'Well, it isn't ghosts!' I yelled, knowing I'd have seen them. 'Nor mice!' thinking that if it was, they must be wearing hobnailed boots and slugging back the whiskey each night.

One hefty female resident was sporting for a fight when she snarled out, '*I* don't know nothing about it!' I stepped back and she slammed her door in my face.

It was difficult for me to locate the troublemaker because the flats were built in a most peculiar way: everyone slept at the back, but lived at the front.

All the rooms were piled high on top of each other, but certain living-rooms were lower than their bedrooms, and some stairways connecting the backs to the fronts were also criss-crossed in an impossible-to-untangle maze. If it sounds confusing, it was. I hadn't a clue whose bedrooms were above mine; so I wrote off to the Housing Department complaining about the din, then crossed my fingers and hoped for the best. But time dragged on and the noise grew louder, earlier, and it became more belligerent.

Then it entered a new phase: vocals. Between the knockings, occasionally there'd come a shout – a kind of wordless grunt or angry cry.

I then became quite concerned, thinking that a distressed child might be involved. But why didn't he or she speak?

As usual, the Civil Service produced a quick and resounding silence, but by now I was at my wits' end; so I tried a spot of Other-World medicine: *the power of prayer*.

My spirit guide had often taught me:

Prayer is a stream of Living Thought: it radiates outwards, rippling the atmosphere, and it is then registered by people in the world of spirit who exist on roughly the same frequency as the person who is praying.

Prayer is 'heard' by sensing the Language of Thought. If a prayer contains good and noble requests that, if granted, would benefit the parties involved, we will do what we can to materialise the desired results on Earth.

However, selfish and greedy prayers are often ignored by evolved souls in my world.

Thoughts are *alive*, and great care should be taken to regulate them, for they will certainly draw the response they deserve, when the time is right, because *Like Attracts Like*.

Bearing this in mind, later that night I transmitted a stream of thoughts to my invisible friends.

(I never bother them unless I'm unable to cope.)

'Well, I've done all I can,' I lamented, 'but I think someone needs your help. And if you can also solve this dreadful noise problem, I'd be grateful.' It was a simple request for aid, which I entrusted to the spirit world; but I knew from past experience that I would now need to be patient while waiting for a reply.

A few days later, someone knocked on my back-door; I heard it because I was sitting in a makeshift living-room which I'd set up in one of my bedrooms at the rear of the flats, because in my proper living-room the sound of the residents' televisions was too loud to bear.

Gingerly, I peeked round the door – and was greeted by a cultured, mature woman, beautifully-dressed in pale matching colours. She looked quite out of place on our estate.

'Hello,' she smiled. 'May I please speak with you, Mr O'Brien?'

'Certainly,' I replied, instantly warming to her gentle manner. 'Please, come in.'

She settled comfortably on the sofa and then intro-duced herself, but I shall call her Mrs Smythe.

'What can I do for you, Mrs Smythe?'

'Well, I've come to ask if you've heard anything unusual, anything at all, any small disturbances in the area maybe? Or, anything else...?'

Her kind voice trailed away, as if begging for a response, and her eyes were strangely full of hope.

'Why yes,' I chipped in enthusiastically. 'Have you come from the Housing Department? I complained to them recently.'

'Really?' she said, quite surprised and moving to

the very edge of her seat. 'Can you tell me why?'

'Well, because of the dreadful noise that's been going on above these bedrooms for the last few months,' and I pointed to the ceiling.

As I gave a blow-by-blow account of the problem her face seemed to light up and she heaved a shivering sigh; then she raised her eyes to heaven and murmured, 'Thank God. Oh thank God. I can't believe it...' She'd obviously been stunned by my remarks.

I was more than intrigued. 'Is something wrong?'

'Oh no, Mr O'Brien, quite the opposite,' she said, regaining her composure, 'everything's *right*. I'm a social worker assigned to a problem family here, and for months now my department's suspected them of maltreating their son. He's three years old but he looks only about eighteen months – he's so painfully thin and neglected. And he can't speak a word because no one's ever communicated with him properly, or tried to teach him anything. Then, last week we found a cigarette burn on his little body –'

'My God, you mean – '

' – Yes. But cruelty is very hard to prove. You see, we have so little evidence. Whenever we confront the father he just shouts back at us: "How do *you* know what goes on in my house?" Our hands have been tied.'

'Until you saw what I wrote in my letter at the Housing offices?'

She frowned. 'No. What did you write?'

'But I clearly said that I thought a distressed child was involved.'

'I'll get on to it straightaway,' she declared, rising

urgently.

But before leaving she obtained my promise that I'd report any further noises, for the sake of the young boy, and that I'd visit her superior about the case, which I did.

I was interviewed by a benevolent official, whom I shall call Mr Davis, who profusely thanked me for my help. 'Your report is invaluable,' he beamed, 'for now we have something concrete to go on. If this case proceeds to court, would you be a witness, Mr O'Brien?' I said I would, because the thought of that poor child being imprisoned in his bedroom haunted my mind.

Mr Davis added, 'We've been unable to prove the father's aggression, you see; until today, that is. Our suspicions are now substantiated, thanks to your concern.'

'Whatever you do,' I implored him, 'please don't close the files on this case: anything might happen to that little boy. I'll give you all the help I can.'

'I can now reveal,' he said, consulting his notes, 'that we're trying to get this difficult family moved to a more conventional dwelling – to a house where all the bedrooms are at the front. In such a place, these problems would never have occurred: the toddler's cries would have been reported much sooner than this.'

I was delighted that something was finally being done.

A few days later, the warm-hearted Mrs Smythe called again to inform me, 'They've been locking their son in the bedroom all day. They've not been changing his wet underclothes, and he hasn't been toilet-trained. Mr O'Brien, these flats are death-traps for children in underprivileged families. If it wasn't for your conscience we'd never have known the truth.' She sighed deeply. 'God alone knows what might have happened to that little boy. He's well underweight now, but he could have starved to death, or something even worse.'

We sat quietly for a few moments, quite unable to understand how people could be so cruel to the little ones who are sent from heaven to bring us joy and happiness. We were united in the belief that people are supposed to show love and respect to one another, all of their days.

When the kind woman discovered her speech again she said, 'Thanks to you, these people will soon be moving to a better house, where we'll be able to keep an extra-special eye on the their son. He'll even get nursery-school training and speech therapy now.'

I was overjoyed.

'Tell me, Mrs Smythe: I had such a surprise when you called on me the other day; what made you knock my door?' I asked.

'Well, I'd almost given up hope on the whole case, but I...' She fidgeted with her handkerchief, then raised her face and looked into my steadfast eyes. 'It was like this. You see... the night before making my housecalls, I'd prayed for some help. It was a last desperate hope, really, a final plea in the hope that something might be done.

'Then, as I passed your back door the next day, I suddenly felt inspired to knock; and I'm so glad that I did. Does that sound very silly?'

'No. For you see, I too prayed for help.'

We looked at each other, then I added, 'It seems that someone, somewhere, heard our requests and granted them, thank God.'

'Do you really believe that's possible?' asked the gentle lady.

'Yes, I do. Even the young boy's cries were heard and answered, weren't they?'

A long, respectful silence fell between us.

'It's amazing really,' she said at last, her big eyes bright with realisation.

I smiled. 'Tell me, Mrs Smythe: do you believe in the power of prayer?'

And there was only a moment's pause while she considered my question, after which she smiled back at me, leaned forward slightly in her seat and said quietly, 'You know something, Mr O'Brien... I think I do.'

# 12

# 'O, Great White Spirit...'

*(White Owl delivers an Invocation,
prior to rendering service.)*

O, Great White Spirit,
we open our hearts and souls unto Thee
in innocent trust, like children
seeking refreshment for our spirits,
knowledge for our minds,
and light for our pathway.

We are grateful for the challenges that beset us
and test us through life,
for these are the priceless jewels
of spiritual progression –
disguised as torment,
trial and hardship –
which,
when faced, overcome and defeated,
have made us richer in the spirit.

Through pain we have come to know compassion;
through sorrow, joy;
through blinding darkness, effulgent light;
and through wandering in confusion and despair,
we have come to know Thee.

We thank Thee for the great truths
so far vouched-safe to us,
and now reaffirm our promise
to shine them into the Mind of Man
through any means at our disposal.

May channels for the Power of Thy Spirit
present themselves for service,
with hearts full of gentle compassion,
so that together we may spread
the love of brotherhood
wide throughout the Earth;
destroying barriers of
materialism, creed,
racialism, intolerance,
and ignorance and selfishness,
(which steal away freedom and happiness).

Sweeping these aside
with Thy Mighty Understanding,
we pray for strength to deliver these revelations,
and to encourage minds to
love all,
help all,
and care for all Creation.

May peace reign
in the hearts of all your Children,
wherever they may be.

O, Great White Spirit,
may the time come quickly
when men will know Thee for what Thou Art:
not a vengeful Deity, shaped as a jealous man,
but a Great Power of Consciousness which
Sees, Hears,
and Knows all things.

Thou Art in the burning sunshine,
behind the sparkling eyes of a little child,
in the beauty and splendour of flowers,
and in flights of feathered birds.
In Majesty, through Immutable,
Eternal Natural Laws
are Thy wondrous works seen:
Laws which wheel the stars in spiral courses,
and ebb and flow the endless tides;
Celestial Rulings
which fill us with wonder
at the secret forming of a child,
and at the miracle of its birth;
and at the Mystery of how Thy Consciousness
breathes into common clay,
begetting Life.

Thou Art within,
and without;
beneath, above, alongside,
and through all forms and expressions of Life.
Thou Art the Divine Architect;
The Lawgiver;
The Unfolding Creator;
Our Father
and Our Mother –
and we are all Thy Children,
each one.

And for all Thy many blessings,
both hidden and seen,
accept now
our grateful thanks.

# 13

# Circles of Light

Tuesdays and Fridays were special nights up North because my friends and I sat in two psychic circles, surrounded by the power of the spirit.

Each week, in the stillness of the séance-room, we awaited any Other-World manifestations, in much the same way as Jesus and the prophets of old did in Biblical times.

Because I was asked to lead both sessions, every Tuesday at teatime I'd travel from Gateshead to Jarrow on the Metro train, to my friend Sheila's home. Carrying an overnight bag and swinging a lethal cardboard box (with my cat Sooty inside it, clawing to get out), and brandishing a massive golf-umbrella (which usually knocked everyone sideways off the platform) I'd arrive flustered, then fall onto Sheila's sofa, exhausted by the long trek.

After tea, the other three sitters arrived and we'd exchange amusing gossip about the latest 'goings-on' since last we met. After spending a miserable week on my filthy estate, I really looked forward to these soirées.

Laughter was always present, but the serious business of the Physical Circle followed, during which the spirit people drew much closer to the Earth than they would normally do.

Our group was psychically strong: each of our five sitters was a powerful platform medium, so the circles were never boring; in fact, they were always lively and fascinating, and they also produced some startling results.

At precisely eight o'clock, all freshly bathed and wearing comfortable loose clothes, we'd enter the blacked-out séance-room and sit in a semi-circle. Having unhooked the telephone to avoid being disturbed, I'd turn off the white light and switch on a soft-red lamp. The vibrations emitted by red light are some of the lowest-frequency energy-waves visible to us on Earth, and they don't disturb the delicate psychic powers generated by the spirit people during the séance.

After a while, I'd then dim the red lamp and plunge the room into pitch-blackness, because specialised spirit manifestations are best created in the dark. Photographic images need darkness in order to develop, and babies need darkness to form inside their mothers' wombs; similarly the spirit operators usually need darkness to manifest their physical forms.

One of the group always started the circle with a sincere prayer, asking that sensible and intelligent guidance would reach us, and that our spirit guardians and friends would gather around to protect us from any undesirable souls or forces that might be near the séance-room.

Then we played soothing taped music to help us all to relax.

Have you any idea what it's like to sit in absolute pitch-darkness? Your eyes are open, but they see nothing: an impenetrable black shroud surrounds you. There was never any firelight in our séance-room, and on cold winter nights we were each so tightly wrapped in woolly blankets that it's a living wonder we sensed anything at all!

After a while, the music was switched off then we entered a period of utter silence, which no one was allowed to break. Voicelessly, we prayed. We also sent out healing thoughts to the world, and to the animal kingdom: to anyone, anywhere, who might be suffering and in need of God's healing energies. At these quiet times, we tried to keep our thoughts as spiritual as possible. Then we sat and waited for the 'Angels', 'the messengers', to arrive – and we were rarely disappointed.

Supernormal sounds and visions often came to us: spirit messages, raps, small coloured discs of spirit-light floating the air – we experienced all of these phenomena, and more. Bright columns of silver energy 'built up' then slowly dissolved into nothingness; spirit gifts 'arrived' for us; and disembodied hands touched our faces and moved around the room. Our invisible friends always tried their best to materialise themselves, so that we could experience the same phenomena which must have astonished the twelve disciples, twenty centuries ago, when The Nazarene appeared in their midst after his 'death'.

I frequently reported that someone had touched my shoulders: our invisible friends often withdrew sufficient psychic power from us to clothe their hands in what is called 'ectoplasm' – a substance derived from the body-fluids and tissues of the sitters. This borrowed psychic 'power' was always returned to the mediums, of course, after the spirit visitors had departed.

One poor sitter was often plagued by an odd occurrence, and she'd whisper, 'Stephen? Did you just get up and walk past me?'

'No, I haven't moved.'

Then out loud she'd declare: 'Well, I'll eat hay with a donkey! Who was *that* then? Somebody's been hoofing it around here again tonight: the little blighter went right past my face. Blooming cheek!' And we'd laugh because none of us had shifted an inch.

She often felt a spirit person's breath warming her face, and heard a man's deep breathing as he 'glided' around the room. 'If I never move from this spot, that heavy-breather was here again, snorting right into my left ear! What a nerve!' she quipped, and there were more smiles all around. She was a marvellous tonic, and so good-humoured about the Other Side's frequent pranks, especially when they tickled her nose. 'I don't mind you *itching* it,' she'd announce haughtily, 'as long you *scratch* it as well!'

One evening, we heard a scratching noise coming from above the fireplace, and a sitter remarked: 'Sheila, I think they're scraping the wallpaper off the walls.'

'Oh good! They can re-decorate them if they like! They need doing!' she grinned.

Then I was quite startled: having eased off my

shoes and extended my legs to get my circulation moving, I was aware that my foot had touched something hard, lying on the floor in front of me. Using my toes, I outlined a large man's foot where seconds earlier there'd been an empty space. I withdrew my leg, but no spirit voice said 'Ouch!'

But we were all a surprised when the Other Side brought us a tangible gift. One evening after the séance, we were tidying the room when I found a small piece of blue paper on the floor: about the size of a postage-stamp, it was quite old and worn, and there was German writing on it.

We knew this paper hadn't been there earlier because before each séance started the room was always thoroughly cleaned and checked.

A spirit gift is called an 'apport' – a French word derived from the verb 'to bring'. But our gift had the name of a German town written on one side of it, and a single word printed on the other, and this was *Tabak*. Having studied German at school, I thought *Tabak* meant *tobacco*, and it turned out that I was right.

The significance of this apport proved once again that the spirit people were ever-present in my life. On the evening *before* their gift had arrived, with one of our circle, Graeme, I'd attended an art evening-class where we'd had a disagreement with the lecturer. She'd allowed some students to smoke in the tiny room, which made Graeme announce emphatically, 'If *that* continues, I'm not coming back here again!' And I agreed, for the two of us were badly affected by it.

One of the offenders had rammed *tobacco* into a

Young Jamie Allen, seven, died of liver cancer –
but he returned to his father through Stephen's
mediumship with 'remarkably accurate' evidence.

'Don't cry for me, Daddy.
I'm still alive and I love you.'

'As a young child, I vividly recall being visited
by people who were surrounded by a strange
and glimmering light.'

White Owl, a Native American Indian,
Stephen's spirit guide and teacher.

'Take my hand and I will show you
what life is like in the next world…'

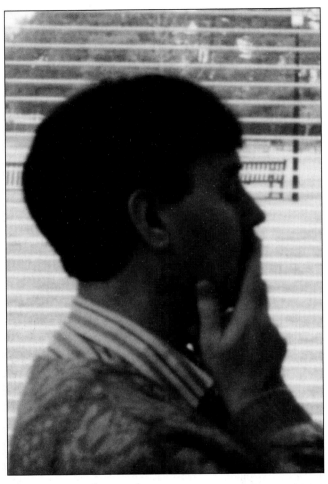

A private moment of prayer.
Stephen prepares to take a theatre demonstration
of clairvoyance.

Stephen pictured outside the old English mansion house where he crossed time-zones and came face-to-face with a woman from the past. 'I could have reached out my hand across the centuries, and touched her...'

Stephen O'Brien 'caught in action', delivering from the next world one of the thousands of evidential messages that he receives each year.

'Dedication, commitment, and a willingness to serve.'

Two full-houses listen intently
to Stephen O'Brien's celebrated mediumship.

'Goodnight…'

Stephen and his now-famous cat, Sooty.

'I'm just an ordinary man, who sometimes happens
to hear voices from another world.'

pipe.

Furthermore, the teacher's name was Germanic: she was called *Greta*.

Everything tied-in so perfectly that we couldn't help thinking how clever our spirit friends had been to bring our gift all the way from Germany to Jarrow.

Each week, in addition to these manifestations, we received wise spiritual teachings, counselling from our guides, and personal messages from our loved ones.

But I think one of the more unusual 'happenings' occurred on one bitingly-cold winter evening.

'*Eeee*! It's *freezing* in here tonight!' wailed Sheila, wrapping a woolly blanket more firmly round her legs.

'My feet are like ice-cubes!' chipped in someone else, while the rest of us turned cheerfully blue.

Spirit-draughts cooled the room and turned it into a refrigerator; the temperature often dropped like this when physical phenomena were developing.

After entering the usual silence, we were startled when all at once a flash of brilliant white light blazed through the air and lit up the room, as if lightning had struck the house.

We were blinded for a moment, then darkness engulfed us again; and this was followed by further silence. No one moved; and none of us commented on the phenomenon. Looking back now, I think we were nonplussed.

But after the circle, someone piped up, 'Did you see it! It was definitely a spirit-light!'

Sheila agreed, and so did the others.

But I was unsure: it *was* a manifestation of energy, certainly, but had it come from the spirit world? I wasn't entirely convinced.

During refreshments, I questioned Sheila's son, who'd been in the next room watching television with his girlfriend when the light had blinded us. Pointing to a camera on the coffee table I asked, 'Did you take photographs with that when we were next door, sitting in the circle?'

'Yes.'

'How many?'

'Just the one.'

'And was the camera pointing towards the séance-room by any chance?'

'Well yes, it was. Why?'

The mystery was solved.

The light had been caused by the camera flash – yet solid brick walls and passageways lay between the two places, and we'd been sitting in an utterly blacked-out room: there was no way on Earth that any light could have entered the circle, at least not by normal means.

The next time we gathered, I questioned my spirit mentor about it and he confirmed my suspicions:

It *was* the flashlight you saw.

Not only did it take *you* by surprise, but *we* were also caught unawares! It was unexpected.

When you sit in circle we sensitise the atmosphere, quickening it so that your energies can be used for manifestations. The whole area – even the space beyond the séance-room – is quickened, which is why the light penetrated the bricks and mortar: the light passed through the atmosphere, which was vibrating at a much higher rate than its physical surroundings.

Think of sound-waves. When you are in one room you can sometimes hear speech in the next, reaching you through the walls because the sound-waves pass through them.

In future we will be more careful. But you must remember that we are learning, just as you are.

Afterwards, Sheila wittily mused over her cheese flan, in a mock-refined accent, 'I don't mind them vibrating the walls, as long as they don't knock them down! They're not paid for yet!'

On another evening, my spirit guide treated us to a remarkable piece of survival evidence when I heard him tell me about an acquaintance back in Wales. 'Tell Gladys Brooks that her mother has arrived safely on our Side of Life,' he said; and he followed this with a personal message from her Mum, which I memorised word for word.

Incredibly, later that night I received a telephone call from Wales, requesting future bookings for my services. Quite spontaneously I asked the caller, 'Have you seen Gladys Brooks lately?'

'Yes, she's right here in the room with me.'

'Will you put her on the line?'

'Certainly.'

I had to tread carefully, for I didn't know whether Gladys's mother was dead or alive. But I needn't have feared: Gladys was absolutely *amazed* when I relayed my guide's words to her.

'Stephen,' she said, '*my mother's just passed away with cancer, and I'd asked the Other Side to give me evidence of her survival through someone who knew nothing about it. Thank you so much.'*

And when I recounted her mother's full message, Gladys was over the moon.

The communication was:

*I've arrived safely on the Other Side, and it's just as you said it was. Look after the family – and I'll be through to you again when I'm rested. Love Mam.*

After pausing to gather her thoughts, Gladys said, 'Stephen, that's remarkable, because I'd sat with my mother when she was dying, whispering to her about what I thought she'd find after her passing. So her words, "It's just as you said it was," mean such a lot to me.'

My guide had helped another two souls and their families, and I thanked him.

But he also spoke to me privately at the circles, leaving me in no doubt that he knew just how trapped I felt in my miserable living conditions in Gateshead. 'Be patient, my son,' he said, 'and all will be well; but you must be patient.'

But I couldn't settle down in such a lawless estate, which robbed me of many nights of sleep and rest.

With what seemed like agonising slowness, the months tumbled over one another, and I watched the seasons come and go, but I couldn't rise above the depressing atmosphere shrouding the estate; so I threw myself into my mediumship, one-hundred-and-fifty per cent. I kept busy all the time.

I did anything to occupy my mind and get me out of my miserable circumstances.

I immersed myself in service and in the circles; I

took a course on Moral Philosophy at Newcastle University, gained a 'Distinction' in music examinations, and appeared in many public meetings for worthy causes. Hundreds of pounds were raised through the ticket-sales of my meetings and were donated to places such as Mother Teresa's Mission for the Destitute and Dying, in Calcutta. I thought, 'While Mother looks after her patients' earthly needs in the east, I'll support her financially by meeting my audiences' spiritual needs in the west.'

It was a good arrangement and it worked well.

An endless roundabout of work was now whizzing around me so quickly that Sheila offered to ease my stress by becoming my telephone Secretary. She undertook this thankless task and dealt with it brilliantly: forever patient, she was the epitome of courtesy.

My new friends rallied round and supported me through my darker days, and I'll always be grateful for the love and kindness they showed. Whenever they could, they cooked me meals, invited me to join them at the warmth of their firesides, and expressed true friendship to someone who often felt like a fish out of water.

I shall never forget their greatness of heart.

Even though I was in my early-thirties I'd often curl up at night, with Sooty purring away, crooked into the back of my knees under the duvet, and simply say, 'Thank you, God, for the love of my friends, and for my warm bed. Thank you for not forsaking me... As troublesome as my life is, at least I have a roof over my head tonight, which is more than some of your children have.'

Then I'd drift into a troubled sleep, warmed only by the dream-voices of my friends: 'If ever you're in the area, don't walk by, Stephen. Pop in and see us. Never feel alone, so far away from home.'

Seeing that I was on edge, Graeme introduced me to nearly every spiritual organisation in the North-east. Sometimes we'd trudge through ankle-deep snow or battle against piercing winter winds, which drove rain as hard as ice-bullets into our faces, to reach what seemed like the outer edges of the known universe just to help out at a meeting. Some societies were housed in nothing more than ramshackle tin sheds set in barren fields – but the welcome was always big.

I remember on one snowy windswept night when I asked a church Secretary where I could find the toilet and she said, 'Straight through the broken doors and it's in the field round the back. Oh, and don't take any notice of the horse: he won't bite you!' And he didn't.

I lost count of how many spirit messages I gave to seekers all over the region, which heightened my profile, of course; and wherever I went the public stared at me, and treated me like some kind of celebrity, which made me feel most uncomfortable. I was already well-known in the UK, but I didn't want this extra attention.

All I needed was a friendly smile.

Sometimes when I visited societies, chairpersons would point me out in the crowd and cause an embarrassing fuss. One man made an upsetting remark to a full church: 'Welcome to you, Stephen. We're so pleased to have a famous medium in the

North. I understand you live in the swish part of Jesmond and run a guesthouse there. Is that right?'

'No,' I replied quietly, thinking: If they only knew just *how* I lived.

But the Spiritualists were convinced that I was wealthy, joyously happy, and that I wanted for nothing. Isn't it amazing how people make such incredible assumptions? Just because I'd appeared in *Psychic News* and other publications, had turned out well-dressed, and had spoken eloquently, they thought my life was charmed.

But back on the home-front, nothing could have been further from the truth. The grime and filth of the estate hadn't improved: in fact it had worsened. Vandalism was rife, and the cruelty of the children completely horrified me.

I daren't let Sooty go outdoors for fear of her life. The local newspaper had front-paged a story about a woman who'd caught some children throwing large bricks at a kitten, which they'd half-drowned in a pool of muddy water. According to the report this had happened just outside my block of flats.

Loving animals as I do, I was sickened by this torture.

'If I hadn't frightened them away,' the woman said, 'they'd certainly have killed it. This society's *ill*.' And with a heavy heart I agreed with her, for only the previous week there'd been a blazing fire-ball at the top of the bank outside my window: malicious, idle teenagers had set a car alight. The vehicle was totally gutted, leaving only a blackened steel shell. Thankfully, it had been empty and no one was hurt.

Behind the car there was a government building, a

recently-vacated modern extension that was attached to brick offices, and as soon as it was empty the thugs moved in and literally kicked it down. As incredible as it sounds, they actually *kicked* down the walls until there was nothing left but a huge pile of bricks and rubble.

They destroyed everything: they tore out all the electrics, made off with the radiators, and stole the lead and copper-piping, and the venetian blinds. They even ripped out the doors, presumably to use as firewood; and just as they'd done to the burnt-out car, they left nothing but a useless, gutted ruin. I couldn't believe my eyes. But worse was to come.

When I asked some noisy ten-year-olds if they could, 'Please go and play in the park, away from the corridors,' I received an unrepeatable gush of foul-mouthed language, and my punishment was delivered the following morning. At first I thought Sooty had had an 'accident', but in fact the vandals had pushed dog excrement through the letterbox.

I had to throw away the hall mat and scrub everything with disinfectant and boiling water until the landing was spotlessly clean again.

But what would be the use of complaining? Who would care? Who would do anything about it?

No one.

And this was how I lived.

(So much for the swish guest-house in Jesmond.)

During this time, at each psychic circle my spirit guide's advice kept coming. 'Be patient, and learn. You are never given a cross to bear, without the strength to bear it.' And although I respect his wisdom, I found his advice of little comfort. I knew that when in the midst of stress, a man must try to see his problems as only a passing phase (which is indeed what they are), but this ability is rare.

Remembering the policeman who advised me a few months back 'to move as quickly as possible,' I decided I'd had enough. I was going to find a new home.

But a council official shocked me when he said, 'Some people have wanted to leave your estate for more than sixteen years, Mr O'Brien, and they're still waiting.'

My heart sank into my boots. He was telling me I was stuck with it, that there was no way out.

But with characteristic determination I vowed, 'Well, not me – I'm *moving*.'

I then took matters into my own hands and sought to exchange my flat for a house in any decent area. I walked miles and visited every Housing-Scheme office, made notes of anyone who was looking for a transfer, then tramped the streets for weeks on end until my feet were sore and blistered. I walked and walked until I was fit to drop, having knocked on countless doors and tried for an exchange, but all in vain.

'Where do you live?' the tenants asked. When I told them, the usual reaction was cynical laughter and, 'You must be joking! I wouldn't live there if you paid me!' And they meant it.

On what seemed like my hundredth freezing-cold misty-day excursion to some seedy-looking flats in north Newcastle, I bumped right into one of my circle members. '*Eeee*, Stephen! Fancy seeing *you* here! Where are you off to then, with your A-Z tucked under your arm?' she asked.

When I spilled out the whole sorry tale she cooed sympathetically, 'That's a dreadful place! What on earth are you doing there, man?'

'All I want is a quiet, decent home,' I groaned. 'I've walked the roads for weeks, and feel as if I'm going round and round in circles – and getting nowhere fast.'

We sat on a grey wall and rested our aching feet. '*Whey*, cheer up, Stephen, there's a cemetery up the road, that'll be nice an' quiet!' she joked in her Geordie accent, trying to cheer me up.

But I couldn't raise much of a smile.

'Stephen,' she said seriously, 'you'll *never* get out of that hell-hole, man. It's my job to collect debts from places like that, and I'm telling you it's a dead loss.'

A dark cloud of hopelessness gathered around me and I feared the worst.

Defeat set in, and I replied in a pathetic voice, 'I feel so miserable, and trapped.'

'Listen, I'll keep an ear open on my travels for news of anyone wanting an exchange. But it doesn't look very hopeful, does it?' she sympathised.

'No, it doesn't,' I sighed, 'and it looks as if... it looks as if I'm stuck with it.'

She patted my shoulder and we parted.

I can't describe the awful feeling of helplessness that swept through me as I watched her go: it was as if my whole world had collapsed at my feet.

And I recalled the apparition that had appeared in the white light in my bedroom, saying, 'You are here in England to represent our world, and to work for it.'

Heavy-hearted, and with stooped shoulders, I turned towards Gateshead and dragged my aching feet all the way back to my 'home' – where the grime, the graffiti, the rotting trash, and the self-centred thugs and vandals awaited me.

# 14

# Time-Slips

It was a roasting-hot July day, especially inside Newcastle Cathedral. Noticing its ancient doors were open, I'd gone inside, drawn by the peaceful tranquillity. It was as if I'd entered a sound-proof box, and the busy traffic and bustling shoppers didn't exist any more. All around me stood towering stone pillars; and many centuries-old brass and marble plaques, relics of times long past, decorated the walls in silent tribute to the famed of yesteryear; and their mortal remains were covered by grey slate tombstones paving the ancient floor.

Bright sunshine streamed through the stained-glass windows, and shafts of rainbow-light fell across the old wooden pews and veiled the distant altar in a glowing mist. But it was the tangible silence that struck me most: the empty church seemed immersed in it, until I heard some clicking footsteps. Turning quietly, I saw a young man enter the organ loft, and I decided to leave him in peace. But just as I reached the exit a spirit voice said: 'Rest awhile.' So I did.

I sat next to the aisle at the rear of the church, near the flat blue tombstones.

Suddenly the magnificent organ-pipes burst into life and played a most wonderful hymn. It was a very old piece, composed and sung in a bygone age, and its melodic strains, coupled with the peacefulness and my exact location in the church, triggered off a Time-Slip – a quite unexpected journey way back into the past.

Vibrant chords echoed the still air as my eyesight blurred and the Present Now slipped away, and I witnessed some remarkable sights and sounds from long ago...

All at once the empty pews filled with worshippers who stood tall in the packed church. While the music burgeoned, these people – who were from another time, from another age – raised their voices in joyful praise. The women wore long capes which had many folds in them, and their bonnets were adorned with coloured ribbons; and the men were dressed in darker, rougher clothes. I sat transfixed, afraid to move in case I disturbed this unique experience. Above the singing I could hear the blood pulsing in my ears and throat.

Then I saw the procession. Thirty silent nuns were walking slowly up the aisle towards me. Each sister was dressed in a thick black habit and she carried a lighted candle, held either in a brass holder or in a glinting lantern, as the procession gradually approached the back of the church.

I was struck by the tranquil majesty of the scene, but couldn't help wondering why I was seeing nuns in a Church of England Cathedral.

Nevertheless, here they were, with their heads half-bowed in reverent prayer as they gracefully walked forwards to the stirring music.

Then a curious thing happened: one of them, a tall woman, turned her head and looked directly at me. She stared at my face in surprise – no doubt bewildered by the sight of my modern clothes – and instantly it dawned on me that I'd been *seen* by this woman from a time long past.

*Both of us were occupying the same place, but the shadows of ourselves had crossed Time Zones.*

She was witnessing a Future scene, while I was looking into the Past.

Then the oldest nun, who was supported by two others, felt her leg give way and she dropped to her knees directly in front of me. I half-leaned forward to assist her, but then restrained myself, fearful of breaking this contact, and watched as others helped her to her feet again with dignity. The halted procession then continued on its winding way, lanterns and candles glimmering, habits gently rustling, as the nuns filed steadily past me...

In a twinkling of an eye the Past suddenly slipped from sight, and I was back again in the modern world.

Strangely affected by my experience, I sat perplexed, stroking my chin and gazing around the empty church. All the 'ghosts' had vanished and the aisle was now deserted. The rich organ music had stopped, and I was firmly back in the Present.

Puzzled by why I'd seen nuns in the time-slip, I asked a Cathedral official to provide an answer, and he did.

'This has been consecrated ground since 1091,' he said, 'which was when the first church was built on this site. But before the Reformation, when Henry VIII ransacked the churches in the early 1500s, this church was a Roman Catholic place of worship.'

There was the answer.

Somehow I'd travelled back into history; but I hadn't seen a 'dead' picture, I'd seen a 'living' event that had occurred in the Cathedral's past.

I reasoned then that what we think of as the Past, isn't over and gone – how could it be if I'd just seen it, and furthermore been seen 'in it'?

Man's concept of Time has to change.

But that isn't the only time-slip I've experienced. Another strange step backwards came to me one peaceful night when I was near the mystical Cotswold Hills and the rambling Severn River valley, in Gloucestershire, in South-west England.

I was staying with friends in a stunning mansion house that had been built in 1584 but which still retained much of its original structure, despite having been converted into apartments. One hot August night when I was sitting in the gardens and relaxing, I marvelled at the mansion's dramatic silhouette set against the darkening sky. Brilliant stars pierced the dying light, and the old towers of the house jutted up towards them as if to say defiantly, 'I've been here for centuries, while fickle humans have come and gone.'

And then it happened:

Fading up within in my mind I heard the sound of violins playing waltz music, and the dark ballroom that overlooked the gardens was now brightly lit inside. An orchestra was accompanying ladies and gentlemen of fine breeding as they danced romantically together. The house was full of laughter and conversations that drifted gently across the lawns.

Near to the weather-beaten stone balustrade where I was sitting, I saw two exquisitely-dressed young women sauntering along the grass, each occasionally supporting herself with one hand on the stone – but the stone was no longer ancient and crumbling: it was now in perfect condition.

The pretty young belles giggled, and wafted the hot air from their faces with delicate bamboo fans. One of them particularly caught my eye: she was very slim and had sandy-coloured hair, parted in the middle and pulled back into bouncy ringlets which cascaded over her slender white shoulders. Her tight-fitting apple-green bodice shimmered in the fading light, and her wide skirts swayed gently in the evening breeze.

I felt I could have stretched out my hand across the centuries, and touched her.

The vision was so remarkably clear that beyond these ladies I could even see the silhouettes of the dancers in the distant ballroom as they waltzed in time to the music.

And then, for a fleeting moment only, when the woman glanced in my direction, our eyes met: and a strange, quizzical look flickered across her face. She turned away self-consciously, because she'd seen the 'ghost' of my reflection – as I had seen hers – on that sultry Autumn night. Then we both faded out from each other's world...

My host later informed me that the old mansion house had indeed smiled through many fine soirées. In those far-off days an extremely wealthy family called the Marlings had owned it, and pretty young women and dashing young men had often partied in its fine grounds.

I was fascinated by this experience because: if we can visit the Past, what then of the Future? Can that also be glimpsed? Is the future a random set of haphazard and changeable circumstances, or is it preordained: fixed and unchangeable? If so, then someone, somewhere, would be responsible for planning all the horrific acts, such as air and sea disasters, child abuse, torture, rape, and countless murders – and who among us would dare to undertake this gruesome task?

But if the Future *isn't* preordained, then how on earth can this next experience be explained?

Suddenly the department store faded away and in its place I saw the Shuttlecraft launch-pad in America, and heard the Mission Controller's voice saying, 'three – two – one – *ignition*! Lift off! We have lift off!' And I watched the gigantic Space Shuttle rise majestically from the ground. I could almost smell the burning fuel, and sense the great excitement in the distant crowds, as if I were there – it was a wonderfully clear psychic vision, a truly magnificent sight.

The huge shuttle climbed high into the cold blue skies, leaving a long white smoke-trail behind it. Every detail was so well-defined that it took my breath away: I could even see the yellow-white fire shooting out from its exhaust rockets.

Then suddenly two giant numbers superimposed themselves over my clairvoyant vision; these large golden numbers were: 25. They hovered there for a moment, then I felt sickened as I spied trails of igniting fuel running up the Shuttle's fuselage, only seconds before the craft exploded into a fireball before my horrified gaze. I was so stunned that I couldn't speak – and the dreadful vision vanished, leaving me back in the department store where I worked.

An assistant asked, 'Are you all right, Stephen? You look as if you've seen a ghost.'

'No, I'm fine,' I muttered.

But when I explained what had happened, she didn't believe me. 'Perhaps you imagined it. Try to forget about it.'

'But I saw it clearer than I can see you now,' I replied. 'But what did those numbers mean? Why 25?' However, the subject was dropped.

The first major ground-launched voyage of the *Columbia* Shuttlecraft was scheduled for that week and I felt so sure it was doomed to explode 25 seconds into the flight that I couldn't bring myself to watch the news. But when I later heard that the mission was successful a great sense of relief flooded my mind. 'Thank God I was wrong,' I said.

In fact, over the next five years a further two dozen successful flights were made, which seemed to indicate that my premonition was quite wrong – until five years later when, on 28th January 1986, while watching television in Gateshead, my nightmare vision materialised.

I watched in horror as the *Challenger* Shuttlecraft

exploded *exactly as I'd foreseen it, five years previously.* It was correct in every heart-breaking detail. My stomach clenched, along with millions of others around the world who watched the tragedy unfold 'live', and realised that the craft's seven crew members had all been killed.

Countless schoolchildren had tuned-in to the event because they were supporting, a young mother-of-two teacher, Mrs Christa McAuliffe, who was to make history by broadcasting the first educational lessons from space.

Her husband, children, and her mother stood near the launch-site and were stunned into disbelief as they witnessed the horrific explosion.

On that sad day, countless emotional shock-waves travelled right around the globe.

*But the event had solved the riddle of those golden numbers, because this was the 25th Shuttle flight.*

But how could I have seen it five years *before* it took place? Every physical law prohibits such a forecast, yet it happened.

Having now given the matter serious thought, I can offer only this explanation: *the future casts its shadow before it.*

An interesting footnote to this episode is that many years after this accident, the engineers who'd built the rocket systems appeared on television to claim they'd forewarned Mission Control of the possible tragedy. The designers had stated that the craft might not function properly in the freezing temperatures near the launch-pad because some rubber fuel-seals around the solid rocket-boosters could perish on take-off, which could turn the fuel tanks into a giant bomb, just waiting to explode.

But Mission Control still allowed the flight to proceed – and with disastrous results.

Let me now raise three interesting points that may indicate why I was able to foresee this event. Firstly, there were people close to the project who feared that this tragedy might occur. Secondly, if we look at the 'accident' from a psychic aspect: the amount of shock, grief, and anger that was projected into the planet's spiritual atmosphere on that fateful day would have been so great as to psychically 'imprint' itself in the energy-fields surrounding the Earth.

And lastly, the date of the explosion is of interest here because it occurred on 28th January, which is my birthday.

Could all of these 'future' events have combined to somehow project their powerful images 'backwards' into my consciousness? I think this is possible.

It's true that developed sensitives find it easier to register traumatic and emotional events, rather than ordinary every-day occurrences. This might explain why I'd foreseen the tragedy so clearly, but it doesn't explain why I'd foreseen it *five years* before it took place.

I know what I'm about to say is difficult to grasp, but it seems to me that somewhere, right now, the Future is already taking place.

And if that's correct, then we should be able to forecast anything: the time of our own death, for instance.

But can we?

Is our moment of transition known? Is each death recorded somewhere in spiritual minds that are far in advance of ours?

I believe it is – and this next amazing 'happening' provides evidence to support my claim. One of my dearest friends, Phyllis, who was an honest and kind woman in her late sixties at the time of this event, underwent a spiritual experience when she was pronounced terminally ill. She'd been placed in a hospital side-room to die, after undergoing five major operations consecutively. The purpose of the main one had been to remove a massive cancerous growth from her abdomen.

Her family was told that she had forty-eight hours to live; so they gathered silently around her bed, and waited for the end.

Phyllis was in a deep coma and, as far as this world was concerned, 'dead' to all hope. But what her doctors and anxious family didn't know was that while she was physically unconscious, in her spirit form she was undergoing either a remarkable Near Death Experience, often called an NDE, or an Out-of-the-Body Experience, known as an OOBE.

I'll never forget her incredible recollection; but she can tell us about it herself:

I remember floating out of my body, light as air, and the next thing I saw was a white marble pathway leading up to a large marble arch, which was covered in green heather.

I was suddenly taken aback when I caught sight of my 'dead' mother and father standing under the archway. They were younger than when they had died. They stood there in the prime of life, very much alive and well – and young, not old.

My Dad was wearing a smart grey suit, and my

mother wore a neat black frock with a lace collar and cuffs. Dad was leaning on a walking-stick, which was something he always took with him on his long strolls.

I walked towards them – or maybe I floated, I can't fully recall that part – and when I got near I was overcome with joy. Dad stretched out his hand and put it on my shoulder, but my mother caught my arm in hers and firmly said, *'Go back, Phyl. You haven't finished your contract yet.'*

Phyllis then woke up with a start. Her surprised family was dumbstruck: their mouths and eyes were wide open.

When the shocked Ward Sister leaned over and asked her how she was feeling, she replied, 'Fine thanks.'

Her astonished consultants couldn't believe what had happened, nor could they understand why their prognosis had been so wrong – but the spirit people knew much more about Phyllis's lifespan than the medics did.

Furthermore, her remarkable psychic experience occurred *over eighteen years before she actually did pass away.*

Up until that time, despite many illnesses that had constantly beset her (including cancer, diabetes, and a very weak heart), Phyllis remained on Earth. Although the medical profession had all but buried her off, for eighteen years she worked out her 'contract' as her mother said she should.

Phyllis was convinced that her spirit family saved her; in fact, after her experience, she often saw brightly-coloured healing-lights floating around her bed at night, especially when she felt unwell.

*The two worlds interpenetrate each other, and are so intricately woven together that it's often difficult to know where one world ends and the next begins.*

Sceptics might accuse Phyllis of having a vivid imagination (an accusation they trot out whenever they're perplexed): but they can't explain her miraculous recovery which defied medical science for eighteen years.

The sceptics must think again.

An invisible web of never-ending love surrounds us, and if we would only open our inward sight, we would see it.

True accounts such as the one above have led me to believe that the time of each 'death' is known: it is preordained.

Over the years, I've met many people who tried to commit suicide, but failed; people like Mrs Killick. She called for a consultation one sunny May afternoon. A radiant woman of middle years, she was wreathed in smiles and was smartly dressed in colour co-ordinated hues. No one would have thought that beneath that fine exterior lay a person who'd led a tortured life.

'Now', she said directly, 'whatever information you get from the spirit world, Stephen, please don't hold back – just give it right from the shoulder.'

'But this might not work at all,' I put in. 'Every consultation is an experiment.'

We both settled back to wait; however, her spirit mother quickly communicated. She gave her name and her manner of passing, both of which were accepted. Her Mum was also on-target when she mentioned her daughter's anxieties, but some of her comments made my sitter cry.

'Forgive me, but your Mum says you've had a dreadful life, full of suffering; a journey through blackness that you thought would never end. It was then that you tried to kill yourself–' I stopped speaking instantly. Mediums should never transmit alarming information – that's an unwritten rule – but Mrs Killick said, 'She's absolutely right. Please go on, and give it straight from the shoulder, Stephen.' So I did.

'She says you wouldn't be alive today if it wasn't for her. She says *she stopped your suicide attempt, even though she was on the Other Side when you took those fatal pills.*'

I stroked my forehead in embarrassment. What on earth was I telling this complete stranger?

I had no idea how she'd react to these messages, but oddly enough the tearful woman simply nodded in agreement.

'I *knew* it was my Mum who saved my life; and now you've confirmed it,' was her astonishing reply. 'You see, Stephen, I did try to kill myself while my husband was at work and my thirteen-year-old son was packed off to the cinema. I locked all the doors and windows, went upstairs and took a massive overdose of tablets. I lay down on the bed, praying for the end, ready to die. I must have slipped into a coma.

'But the next day I woke up in a hospital bed and I went hysterical; and I kept shouting: "*Why I am still alive? I should be dead!*"

'But do you know what happened after I took those pills?'

I gently shook my head.

'My son felt a sudden impulse to rush out of the movies and run home. To this day he doesn't know what came over him. He ran home as fast as his legs could carry him, only to find that the doors were locked. Somehow, he turned the key with a stick and poked it out. Then, with a thin twig, he hooked it under the back door and let himself in. He flew upstairs, and found me close to death on the bed.'

Mrs Killick stopped, her eyes filling with emotion.

She slowly regained her composure then added, 'They just managed to save me by pumping my stomach and massaging my heart. I was nearly gone.'

She leaned towards me and said emphatically, '*I should be dead*, Stephen, not sitting here talking to you today. But what you've just told me has confirmed my intuition. Deep down, I always felt that my mother in the next life had impressed my son to save me. Now I *know* I was right.

'And I'm glad that she did, because now I can see that taking my life wouldn't have helped anyone, least of all me. And I'm much happier today than I've ever been.'

I pondered on her experience for a moment, then asked if she thought it were possible that she, herself, could have sent powerful cries for help to her son, subconsciously (a tiresome psychologist argument), but she firmly ruled this out.

'No. I *wanted* to die,' she stated emphatically. 'I didn't *want* to be saved, and I'd made sure I was alone. I had no intention of being discovered.'

This story is an incredible example of how a compassionate spirit mother expressed her tender loving care from the other world: death was no barrier to her love, no barrier to her thoughts at all.

How many other times, I wonder, have people in the next world intervened in our daily lives, mingling their thoughts with ours, and inspiring us towards a more peaceful and loving existence?

How many times has an inexplicable 'chance' thought opened up a completely new direction in your life?

*We're surrounded by invisible Angels who envelop us with their love, and often we don't even know it.*

Now, back to time-slips and the subject of the future.

Perhaps the most surprising prediction I've been given came when I was feeling quite low. I was out walking, and thinking, 'When will things brighten up for me?' when all at once a clear voice spoke through the sunlight, about three feet above my head: 'When Thatcher goes to War,' it said.

I stopped and looked up into empty space.

Passers-by stared, because they hadn't heard those prophetic sounds from another world. But being a rather sensible man, I shelved this prediction as 'only a possibility', not having heard of any serious disputes between Britain and other countries.

But two years later, just when my life did begin to straighten out, the Falklands Conflict rose overnight and claimed world attention. Britain's then Prime Minister, Margaret Thatcher, dispatched a taskforce to Argentina, and the prophecy was fulfilled.

How can the spirit world's foreknowledge of this event be explained?

Could science account for it? I think not. But psychic science may offer us an explanation. It's possible, of course, that the Argentine Military Junta had planned their attacks on the Falklands two years in advance. Or perhaps – and this is what I believe – the spirit inspirer who delivered that prediction to me had glimpsed the future.

My other-world friend has said:

When people from Spirit transmit news of an event to you, they are not always certain whether it has already happened, is taking place now, or is just about to occur.

This is because we deal with the Language of Thought, which relates differently to Time in my world than it does in yours.

Thought exists in a dimension of its own, and different rules apply.

Being scientifically-minded, I once took part in some fascinating Time experiments at Stansted Hall College of Psychic Studies in Essex, England. In addition to giving lectures on psychic science and demonstrating my mediumship there, I agreed to join three lecturers in some thought-provoking research.

The test involved two of Spiritualism's renowned mediums, Mary Duffy and Gordon Higginson, and was undertaken in absolute secrecy. Unknown to our hundred students from all parts of the world, we gathered in the stately home's library on a misty afternoon. Eric Hatton, who was then the Vice-President of the Spiritualists' National Union, crept in to meet us, armed with a wicked grin and a tape-recorder. We'd no idea what he had in mind.

'Now, I'd like you all to tune-in to the spirit world and to receive one message each, then deliver it to this empty room,' he instructed us. 'Allow the Other Side to place the connection by selecting the exact seat of the recipient, if possible, and I'll tape the messages; then we'll call the students together tonight and let them sit where they wish.

'When the tape plays we'll see if the links fall to the right people, in the correct seats. If they do, this would demonstrate that the Other Side can see into the future, that they can foresee who'll attend, and possibly even where they'll sit.'

Such a fascinating challenge couldn't be refused, so without hesitation I received the first message.

My communicator mentioned a place known as 'Tunstall', gave a few family names, then revealed that my female recipient had lost a young son.

More precise details came through concerning her health: the communicator stated that she'd 'undergone surgery to remove her womb'.

Normally I would never mention such personal information, but this was a scientific test and we needed to be as specific as possible.

Gordon and Mary then followed suit, each pinpointing the exact seat of their absent recipient, as I had done, and delivering spirit-supplied facts about him or her.

But would we three be successful? Always ready with his wit, Eric declared, 'Only time will tell!'

Outside the library later that evening, Eric had written an announcement on the blackboard: *A Surprise Experiment in Time – Stephen, Gordon, and*

*Mary lay their reputations on the line.*

'He can say that again!' I said to elderly Eva French, a witty cackling Londoner who was a regular feature at the college. She grabbed some chalk, raised a wicked eyebrow, and scribbled underneath: *'Heads will roll!'* Then she shook the hall with her infectious guffaws. We sloped off into the library, where she plonked herself down in the front row and knitted furiously, like Madame Defarge eyeing up the guillotine...

I gingerly took my seat on the platform alongside Gordon, Mary and Eric, and the test got underway. While Eric explained the plan to the students, my throat contracted when I glanced at the audience – *my target seat was empty.* I whispered to Gordon through the side of my mouth, 'It's all right for you to smile, yours is occupied: mine's vacant.'

He grinned from ear to ear. 'We haven't started yet; Stephen.'

Seconds before Eric switched on the recorded messages, there was an almighty fuss at the back of the room as an old woman bumbled in, weighed down with shopping.

'I'm sorry I'm late,' she spluttered, and she was shushed by the crowd, and people ducked when her bags swung all over the place. 'Move up please!' she ordered, and everyone shifted along one seat – and my target chair was now taken.

What's more, my message fell to the correct lady, sitting in the correct seat; and, astonishingly, all the information was accurate.

We were astounded.

My recipient told us that she lived in Tunstall, the

place I'd mentioned, and that she had indeed undergone a hysterectomy, and that her son had died. The other facts were also correct.

Eva French dropped a few stitches, lowered her knitting, and gawped up at me with her chin on her chest, comically miming in exaggerated silence, 'P'raps 'eads won't roll after all, Mr O'Brien!'

Gordon and Mary had similar successes.

But how could the spirit people have foreseen these events in such detail? None of us could have known where anyone would sit on that night. What is the explanation? Could the people in the next world have guided the students to their seats? Or had our spirit friends jumped forward in Time and foreseen the shadows of what was to be?

I think they did.

Here's White Owl on the mystery of Time:

Time, as you know it, is an illusion.

You are trapped in a three-dimensional world, seeing events from only one restricted viewpoint. You are limited by the slow-moving physical brain and its sluggish perceptions.

It is therefore beyond your current abilities to appreciate the intricacies of Time in all their fullness. It is also difficult for me to explain, from my vantage-point, how Time is experienced by us. But I will try.

Time does not run in a straight line, from the past to the present, then on into the future, as many with you suppose.

Neither is it a question of the past having gone, the present being with you now, and the future waiting to come.

Nor is Time a circle or a spiral. None of these geometrical figures describes it adequately.

Time is not a shape, it is an Entity; a Living Being; a Consciousness on its own, delicately interwoven into every facet of Being in every known and unknown world.

It is Past, Present, and Future, all combined into One.

It has no fixed boundaries; it has no clear-cut demarcation lines, as many think.

It is an integral part of Immortality Itself.

The Past is not dead and gone: it is alive. Neither is the Future yet unborn: it is with us Now.

Understanding these concepts is not easy while you are still encased in flesh – realisation dawns with growth and development; and only those with eyes to see can perceive these inner realities, when they are ready to see them.

Many spirit people know nothing of these ideas; to them, Time still remains a mystery, or a straight line: Past, Present, Future.

I cannot be clearer at present, for these truths can be fully experienced only by the true Seeker who can release his Spirit and appreciate the workings of Thought.

\*

## The Dance of Time

Old grandfather clock
By the peaceful wall,

Tick tock,
Tick tock;
Clicking out your endless seconds,
Swinging out your days,
And smiling at the man who winds you
In his foolish ways.

Old grandfather clock
Tick tock,
Don't mock:
Time does not exist –
She's just a clever mind-trick
And you are her accomplice.

Old grandfather clock,
Don't mock –
Time like a Spanish Flamenco Dancer
Wears a scarlet frock, and spins and prances
Clicking castanets and swirling crimson skirts
In fast hypnotic dance;
Her sultry eyelids flutter and entrance
Till reason's locked and shuttered,
Then stamping out her flamenco rhyme
So rhythmically, so sneakily,
She clasps her victim fast:
To age and to decline,
To suffer and never know the wonder of
The freedom from Time.

Grinningly she's tricked you,
And wooed you with her Power
So that close to her gyrating dance
A boring minute's like an endless hour.

And as Spanish music swells with tensions
Trapped are you in three dimensions.
And Scarlet Time tosses her gypsy locks
And slyly turns the countless clocks,
And spins the stars and marks your birth
And times you as your death unfurls:
Clicking and dancing, swirling and prancing;
Wheels within wheels,
Worlds within worlds.

'Come dance with me!
Come dance, come dance!
Come near and kiss your youth goodbye!
Come shake a tambourine with me!
Come count the days, come age and die!
Come hold me close and grip me fast,
And let me show that nothing lasts!'

Then lured by her encircling palms
A fine young man fell into her arms,
And twirled and danced and became entranced
By Scarlet Time and her gypsy charms.
And around and around the floor they sped
As Spanish music upwards climbed;
And gypsy Time, she stamped and rhymed
And held the youngster to her breast
And danced and spun without a rest,
Until her laughter drowned his cries
As his spinning flesh sunk on his frame and dried:
And all the watchers near them cried
As the muscle-bound youngster aged and sighed,
And crooked his back, and lost his sight,
And forgot his name, and groaned and died.
Like an age-old corpse, battered by strife,
His dry flesh powdered to dusty life.

And Gypsy Time laughed as his skeleton fell
And she spun herself free to continue her spell –
Faster and faster and quicker she swirled,
Until she saw me – and then she called:

  *'Come dance, come dance!*
  *Come step with me!*
  *Come waltz and let me clasp you tight!*
  *Come age and die and twirl with me,*
  *Come hold me fast with all your might!'*

And into her arms she pulled my form
Against her body, soft and warm,
And tightened up her vice-lock grip
  As the watchers gasped and prayed I'd slip
  Away from her 'ere magic starts –
But the pounding music thumped my heart.

Then gazing into her sultry face,
Something within me started to race
And make me see she was just a 'mask' –
A shadow-dance
That covered a truth beneath her stance.

So I raised my angered fist aloft
And struck her painted china face!

And suddenly the music ceased;
  And the watchers gasped in the deafening peace,
Broken only by the glittering falling glass
As onto the floor her body smashed:
Time shattered to a thousand slithers
Like a broken Dresden doll with tousled locks;
Time turned to dust and sighed, and finally died –

And all the watchers smiled
At her empty dress 'neath the ticking clock.

Old grandfather clock, tick tock:
Don't mock.
Time does not exist –
She's just a clever mind-trick
And you are her accomplice!

I've broken the spell, I'm free at last!
And I'll give my truth to all who ask.
My life is cleared of apprehension,
No longer trapped in three dimensions.
I've broken free. I've seen the light!
I know there is no day or night;
No Past or Future yet to be –
*Just this Living Moment Only.*
And I'm free, my friend! At last I'm free!

And then, through the mist, the tick tock stopped,
And bellowing low came the voice of the clock:

*'Break the spell, you surely did,*
*But more than you know is currently hid:*
*Now, ceasing all my endless tocks*
*I'll give the secret Time unlocks.'*

And all the room fell deathly still,
The birds stopped singing on the windowsill,
And every soul held his breath and listened
To the mellow voice that glistened:

*'Exist for Now*
*And Time will smile on you,*
*(For she knows well her lie)*

*But break her face, and crack she will.*
*Time measured by decay: Untrue!*
*That is an Illusion,*
*Which grins at those who fail to see*
*And frowns at those who do.'*

Old grandfather clock, tick tock:
Tick away ever, I care not!
I'll not be bound by transient things:
In Ever-Nowness my song I'll sing –
And to my life I'll constantly bring
My Own Time.

And once again the clock-voice croaked,
Shimmering the stillness as it spoke:

*The Ever-present Now holds fast*
*The ghosts of all the seeming Past,*
*And the seeds of Future yet to be*
*Floating through memory:*
*For Past and Present, and the Now*
*Are all One and the same;*
*A marriage of All Three*
*(Hard I know to see)*

*But somewhere Now, you're dying.*
*And somewhere Now, at birth you're crying.*
*Can you follow me?'*

And instantly a bright light flashed my mind –
And suddenly I realised
What I sought to find
Was right before me,
And I'd been blind.

Old grandfather clock, tick tock,
Tick tock:
Tick away endless, I care not.
For Time is but the Ghost of a Great Illusion
And I'm no longer trapped by her Delusion.

# 15

# Questions and Answers

Many thousands of intelligent questions have been asked of me over the years. Seekers have always been full of bright thoughts and, while I'm the first to admit that I don't have all the answers, I do try to share whatever knowledge I've gained on my own quest for Truth.

By popular request here's another varied and, I hope, thought-provoking selection of questions that have been asked quite frequently.

*How do you hear your spirit voices?*
All spirit voices are heard within the Mind. Communicators don't have physical voice-boxes; so even when their voices sound completely objective to a medium, and as audible as mine is now, they are still heard within the mind. The brain conveys sound-waves to the mind, which recognises them as speech. A similar principle applies to physical sight and sense. Everything is a mind-experience.

*Where is the spirit world?*
Eternity is everywhere. There are many worlds of spirit, all interpenetrating one another.

Just as television and radio signals are passing right through us now, unsensed (when we've no instrument to interpret them), so the spirit worlds are also with us here and now, but they exist at much higher frequencies than our world, which is why they remain mostly unregistered.

Imagine the Universe as a tank of water, and the Earth as a sponge, submerged in the tank. The water represents the worlds of spirit.

The spirit worlds are simultaneously all around us, and moving through us.

We'll never be more eternal than we are at this moment. We are Spirit now.

*Do children grow up on the Other Side?*
Yes. Children reach the full bloom of youth in the spirit world and then remain in young adulthood.

The ageing process belongs only to the physical body, it doesn't affect the spirit body.

*When old people die, do they stay old?*
No. The spirit body reaches adulthood and remains in that state, provided, of course, that this is what the individual desires. Simply by taking thought a spirit person can alter his or her appearance.

Although the physical body wears out, decaying day by day, inside it there's a fit and healthy spirit- or energy-body.

When death occurs, the old will be young again, if that's what they wish.

*Why have you described 'old' people returning to us in tonight's meeting?*
In order to be recognised, your loved ones project into my mind images of themselves as they were when you knew them.

*Are 'accidents' meant to happen?*
I'm not happy about the word 'accident' because everything is governed by the Natural Laws. The law of Cause and Effect cannot be cheated.

If the brakes of a car fail, sending a driver into eternity, 'hidden' causes can explain why this effect has happened.

There's no such thing as an 'accident' because all happenings conform to the Laws of the Universe: in this case, the cause would be a mechanical fault.

We should also take into account another factor: Time. In mass tragedies large numbers of people cross over into the next world – why? Why were those people there at that particular time? Why weren't *we* there?

The answer is simple: a long chain of 'hidden' *causes* has carried those souls to connect with those precise *effects* – their time to pass over had arrived.

In this respect, no death can be viewed as an 'accident'.

I don't believe in 'coincidence'.

The Universe is a highly organised place.

*I have prophetic dreams that come true. Where does this information come from?*
Premonitions will most likely reach you from within your higher self: your own spirit can receive details

of future events, you don't have to be given these by a third party. Your own future can project itself 'backwards', so to speak, into your present awareness and you can see it, provided that you've developed a certain sensitivity.

But on many occasions what you perceive as future events are often only sets of possibilities.

But never forget that your soul knows where it's going, why it's come here, and what it's hoping to achieve in this life.

If you could get in touch with the higher part of your mind you would never fear tomorrow, for you'd see your pathway clearly before you.

*One night I floated out of my body, panicked and couldn't get back in for a while. What should I do if it happens again?*
Don't panic! Out-of-the-body experiences are very common occurrences.

During an OOBE your spirit body, which is more or less a replica of your physical body, exteriorises a little and you become conscious in the next world.

If you panic when you're returning you create strong whirling vibrations in your mind, which momentarily hinder your re-alignment.

Returning is best done gently. Next time, keep calm – there's nothing to fear. You are always in control.

*Do we have any privacy?*
Yes, of course.

We don't always know what's happening on the Other Side, and they don't always know what's happening here. Unless either party tunes-in to the other's existence, each world remains unsensed.

*Can the spirit people see our thoughts?*
Yes. If they've mastered their natural telepathic abilities the spirit people can see into our minds; but even then they don't see everything.

Telepathy comes easily to them, once they've learned the skill.

*What language do they speak?*
The true language of the spirit is *Thought*.

When Thoughts are transferred from one mind to another, physical language is unnecessary, because at its deepest levels the mind works with images and feelings. Our words simply clothe those deeper impulses.

A spirit person can speak his mother-tongue, of course, or even learn another language if he wishes to.

*What work do they do Over There?*
Many avenues of work are open to people in the next world: they can teach, heal, study the arts and sciences, or follow any pursuit their imagination can create.

*Do they earn money?*
No, there's no monetary system in the Spirit World.

However, if people want money, then they can have it – for all the good it'll do them!

The coin of the spirit is service.

Real progression comes through service, which

allows your spirit and character to deepen and grow. Service brings you a sense of self-worth and achievement.

Happiness is a state of mind. Your outlook and attitude will govern your life in the Beyond.

*Is it true that we all have a Guardian Angel?*
In a way, yes. We're certainly observed by many souls in the next world, but I disagree with traditional thought in this respect: I don't believe we all have *one* specific soul who 'guards' us in a specific way. I accept the Law of Personal Responsibility, which states that we're in charge of our lives, that we must be responsible for planning and executing them.

Although help is always available, I don't think we're all led or guided every step of the way.

*So what is your own guide's task?*
My spirit guide is in charge of the spiritual work we're doing. I'm responsible for all its aspects on Earth, and he's responsible for all its aspects in the Beyond. Ours is a willing co-operation; it is never a domination. We're partners, good friends. Love and respect binds us together.

He doesn't interfere with my daily life, nor I with his. However, because he loves me he often imparts some sound advice.

And, of course, he isn't the only spirit person who helps me: over the years several Spirit Controls or Helpers have guided me, and willingly added their expertise to my work.

*Will your guide use another medium after you have died?*

No, I don't think so, because it isn't easy for two minds to blend closely together, especially when they live in different worlds. He's often said our work is a unique mission, and that it'll finish when I cross over into the light.

*Is reincarnation a fact?*

It all depends on the mind you're questioning. Even in the spirit realms they're divided on the issue of reincarnation: some spirit people claim it as a fact, while others hotly deny it.

I believe that with God all things are possible, and therefore these opportunities would be available. But you, as a personality, as a characterised soul, will not reincarnate. However, what *can* return to Earth is another aspect your eternal mind. There are vast differences between your Personality and your Spirit.

Your Personality comprises everything that you are in your physical consciousness – whereas your Spirit is the everlasting *essence* of you, the direct Life-Force that links you to the Great Spirit.

In your current form you will not return. Your soul will pass into Eternity, there to live for ever.

However, at some future time another portion of your spirit, another part of your vast mind, might again characterise itself into flesh and create a new personality.

Your individual survival is assured.

It isn't easy to grasp these mystical concepts, which liken the spirit to a many-faceted diamond whose segments are materialised into Earth consciousness as different personalities, and yet each segment has sprung from the same spirit source.

The existence of reincarnation cannot be proved to sceptical minds. Sceptics will always offer alternative explanations which nullify any memories that are presented as 'previous lives'.

Neither do I think reincarnation is as common an occurrence as some would have us believe.

If it happens, it occurs because your spirit realises there are lessons to be learned on the Earth, and special tasks still to be accomplished.

Because you have free will and personal responsibility, you alone will decide whether or not to undertake another incarnation.

*How can I develop my psychic powers? Can you offer me some comprehensive advice?*
Look at your true motives for undertaking any spiritual work: if they're based on a genuine desire to help and serve others, that's a good starting-point. But if your motivation is centred on inflating your ego, then you're heading for humiliation, heartache, stress and disappointment.

Remember the Universal Law of Like Attracts Like. From the next life you will draw to yourself people who will share your motivation. That's fine, if your motives are helpful, loving, and sincere – but if they're not, you'll receive exactly what you've earned. We get what we deserve.

That's the Law.

Psychic development excites the body's nervous energies, and delves into areas of the mind that can

237

be best endured, understood, and dealt with, only by people whose personalities are stable in all senses of the word.

If your emotional or mental health is in question, leave psychic unfoldment well alone. Otherwise, join a group. Don't develop these skills in isolation. Find a development class, preferably conducted by a well-trained and respected medium who'll be aware of all the dangers and pitfalls that lie ahead of you.

Many times in your formative years, you'll need the sensible guidance of an experienced medium. You cannot develop these gifts overnight, in a few weeks, or in a few months.

There are probably psychic centres or Spiritualist Churches in your region, where you can find experienced tutors. Ask at your Central Library for addresses; or search the Internet for helpful information.

Never remain in ignorance: read as much as you can. Sift through the material, and accept only what appeals to your intellect and intelligence.

*Question every teaching – accept nothing blindly. There's no room for a blind faith in your search for the Truth.*

*There's room only for a faith founded on knowledge, on research, on fact and experience.*

*Even when guidance and information reach you from the Other Side, this doesn't mean they are valid – you must question everything, always.*

It's easy to fall into the trap of self-delusion if you try to unfold your talents in isolation. To succeed, mediums need constructive, objective criticism, and above all: education.

As with any other learning process, you should be trained by recognised authorities.

You wouldn't dream of re-wiring a house unless you were a properly-trained electrician: the dangers are obvious. The same principle applies to psychic development: never meddle with the powers of the mind unless you're strong-willed and self-governed, very disciplined, and, of course, emotionally and mentally stable.

*Can I join a psychic development class straightaway?*
Most teachers will want to get to know you first, to assess your emotional and mental stability, and to take into account other factors such as your background, *before* they agree to train you. The development of psychic and mediumistic skills isn't a party-game, it's a serious study; and if you're not serious about studying it or about helping mankind – then steer clear of it.

*I saw columns of light and small coloured lights, the size of a coin, floating in my bedroom. What were they?*
Ethereal lights and mists are usually manifestations of psychic energy, often caused by a spirit person's presence, or by the natural electro-magnetic fields radiated either by the building or by the ground on which it stands.

*How can a spirit person walk through a wall?*
The atoms that comprise the spirit person's body exist (or vibrate) at higher frequencies than the atoms that comprise the wall.
   *Everything exists in a state of constant vibration.*

If the spirit visitor's body 'vibrated' at the same rate as the bricks in the wall, he would bump into them, as we do.

*I prayed that my young daughter would recover from terminal cancer, but she died. Why was she taken from me?*
No one 'takes' a soul away: when a body 'dies' the soul passes back into its rightful home.

We're governed by complex and innumerable Natural Laws, and one of these is Cause and Effect. Illness is the 'visible' effect of a number of 'hidden' causes. Your daughter's body reached the point where it could no longer allow her spirit further expression in this world, and her 'death' occurred.

But don't be saddened; everyone lives on into Eternity. Try to keep cheerful, because your child is still alive.

As to your prayer not being answered: to die is not a tragedy for the person making the crossing; in many cases it's a blessed release.

*Can mediums foretell the future?*
Mediums can occasionally foresee the future, but the principal task of a medium is to relay evidence of survival from one world to another.

*You teach that physical handicaps vanish upon death, but what about mental handicaps: do they persist beyond the grave?*
Mental handicaps don't exist in the spiritual world because they are *physical* malfunctions caused by the brain, which acts like a computer: a thought-

receiving-and-transmitting station.

The mind is perfect. The mind is King.

On Earth the brain can sometimes malfunction; but in the spirit world, once the brain is out of the way, the individual can freely express his thoughts again.

In the spiritual world people have plenty of time to nurture and deepen their thinking.

Divine Justice rules this Universe; and in the worlds beyond this one, a balance is always struck.

*Does cremation in any way affect the soul?*
No. Once death has occurred, the soul is unaffected by anything that you do to the body.

*My husband was buried in a mass war-victims' grave without a religious service being conducted. Will he inherit eternal life?*
Everyone survives death; that is the Law. Burials in 'sanctified ground', or religious services, don't in any way affect your right to inherit eternal life.

Just send out loving thoughts to your husband, and remember he'll be close to you. He isn't under the earth.

*My mother and I argued violently before she died. Do you think she'll forgive me?*
Only your Mum can answer that, but there's a good chance that from her new viewpoint she'll see things differently, and will now forgive you. Forgiveness is a jewel found in souls who are progressing towards spirituality. Meanwhile, send your mother good thoughts and she'll receive them.

*My father was a Catholic and he didn't believe in communicating with the 'dead'. Do you think he'll get in touch?*

It's up to him.

If your father still believes communication to be wrong, he may not try it. On the other hand – and this is the stronger possibility – now that he realises he's still alive, he'll probably try to get in touch. By the way, we can't communicate with anything that's 'dead'. Mediums communicate only with the living.

Catholics pray to their saints, and these are only mortal beings who have passed over.

*Is Spiritualism a dangerous cult linked to the occult?*

No. In Britain, Spiritualism is a State-recognised religion, registered at the Home Office; and its ordained ministers perform marriages, funerals, and naming services (the Spiritualist equivalent of a 'christening').

Spiritualism asks its adherents to believe nothing, but to test everything with their common sense and intelligence. It has no creed, no dogma, no special book, and no set philosophy. It refrains from telling people what they should believe or what they should do.

Spiritualism is, however, founded upon Seven Principles that were mainly received through the mediumship of one of its early pioneers, Emma Hardinge-Britten.

Ardent Spiritualists claim their belief is not only a religion but also a science and a way of life. The Principles are based upon Universal Laws; and these are:

1. The fatherhood of God.
2. The brotherhood of man.
3. The communion of spirits and the ministry of angels.
4. The continuous existence of the human soul.
5. Personal responsibility.
6. Compensation and retribution for all the good and evil deeds done on Earth.
7. Eternal progress open to every human soul.

Many Spiritualists will accept these guidelines only if they remain open to liberty of interpretation.

Others believe that man has evolved and that these Principles are now outdated.

Feminists want the masculine references changed; and compassionate vegetarians want the souls of animals included in the open road to progression; which, of course, they are.

*Which is the most important Spiritualist Principle?*
The 5th Principle, Personal Responsibility, is probably the most important one because it teaches that we can blame no one but ourselves for our actions and thoughts. We alone must carry the burden of our mistakes, and we alone must rectify them.

*There is no 'vicarious atonement': no one can take away from us the mistakes that we've made; only we ourselves can do this.*

Spiritualists find this concept morally sound and Just because it speaks of a Divine Justice which cannot ever be cheated.

*As we sow, so shall we reap.*

If we plant a rose, a lettuce will not grow. If we

shine forth love, love will eventually return to us. This same law applies to all the negative aspects of hatred, anger, intolerance, and selfishness.

*What happens in a Spiritualist Church?*
Most church services include hymns or spiritual songs, followed by a prayer, delivered from the heart of the speaker. There's often a reading taken from any book belonging to any faith or set of teachings.

The main part of the service is a demonstration of clairvoyance, message-relaying from the spiritual world.

Nearly all churches hold separate services where spiritual healing is administered to the sick, either through the laying-on-of-hands or through prayer.

Churches usually advertise in local newspapers, or their addresses can be obtained from your Library or on the Internet. Spiritualists are quite friendly folk, and their churches are often good places in which to start your investigations; I began mine there.

*I had a vision of my husband while he was physically hundreds of miles away, but he was still alive. What did I see?*
You saw your husband's double, or Phantasm of the Living. A person doesn't have to be 'dead' in order to be seen in another place, or in another time.

What's seen is usually a thought-form of the loved one, but sometimes a spirit body can be glimpsed, because it has travelled out of the person's physical frame while he's asleep or resting. There are many documented cases of bi-corporiety: instances in which a person has been seen in two different places at exactly the same time.

It's been reported that the two forms can even hold separate conversations simultaneously.

I've received many letters from people world-wide who have either 'seen' me in their homes or 'glimpsed' me walking down their streets, when I was resting or sleeping in Britain.

*When I attended a 'Transfiguration' meeting, other people saw the medium's features change as the spirit people purported to make themselves visible; but I saw nothing. Why was this?*
You didn't see a genuine Transfiguration medium; these gifted people are extremely rare.

If the physical mediumship is genuine, *everyone* sees the startling changes as communicators build up their features over the medium's bone structure, thereby making themselves visible to *all* of the witnesses.

What you saw was probably a deluded 'medium', or even worse than this – a charlatan.

*How does a spirit person possess a human being?*
Spirit people cannot 'possess' physical people; they can achieve a close proximity to another's mind, but this can't be accomplished successfully without the full consent and co-operation of the medium.

Your body is your own, and you alone can open your doors to the spirit people, because only you have all the keys.

*Do your communicators ever get things wrong, or get*

*their facts mixed up?*
The spirit people frequently make mistakes; they
are fallible human beings, just as we are.

*There are 1,000 people in here tonight, but you can only
give relatively few messages.*
  *Is it worth the effort?*
Ask me that question again when you've been one of
the people who were helped.

*Truth builds her Nest*
*only in the Branches of an Open Mind;*
*and as a Gift to those who Love her,*
*she will set their Spirits Free*

Stephen O'Brien

# 16

# Spiritual Reflections

Many thousands of people have written to say how much they've been helped by my teachings, and have asked me to publish my lectures.

'Perhaps one day I'll get them printed,' I replied.

Meanwhile, by public request, here are some interesting reflections, culled from the millions of words I deliver each year through my writings, public appearances, and media interviews.

I think the following sayings will strike a spiritual chord in readers because they touch upon some of the important aspects of our lives, and attempt to endow them with deeper meaning.

## God and the Natural Laws

God is a Great Spirit, a Force, a Breath of Living Consciousness. The Creative Mind is not a man, but a Power of Life Itself.

We're all Children of the Great Spirit. We are small sparks which have been struck from the Great Spirit's Life-Force. The Divine Spark motivates us, gives us a conscious awareness of our own Being, and links us to the Creative Mind, for ever.

We can never be separated from our Creator – the link remains eternally unbroken. We are Sons and Daughters of the Living Mind, and therefore we're all Brothers and Sisters.

People say God is perfect; but how do they know God is perfect? The Spirit of God may be slowly evolving, just as our spirits are.

We are governed by Eternal Natural Laws, not by laws made by man – for they are transient – but by the Natural Laws which are born in the Creative Mind; in the Lawgiver, whom some men call God.

The Natural Laws reign supreme in all areas of Being: in emotional, physical, mental, and spiritual kingdoms.

We are personally responsible for what we think, say, and do, and no one in this world or in the next can take away from us the mistakes we've made. We ourselves must rectify them and learn from the growth-experience of facing our challenges and conquering them.

We have free will: freedom of choice, the right to govern our lives as we see fit; and this knowledge brings with it personal responsibility for our thoughts and actions. But our free will is limited.

For example, even if we wanted to we couldn't drink the oceans dry in one gulp.

The Natural Laws are continuously at work, forever limiting our power, restricting our choices, influencing our lives, and curtailing our freedom.

We have the power to create beauty and joy, or to wreak havoc and destruction. The governing of our lives is our responsibility – there isn't a personal human-being-type God who will interfere when we make our limited choices.

There's only one Eternity but there are many worlds within worlds, within which we may exist.

All states of life *interpenetrate* one another; so, at any one point in space we could be standing in millions upon millions of different worlds containing countless life-forms. Each world is separated from the next because it vibrates (or exists) at a different set of frequencies to its neighbour.

'In my Father's House there are many mansions'.

And now consider 'The Judgement Day'.

We are our own judges and juries: there is no celestial panel awaiting us when we pass over.

Judgement is immediate. Our minds confront us with the vivid memories of our acts – whether 'good' or 'bad' – and we will pay the price which our highly sensitive spirit-consciences will dictate.

Atonement, or reparation, is usually achieved by seeking the forgiveness of those we've wronged;

then by rendering service to them, and others, until every debt is paid. We will continue to serve until we feel that the records have been put straight, and that we can live in peace with our neighbours, and be at peace with ourselves.

Mediums don't always find love and light in the Beyond. Everyone survives death, and there are places which hold all kinds of people in all manner of conditions. The Golden Rule is *Like Attracts Like*.

'Birds of a feather, flock together'. In Eternity, those of a similar spiritual nature will inhabit similar spheres of existence.

Whatever you think, even unknowingly, is sent out into the Universe by the power of your mind.

Your thoughts are energy-waves which cannot be destroyed; and one day these energies will return to you in full measure.

You will reap exactly what you have sown.

You will receive only what you have earned, only what you deserve. This Law is unchangeable and mathematically precise in its operation.

This is Divine Justice.

## Ghosts and Poltergeists

Ghosts are energy-pictures captured by the psychic fields of activity permeating and surrounding the walls and atmospheres of buildings.

Ghosts are different from spirit people. Ghosts aren't real spirit people making a visitation; they're merely 'psychic snapshots'.

Ghosts cannot communicate with us in the way that living spirit people can.

Ghosts have no conscious personalities because they're merely 'energy pictures'.

Sadly, many mediums still don't understand the difference between thought-forms and spirit communicators, and fall into the trap of confusing the two.

'Poltergeist' means 'noisy (or troubled) spirit', but most poltergeists are nothing of the kind.

Telekinesis, or the supernormal movement of objects, usually occurs when the physical people in a house radiate excess psychic energy.

When teenagers reach puberty they often throw off tremendous amounts of psychic power as their hormone levels rise.

A real poltergeist – a troublesome visitor from another world, bound close to the Earth by powerful desires – is a quite rare phenomenon.

A genuine poltergeist moves physical objects by drawing on the energies radiated by individuals and life-forms living in the vicinity.


### Suicide

Taking your own life doesn't extinguish it. If you take your life, you merely terminate it here and place yourself in another world.

If you can't cope with life here, you won't be able to cope with life Over There, because you'll take with you this 'inability to cope'. Nevertheless, in the Beyond all suicide victims are helped by compassionate and qualified specialists to achieve a state of spiritual health and well-being.

Peace of mind must be earned by those who desire it.

I wouldn't advise anyone to take his own life because the reason for life is growth; and soul-growth cannot come only in the sunlight – it also occurs in the shade.

## The Animal Kingdom and Survival

Many people are distressed when their beloved pets pass away, and want to know if they survive death. I can happily report that they do.

I've lost count of the animals who've returned to their loved ones through my mediumship. In nearly all cases, spirit animals bring feelings of warmth and gratitude for the love and concern shown to them when they lived on Earth.

Animals have souls: they survive death. In Eternity, kind people care for our animal friends.

Over the years, as well as cats and dogs: giraffes, elephants, horses, birds, and ponies, and all kinds of creatures have successfully returned through my mediumship to the people they love.

When animals share a close bond with us, we've helped them to achieve a greater awareness of their individuality, which in turn assures not only their survival but also their spirit return.

Even creatures other than domestic pets live on in Eternity.

People often ask if their pets are psychic, and the answer is: *yes*. Animals' minds are so uncluttered and free of prejudice and social etiquette that even the most humble of pets possesses the ability to see or sense the spirit people – a skill that eludes countless humans.

Man experiments on animals because he foolishly believes himself to be higher in importance than them. Man would do well to remember that he is also an animal.

Humankind will never advance spiritually while it subjects animals to unspeakable torture in the name of science and medical research.

*Abattoirs run red with innocent blood.*

The horrors of vivisection perpetrated in laboratories add nothing to man's spiritual stature, for these acts are not born of love and compassion.

In the name of vanity, oceans of innocent blood are shed.

Help to free our animal brethren by purchasing only 'untested-on-animals' household and cosmetic products.

If you become a vegetarian or vegan you'll gain greater health and develop a more compassionate character.

Animals are our brothers and sisters, and we can help them to evolve their natures by showing them what compassion is.

I feel deeply sorry for caged creatures; it must be a far from ideal life for them, being confined in those small spaces. I know *we* wouldn't like it.

We put people in cells as a punishment, but what have the birds and animals done?

Soul power, or psychic power, resides in every living thing.

Animals are extremely sensitive beings: they can register human emotions quite easily because their psychic abilities operate more freely than ours do.

They, like us, are spirits working through physical bodies.

Everything Man has done to the Animals, he has already done to himself...

### The Spirit Body

The physical body exists only because it is built around the blueprint of the spirit body. Take away the spirit body permanently, as in death, and the physical frame begins to decay because it has lost its binding and animating force.

When we discard the physical body we will register through a much finer vehicle of expression: the spirit body, which is the counterpart of the mortal body. In its own world, the spirit (or energy) body is solid and real: it can be touched and sensed, and it occupies space and dimension.

There is no physical handicap present in the spirit body: it functions in perfect health.

If a man loses a limb or suffers from a deformity of the physical body, he need not worry unduly: his inner energy body will be unaffected.

The spirit body cannot be harmed.

Clairvoyantly, I've seen the spirit bodies of several of my friends who were fast asleep in bed at the time. I knew they hadn't passed over because their energy bodies didn't radiate bright lights around them, as the energy bodies of permanent spirit denizens do.

## On Being Met at the Crossing

We're all met when we die, but not necessarily immediately or by the people we might think will be there to greet us. But no one is forgotten in the scheme of things.

In the next world there are Watchers who scan the Earth for 'new arrivals', for people crossing over into the light. Irrespective of how someone 'dies', the spirit people will soon be present.

The Watchers are particularly evident in places of sickness and suffering: they gather in hospitals, in war-zones, and in the vicinity of all large-scale tragedies.

Evolved souls in the other world know when a passing is to be taken; but not all spirit people have access to this information. Some spirit friends can be just as surprised by the news of a passing as we would be.

## Children in the Spirit World

I maintain that a person's life begins at the moment of conception.

Stillborn babies, and children who aren't carried for their full term of pregnancy, all survive death and grow up on the Other Side. In the spirit realms children are loved and cared for by people who dedicate their lives to rearing them, just as good parents do here.

As a general rule, close family members in the next life will bring up your spirit children.

Children grow up on the Other Side until they reach the full bloom of youth. Parents will be able to recognise their spirit offspring because sleeping adults can project out into the astral worlds and meet their children.

Spirit children are often brought to visit their families on Earth, and as the years unfold there will be no separation; and one day there will be a happy reunion.

In the Beyond, children attend schools, learn, play, and grow, as youngsters do on Earth.

Don't worry about your child who has passed: your child will not forget you.

When spirit children visit the Earth, they bring with them feelings of light and energy, and quick, fine vibrations of youthful enthusiasm.

Their eyes are bright and shining, yet behind them there's an inner-knowing that very few Earth children possess.

Spirit children often speak with incarnate youngsters. Many a child has known a real invisible friend.

Spirit children are attracted to our world either by ties of family or by ties of friendship – and sometimes they come just to play with our young ones, and to learn from the experience.

## Religion and Belief

All roads lead to God. The way in which we live our lives is more important than the name of the road we're travelling on, for we shall change direction many times in our search for the Truth.

Religious beliefs carry little weight in the Beyond. In the spirit realms, your life will be governed by immutable Natural Laws which will operate no matter what you might believe.

Never once did my spirit people decry anyone's religion. About your religion they say:

'If it makes you a better person, then it is right for you. If it teaches you to love, then it is a good set of instructions.'

If you believe in anything one hundred per cent, this is dangerous: it's unhealthy because your mind is then closed to any new possibilities.

The Other Side isn't one bit concerned with titles, religions, or lip-service codes of conduct, they're concerned with people: souls, not labels.

Before helping people I never ask what religious faiths they hold, for these are not the most important facets of their lives.

## Thought and Prayer

Just like a pebble dropped into a pool of still water, thoughts, which are all born of energy, radiate outwards. *Thoughts are living things.*

Prayer is a stream of spontaneous living thought, born of desire; and someone, somewhere, will hear those thoughts.

People's prayers *are* answered – but not always immediately, and not always in the way they expect them to be answered, or in the way they wish them to be answered.

The Universal Laws stipulate that by the very act of prayer, by opening up the spiritual heart and recognising a Higher Source and seeking help from it, the petitioner automatically receives an influx of spiritual strength and inspiration.

Viewed in this way, prayer is a personal exercise of one's own spirit, seeking refreshment, guidance, and help from those in Eternity who are in attunement with it.

Mass prayers, frequently read or recited by rote, don't impress evolved spirit-guides because they're not born in the heart and soul of the petitioner.

But a sincerely-meant prayer, filled with emotion and desire, will reach far into the worlds of spirit and bring a fruitful reply.

Selfish prayers will not bring good responses from evolved Beings in Eternity.

But prayers delivered for the good of others, and for one's own spiritual development, will draw the positive help and sensible guidance that the seeker deserves.

We will gain only the rewards that we've earned for ourselves.

## Telepathy

Telepathy is a fact – I've experienced it too many times to deny its existence.

Telepathy is a mind-to-mind contact.

Sceptics often claim that a medium's evidence of survival doesn't come from the spirit world at all: they say it comes purely via telepathy, but this is a presumptuous statement to make. If only *one* case for survival is proved, then the mediums' claims are justified.

The recipient of a spirit message could find that it contains pieces of information which they can't immediately 'place': all such evidence should be thoroughly researched.

If the facts are later proved correct – and there have been many instances in which this has been the case – the theory of telepathy on the part of the medium has to be ruled out. Mediums cannot read facts from a recipient's mind if those facts aren't there.

We have a psychic link with those we love, whether they live in this world or in the next; it's a kind of magnetic link that can never be broken, a thread of awareness that ties us to one another. When loved ones are distressed, a sensitive relative can register this; and distance is no obstacle to this power.

Mediums can use their own soul-powers (or psychic energies) to register vibrations of sight, sense, and sound that don't necessarily reach them from the spirit world. They can scan the electro-magnetic fields of swirling energies – known collectively as the aura – which surround a person, and become aware of all kinds of 'secret' information.

A psychic or medium is quite capable of wrongly interpreting clairvoyant visions.

If a sensitive tries to 'read' a person's auric fields he must never deceive himself into thinking that his perceptions and judgements are always correct, because they may not be.

Years of careful development are needed to perfect these difficult skills.

## Psychic Communication

I can't 'bring people back' or make anyone in the Beyond communicate with us. Firstly, they haven't gone anywhere: they're still near to us, living in a soul-world that interpenetrates ours.

Secondly, no one on Earth has any power to force the people on the Other Side to do his bidding. The spirit people exercise their free will, just as we do.

Communication between the two worlds, even at its best, is always an experiment because so many processes can go wrong.

Mediums don't easily achieve perfect spirit communication. Mediumship has to be developed over a period of years; it has to be channelled correctly, and nurtured carefully like a growing plant or a delicate child.

In order to deepen and expand his gift, a medium must undertake his development seriously. He must be patient; he must take time to study his subject and to experiment with his psychic powers; he must question all kinds of spiritual teaching, and think deeply about why he wants to unfold his gifts.

In order to operate proficiently, with intelligence and sensitivity, a medium should be trained by experts who have walked the ancient path before him. To dabble in anything is unwise; to master anything is sensible.

When a breakdown in communication occurs, the medium is probably at fault – but not always. After all, a medium is tuning-in to the higher frequencies of his mind, and that isn't an easy task.

A medium is rather like a human radio-set; but whereas radio-tuning is more or less fixed, the medium's mind is trying to register constantly-fluctuating spirit-wavelengths.

## Spirit Messages

Spirit messages are prepared in the other world before they're transmitted. In the majority of cases the spirit people know what they wish to say before they make contact.

A spirit message can be fully understood only by the person who is transmitting it and by the person who is receiving it. Information which might sound trivial to others, can, in fact, convey a wealth of hidden meaning to a recipient.

For example, the link might contain code-words or significant personal references known only to the two people involved. Who can say?

Most messages are direct and to the point.

They're usually simply worded, but on occasions they can be so complicated that only the recipient can possibly unravel them and understand them.

Spirit communicators will bring specific information to help us recognise them: their aim is to prove their survival to us.

But communicators might also mention intimate parts of their lives or remote family details, about which the sitter knows nothing; when this happens, recipients are asked to do some research, to check if the information is correct.

Often I catch everything that is transmitted to me by my communicators, but sometimes I miss small pieces of their messages. It isn't easy for the spirit people to make themselves heard in our world.

I've learned to trust and depend upon the voice of the spirit, and to flow *with* the stream of evidence reaching me rather than battle upstream and argue over minor details, which might seem important to the recipient but which mean very little to the communicator.

A private consultation is just exactly that – *private*.

## War and Peace

Governments create wars: wars are not created by nations. In a democratic society, people should vote for the personalities they think might be least likely to destroy world harmony and peace, and more likely to create it.

The more people who know about the horrendous effects that a nuclear war would bring, and about the untold misery it would create, the safer our world will be.

Governments take note: in a full-scale nuclear war there can be no victors.

I don't believe that might is always right.

Materialism is a plague upon humanity, a mental disease that leads to greed, selfishness, poverty, and to the breakdown of human dignity.

World peace will come to this planet only when each individual establishes it within his mind.

Only by your example can you teach. Peace starts right here, right now, in your daily life and in your dealings with other people.

Man is constantly at war with himself: his earthly consciousness battles with his higher self, which is striving continually to seek a closer union with Perfection and God.

## Sceptics

Those who don't wish to believe in survival after death will never accept the evidence of it, even if it's so startlingly-correct that it takes their breath away.

It's a source of constant wonderment to us all that the professional sceptics believe that Life Itself depends upon, and revolves around, the fact that we must accept their opinions as the gospel truth.

Every sceptic has a right to voice his views but there's no need to shout them out. God has blessed me with perfect hearing.
'Empty vessels make the most noise'.

## Death

Survival of the consciousness after death is the natural birthright of All: every living thing survives death.

Do not fear the Dark Angel called Death, for he isn't a Dark Angel at all – he's the Brightest One.

. Death is painless: it is simply the release of the spirit from the earthly body; and I often think of it as a happy release, for in many cases it is.

You 'die' every night when you sleep. As soon as your physical body has relaxed, your spirit body (within) starts to loosen from it and you leave your sleeping form: you can then astral travel in the world of spirit if you wish.
Sometimes your spirit body exteriorises only a little way outside your physical self, and it remains

close to your material body in a state of semi-sleep. In this out-of-body state, your spirit can absorb powerful healing energies from all around it, and channel them naturally to your physical body.

Every passing is unique, but in each case the traveller feels no pain. Pain isn't present in the spirit body: it belongs only to the physical form. The physical body is the pain body; the spirit body is the energy body.

Sudden deaths, such as accidents, send many victims into concussion. When the earthly body is knocked unconscious, the spirit body often suffers from a temporary state of sleep; but awareness soon returns to the new arrival in the spirit realms.

After a long and protracted illness, a sick person takes his passing more gently, and his loved ones in the spirit world gather to meet him as he crosses the threshold of death to life.

Death doesn't change the characters of those who experience it. You will be the same person one second after death, as you were one second before it.
  But change is forever open to all souls, and they can progress if they so choose.

Death will not confer upon us abilities or qualities of mind and character that we haven't developed in this life: everything has to be earned.

A person in a coma is already passing in and out of

the physical body. While the body sleeps, the spirit is released into worlds beyond the Earth.

This same principle applies to someone placed on a life-support system. But if the spirit permanently leaves its unconscious body, then that body has 'died' and it is kept 'alive' only in a mechanical sense, and the body is no longer animated by a spirit, but by a machine. Switch off the machine and the body ceases to function because the spirit is gone.

I have stood on the mountaintops of the Shining Lands and experienced countless visions of other worlds beyond death, and I am not afraid to die; for Death is the Great Liberator, the Bright Angel who leads all living things into an eternal life, which is their natural birthright.

## Evil and 'The Devil'

I'm not happy about the word 'evil'; 'misguided' might be a better word.

One man's 'evil' might be another man's 'good'. Your viewpoint depends on where you stand in the scale of spiritual evolution.

I don't believe in the devil: the devil is a myth, perpetrated by the priests and clergymen of yore.

In antiquity, mediums – or living channels for the power of the 'Holy Spirit' – were central to all Christian church services.

But then jealous priests ousted the sensitives,

seized earthly power, and kept the masses living in fear of church doctrines.

To keep their church coffers full, and thereby provide themselves with a secure livelihood, the priests then subjected all 'unbelievers' and 'the ignorant masses' to the constant threat of 'eternal damnation', mythical 'hellfire' and torments by 'demons' and 'the devil'.

To the great shame of the early Christian Church, its history is full of bloodshed, torture, murder, and the suppression of man's right to think for himself: and this is fact, not fiction.

Thankfully, today we live in more enlightened times, and the Church no longer exercises absolute power over man's educated mind.

However, millions of people in the world still remain 'controlled' by outdated theological beliefs, many of which are founded upon pure fiction.

If man wants to see 'the devil' he should look into a mirror.

Man remains the most cruel animal in creation.


## 'Right' and 'Wrong'

I try not to think in terms of 'right' and 'wrong'. Decisions are made according to our levels of understanding. What seems right to one man may seem obviously wrong to another.

The motive for performing your actions, that is the acid test. When all is said and done you will answer to your conscience for the acts you've committed. You cannot escape your thoughts.

If it's 'wrong' for a citizen to commit murder, how can it be 'right' for the State to do it?

That is illogical.

Our minds are such wonderful instruments that I'm surprised when people blindly accept another's opinions, instead of thinking matters out for themselves. After all, what is true for one man need not be true for another.

Always use the power of your mind to its full capacity.

*Be a thinker, not a follower.*

## The Conduct of the Soul

*What really matters is how you live your life.*

When you pass over you will gravitate to the sphere of existence that you've earned for yourself through the building of your character and the growth of your mind here on Earth.

All that you can take with you through the gateway called 'death' is yourself.

There are no pockets in shrouds.

There are no status symbols in Eternity: there is no earthly aggrandisement Over There.

When you pass through death and inherit eternal life, you will take with you your mind and character, your soul-growth and moral attitudes, and all the facets of your true inner self.

In the next life, you will not be the person that *you* think you are, or the person that *the world* thinks you are – you will be the person that you *truly* are.

In the next world you will see clearly that the only things that mattered in your Earthlife were:

> *how you lived your life:*
> *how you thought;*
> *how you behaved.*

Our problems are our own; they don't belong to the people in the next world, and therefore the solving of them is our responsibility.

All life is made up of comparison. We must know tears and joy, happiness and sadness, pain and peace within. We must learn to face our struggles and hardships; we must learn to cope with them, and overcome them: that is why we were born.

It's not what happens to you that matters: what counts is how you deal with it.

This world makes much of pomp and ceremony, and it treasures public acclaim as a mark of importance; but in the Greater Life what you call yourself will be of little account.

What you really are, what you've done with your life, is what matters Over There.

The only eternal treasure that you can possess is what you *are*.

What greater tribute could a man have than this: that his kindness will be remembered.

There isn't enough kindness in this world of ours. But we can change that, you and I: we can start a revolution of kindness in our own corner of the world, today.

And when we stand on the shores of Eternity and look back upon our experiences in Earth life, we will notice how all the things that we did, happened in just the right places at just the right times. And we shall say to ourselves: it is good.

## Love

The greatest power in the Universe is the Power of Love.

Clever scientists in their laboratories can never dissect love, or technically prove its presence in any way; nevertheless, it exists – and what is more: Love is stronger than Death.

If you have tasted the joys of love – and I don't mean physical love, but the deeper true spiritual love – then be thankful, for you are fortunate indeed.

*Only one single thought –*
*just one code of conduct*
*means more than anything else to me now:*

*Without Love, we are nothing.*

Stephen O'Brien

# 17

# Guidance from Beyond

The mind of God moves in mysterious ways, performing quiet miracles that often remain unsensed by us. But sooner or later, something happens and we realise that an external intelligence, some great Hand of Fate, has indeed guided us.

Suddenly a bright light illuminates the mind, and we experience realisation.

It happened to me.

Two long years after I'd moved to Gateshead, my life was still difficult and getting progressively worse. I couldn't move out of the catchment area, and money was scarce. My neighbours continued to be threatening, and kept me awake at night with their noisy television and radio sets. Life on the estate was a great big pain and strain.

Then one day I received a strange spirit message, which came through during a table-tilt experiment that I conducted at a lecture weekend. Supernormal forces moved, danced, rapped, and tilted a sturdy table in response to questions from sixty students.

Using one tilt for each letter of the alphabet the communicator spelled out his name:

*White Owl – Stephen's friend.*

'Ask him what he wants,' put in a student.

'Get a message!' cried one of the twelve people seated around the table. 'Well, White Owl?' I said, more to satisfy the students than myself, 'Is there any message?'

The table gave another shudder and tilted out:

*Home soon.*

My heart lurched.

(Home? *Wales*? Had I heard him correctly?)

'What did he say?' I asked hesitantly.

'*Home soon*,' piped up a young woman. 'Can you understand that?'

I replied softly, 'Well, I think so,' then half under my breath, 'I hope so...'

All at once, thoughts of beautiful green hills and Welsh mountains moved majestically before my inner sight. I could see the clifftops of Swansea, and smell the ozone as the sea thundered in upon the rocks. I saw the faces of people I'd known since childhood, and was filled with a surging desire to go back, to return to my roots. But it was only a dream – and another tilt of the table brought me sharply back to the séance.

Because my guide sympathised with my difficulties and my homesickness, was he indicating that he'd now try to open up another phase of my life?

Was there more service lying ahead of me, a wealth of opportunities for soul growth which could be brought about only by my living in Wales? I wasn't sure; so I waited patiently while the table tilted and tapped out the rest of his message:

*Home soon – Home is where the heart is.*

There was no doubt in his mind. But would events prove him right?

What happened next was strange indeed, and it started with a letter that my father wrote to the Swansea Housing Department back in Wales:

Dear Sir,

I am writing to you to respectfully request your assistance in finding accommodation in Swansea for my son, Stephen, who is now resident in England, in Tyne and Wear.

Stephen is now registered under the National Mobility Scheme and if you could bring him back to Swansea it would be a tremendous help to me, as I am severely disabled and living on my own at present.

Yours faithfully,

Mr R. O'Brien.

Following on from my Dad's request, I left Sooty 'on holiday' with Sheila, didn't buy food, ignored a final demand for an electricity bill, and thereby scraped together £47 to buy a rail ticket to visit Wales. The tedious seven-and-a-half hour journey gave me time to think back and reflect. Dad and I had never got on well, but all our disagreements had long-since been blown away by time, which is indeed a great healer.

On arriving in Swansea I was shocked by my father's appearance: he looked terribly unwell.

Chest problems made it difficult for him to breathe properly, and the extra weight he'd put on was placing a further strain on his heart. He said he was in constant pain and that he found life a struggle.

I already knew something about Dad's condition because my mother had been so concerned about his arthritis, painful gout, and seventy per cent chest-disability rating, that she'd sent me warning messages from the spirit world.

Because Dad couldn't walk very far, the Social Services Department had now provided him with a small car to aid his mobility.

After he and I had had some tea and a chat, I began a round of calls on various Housing Department officials, which took me a few days to complete. I also visited Dad's doctor who kindly wrote a letter to the Swansea Housing Director, supporting my father's request and recommending that I be housed near him.

Then came an interview at the Housing Offices.

'You're on a Priority list, Mr O'Brien. When something suitable becomes vacant, you'll be informed.'

'But my father's ill. How long will it take?'

'Maybe next week, or possibly two years.'

Walking out into the sharp air, I muttered to myself, 'So much for the "*Home soon*" message.'

'Well, never mind, boy,' groaned Dad later, 'we've done our best. But I can't stand much more of these chest pains. Some mornings I can't breathe properly,' he wheezed. In spite of our stormy past, I felt sorry in my heart for him, especially as he still missed my mother very much.

We said our goodbyes and I headed back north, with many doubts clouding my mind.

When I arrived, Sooty went 'bananas'!

She leapt up and down, ran through the rooms like a whirlwind, shot up the curtains, then sprang off the windows onto my jumper and scrambled all over me like a wildcat. Finally, she sat on my head, mewed with delight, and slapped her furry tail into my eyes. 'Did you miss me, sweetheart?' I laughed, tickling her stomach.

And then came a long and silent red-tape wait...

One dusty evening after wandering through Gateshead, deeply uncertain about my future and thinking about my past, I ended up sitting on the grassy Windmill Hills overlooking the River Tyne. An eerie silver-blue moonlight filled the sky and glimmered on the water, and the majesty of the snaking river dwarfed the black slums along its banks.

As the evening breeze drifted where it liked, and my mind floated with it into the splendour of the scene, the night was broken by a quiet male spirit voice. The sound was gentle, and it heralded a new beginning for me (although I had no idea of that then). 'Finish the book,' it whispered.

'What? My life-story? But I only have scraps of paper with faded memories on them.'

But the voice didn't comment.

'Surely I live in too upsetting a place to have the clear thoughts that a writer needs?'

Silence...

The voice did not speak again.

Entranced by the glittering river as it wound its way to the distant sea, I could hear only the droning of far-off traffic in Newcastle city: not another sound came from Eternity.

Way over the Tyne, high above the horizon, flocks of starlings squealed their cries and wheeled in the dying light of day. The sun was setting over the sky-line as I stood up slowly and ambled back to the dreary estate, perplexed and deep in thought.

Although recording my life seemed to be a very arrogant exercise (far too many 'I's for my liking) I was told by my spirit voices that my story would be of great help to many people in both worlds.

My inspirers said that millions would eventually read it, which brought to mind a strange prediction they'd given me years earlier, when they'd said: 'Unto you is granted the Power of the Word.'

In the following cold and uncertain months, I obeyed my other-world voices and my first book, *Visions of Another World*, was born. It was birthed amongst the poverty and unemployment of Gates-head town; written in the early hours of each morning between midnight and 3 a.m., when all the drunks had fallen senseless into their beds, and the thugs were out in another world, and the night was at its quietest.

I'd often received messages through many other mediums claiming that I'd write a book: and now their prophecies were fulfilled.

I spent long and lonely nights working on that manuscript, sometimes typing away into the dawn hours, but it was a therapeutic exercise that took my mind off my miserable surroundings. But only when I finished the book did I realise how truly blessed I'd been by the invisible world during my thirty-odd years: their love and guidance, their protection and encouragement, had been with me all the way. And through my link with them, I'd come to know my God. In compiling the text, I saw clearly that because I'd been through the fires of hardship I had emerged as a much stronger person, and was now better equipped to serve those who stand in need. After completing the first draft and contemplating its possible publication, I thought: 'Well, even if I die tomorrow I'll have left some-thing behind me to help others to travel along the road,' and somehow that thought made my trials easier to bear.

Then I began to experience *déjà vu*: I had the kinds of experiences in which people said unusual phrases and I spoke their exact words at the same time. Sometimes I described buildings in strange places that I'd never visited, only to discover that when I did arrive there, my descriptions were strikingly accurate.

Then my friend Jeff Rees Jones telephoned me from Swansea to tell me of a vacant council flat he'd seen. But when I applied for it, it had already been let. Dark fears of eventually being re-housed in a high-rise tower block invaded my mind; their noise levels are horrific: you can hear neighbours talking, and lavatories flushing. I'd have no privacy in such a place, and I value highly my privacy, and golden silence.

That night I selfishly prayed, 'I'd hate to leave my new friends, but if I must go then please get me a decent house.' I was even cheeky enough to request two bedrooms and central heating: I'd have loved that because my previous flat had been perishing cold in the winter. But after the refusal of my first application I thought:

'Oh God, bang goes my central heating, and I'll end up in a skyscraper.'

Knowing I was disillusioned, my friends Sheila and Graeme invited me along to Jarrow Spiritualist Church.

'Come on,' said Graeme, 'forget your troubles and do a bit of work.'

'Take your mind off it for a while,' chipped in kindly Sheila, stirring the piping-hot tea she'd just brewed to combat the icy weather. 'Besides, we always need help at the church; sometimes it's so full, there aren't enough mediums to go round.'

Reluctantly I agreed; but was later glad that I'd made the effort because I received an excellent message from one of the elderly mediums there.

'Your grandfather's here,' she smiled, then she gave me an accurate description of my mother's father, known as Grancha Price. She even supplied his surname. 'Oh all right, dear!' she gushed at him, 'it's no good pushing me, I'm going as fast as I can!' Then she said, 'He wants me to tell you that he knows about your application disappointment, but you're to hold on and there *will* be a move for you. He promises it'll be to your satisfaction. He says he heard your prayer, and the solution's coming. Can you understand that?'

Cheered up, I replied, 'Perfectly, thank you.'

Later that week another letter arrived from the Welsh Housing Department. But I hesitated before opening it because my faith in the Civil Service had long-since collapsed like a popped bubble-gum balloon.

My doubts were justified. The letter turned out to

be a confirmation saying the Department would contact me whenever something suitable became vacant. But how long would that be?

The bubble-gum hardened on the ground.

Again I couldn't sleep, and anxious thoughts kept flying through my mind; so in the end I sent up another prayer. 'Am I doing the right thing?' I asked. 'Should I stay in England, or return home to Wales? Are there people here in the North that I've yet to meet and help?' With failing trust, I called out to my invisible friends, 'If it's in my life-plan that I should go home: *please give me a sign.*'

In the stillness I waited for a light to guide me. I wanted advice and wisdom from the Beyond.

I waited; but nothing came.

Tranquillity bathed the dark room...

Weeks dragged by and I'd forgotten about my request when, standing at a bus-stop after my weekly visit to my piano-teacher, Miss Smith (who taught me music for virtually next to nothing), I began chatting to a friendly northern pensioner. She was a charming woman with a thick Geordie accent, but I was struck most by her penetrating eyes. But there was something strange about her bearing and features, and she seemed a little too friendly.

Nevertheless, we gossiped about the atrocious weather and the biting-cold snow lying thick on the ground. Then suddenly she launched an amazing remark:

'I'm from Wales, you know,' she beamed, her blue eyes shining.

Startled, I replied, 'But you don't have a Welsh accent.'

'No,' she said, 'but I'm as Welsh as you are!'

I was astounded by how small the world is.

She added, 'And I catch this bus every week at the same time.'

Then why hadn't we met before – because I too had caught that very same bus at the same time each week for the last two years. Why hadn't we bumped into each other?

It didn't make sense. But then came the biggest shock when she declared, 'I come from Swansea,' and she went on to describe districts just streets away from my birthplace. Then she announced, '*And I'm going back to Swansea in a few weeks.*'

I couldn't believe my ears. This stranger had not only named my hometown, but had also spoken of returning to it soon.

Then, quite out of the blue, a voice from heaven whispered inside my head:

*'This is the sign.'*

The very core of me was shaken.

But who *was* this elderly woman? And why hadn't our paths crossed before?

After we'd shuffled aboard the bus and sat down, I turned round in my seat to talk to her again, but I couldn't find her – she'd vanished.

My spine tingled.

In fact, I never saw the old lady again.

Could she have been a Messenger, sent from the Beyond? Had she been a spirit clothed in flesh, appearing on that bright snowy day, charged with a mission to deliver a sign?

It's often said that we walk and talk with angels, yet fail to recognise them.

No matter: the sign had been given.

I got off the bus and dashed into the supermarket to collect dozens of cardboard boxes, which I stockpiled in a bedroom in readiness for the move – and I didn't have long to wait. Within a week the offer was on the mat, and Grancha Price's spirit prediction proved itself correct; and I was more than satisfied with the two-bedroomed centrally-heated maisonette that I was offered. The property was in a quiet area near my Dad – and I couldn't resist a wicked grin at the thought of the central heating!

But now came the heart-breaking part, when I passed through a time of indecision over whether or not to accept the property.

My soul said 'Yes' but my body screamed 'No!' and I spent pounds I could ill-afford, ringing up friends in Wales and begging for advice. At night I paced the floor, unable to make up my mind. It's hard to describe my feelings: only a shadow of the uncertainty and heart-wrenching emotion can be conveyed.

In wanting to leave the North, I felt I'd failed to make a new life for myself, failed to settle down and complete my spiritual work; yet I yearned to return to my homeland.

I was in an anxious state. Where did I belong? What should I do? Where would I be happiest?

Floating back into my mind came my guide's prediction: *Home soon – Home is where the heart is...* and then I realised that it didn't matter where I lived because my heart would go with me wherever I went. We must be happy *inside* ourselves and not necessarily content with our outward surroundings. So I decided to leave.

I knew I'd miss the North, beating with the great heart of its people, but only when I was leaving did I fully realise just how much I loved them. I knew I'd miss poor Gateshead town, with its quaint streets and its Metro trains whizzing across the River Tyne at lightning speed. I'd miss the warmth and kindness of my new-found friends; and I'd especially miss the spiritual people who'd gathered around me, much like children seeking guidance from a father-figure – only I know that I learned much more from them than they ever did from me. They were wonderful people who'd welcomed me into their families.

Nevertheless, but not without emotional pain, I accepted the new flat.

But I couldn't bring myself to pack. Each time I touched a picture I felt as if I were ripping my heart out, and I sat down and cried like a baby. I'm proud of those tears because they fell in tribute to the love and respect I held for the northern people.

With just four hours left to the end of my tenancy, I still hadn't thrown more than three things into a box. Emotionally, I rang Sheila and Graeme who both dropped everything and dashed over to my flat. Then pandemonium broke loose. Everything was chucked everywhere, willy-nilly – and within three hours my home was hidden in bags and cardboard boxes.

And so it was 'goodbye' to Newcastle, which was one of the most difficult decisions I'd ever had to make. Even the thought of it now brings a wave of nostalgia and a lump to my throat.

The silliest things kept crossing my mind as I packed: thoughts that couldn't be dismissed – mixed images, memories of all the happy northern friendships I'd shared; the good days and bad days, all wrapped in emotion.

I was even strangely haunted by the sadness etched on the face of the ragged old woman who came each day to the city's monument to feed the hungry birds; and by the flocks of black starlings that circled and screeched over the cold city buildings at night. Would I ever see them again?

But I could stay no longer. The voice of Wales was calling, and I had to break the news to my friends.

The first I saw were Keith and Elizabeth, the compassionate people who'd brought my cat, Sooty, to me from an Animal Sanctuary.

'Oh Stephen,' sighed Elizabeth, her voice trembling, 'do you really have to go?' And she cupped a hand to her mouth.

'I'm afraid so,' I said, my own voice breaking at the thought of leaving them, especially after all the kindness they'd shown me.

In silence, Elizabeth looked down at the floor, then up again into my face. 'It's like losing one of our own,' she said softly, 'as if a part of our own family were leaving.'

And her husband, Keith, nodded sadly and took my hand. 'I hope you'll be happy, Stephen,' he said quietly. Then I embraced them.

Everyone seemed upset to think I'd soon be out of their lives, but no one was more upset than I was. 'I'll write and telephone,' I promised, 'and I'll never forget your kindness; and I'll value your friendship, for ever.'

I slowly got round to telling everyone.

Everywhere I went, people wished me well but I could see sorrow in their eyes.

'Look after yourself, Stephen.'

'Watch how you go now, Stephen. Promise you'll keep in touch, won't you? We've really enjoyed your friendship.'

'I think the world of you all,' I said.

'Stephen, it's been a privilege to know you.'

I was bereft of words.

My heart was full.

At the psychic circles, some of the sitters cried and couldn't find the right things to say. Next came great-hearted Sheila, without whose kindness I'd have starved in the North-east, and would have been very lonely. She assured me that I'd always be included in her prayers. 'God bless you, Stephen,' she said, 'and remember: I wish you happiness.'

Our eyes were full, and we embraced.

Everyone had been kind to me. I suppose I didn't appreciate what I had until I was in danger of losing it.

But it was Lily, the eldest sitter, who wept freely and cried the most. She held me so tight that I could never doubt her love and concern.

'Take good care of yourself, Stephen,' she said through her tears, 'and don't ever forget we'll all be thinking of you and praying that God'll keep you safe. God bless you, son.'

I began to weep.

She looked into my eyes. 'And you know where we are if you ever need us, don't you...?' then her speech dwindled away.

'Yes, Lily,' I sighed.

My heart was fit to burst. I couldn't speak another word.

'Come back to us one day, love. Please come back, son. You've done a lot of good up here. Now let me tell you this: many people up here think differently now – you've opened their minds; you've helped them, love, more than you'll ever know. Now, take care; and God Bless you, my handsome boy...' and her voice trailed away as she wiped her eyes.

And so my spiritual work in Northern England came to a close. The Hand of God, guidance from the Beyond, had moved me there, achieved its goal, and now pointed my way back down South, back home to Wales.

My last memory of Northern England was of a rented van, with me and Sooty, and my belongings, jumbled in the back of it, bumping and trundling its way down dusty winding roads and out along the highways and byways and off towards South Wales, four hundred miles in the distance.

As England faded out, and Welsh mountains came into view, my mind spun with memories and my eyes filled with tears. Green fields blurred past the windows, and my thoughts ran free. I knew that the hardships behind me had provided me with soul-growth, and that they'd brought me lasting friendships. I knew that I'd faithfully obeyed my inspirers and touched the souls of everyone who would listen to the spirit world's teachings.

I knew too that the younger Stephen O'Brien had been slowly strangled by his struggles, tested by them, and forced by them into becoming a more mature human being.

The thirty-two-year-old man now returning home was a new creature; someone older, wiser, reborn – someone who'd been spiritually enriched by the love he'd shared with the northern people.

Yet this man was also deeply sad in his heart. As he watched England disappearing over the horizon through the dusty truck windows, and turned his face towards Wales, he felt as if he'd just kissed the Vale of Tears, and passed through the Valley of the Shadow of Death.

# 18

# Touching Millions

My autobiography, *Visions of Another World*, was published in September 1989; and although I was delighted to share my experiences with the world, I had deep and long-standing reservations about the media interest that my life-story would generate.

I dislike being interviewed and photographed. I'm a very private man, but I'd signed a contract which stipulated that I'd fulfil any book-publicity interviews. The spirit world had quietly 'arranged' the circumstances through which its message could now reach the largest number of people, and prior to publication-day my enthusiastic publishers had posted over four hundred review copies of my book to the national and regional media: and thus my fate was sealed.

I didn't *want* to do media interviews: I *had* to do them.

When I think back now to those hectic days crammed with nationwide journeys, which I was loath to take because I positively detest travelling, I gasp in wonderment at how I ever survived them and came home again with my head still on my shoulders. My first nationwide book-tour was an immensely stressful experience.

It all started in 1989 with my first publicity engagement, which was a book-signing session that turned out to be absolute bedlam. With just ten minutes to the start, no books had arrived – special copies were coming from London but were delayed on the roads. The frantic Manageress rang all the local shops to 'borrow' more copies, but they'd all sold out. 'What am I going to do?' she kept saying, slapping her worried forehead.

'*Books*!' shouted a delivery-man.

'Oh thank God!' she exclaimed, eagerly shredding cardboard boxes then yanking copies free.

Meanwhile, restless queues peeked around the presentation-stands and muttered: 'Is he here yet? Has he arrived?'

'No.'

'Oh, he's lovely, you know,' I heard someone say as I descended the stairs and was greeted by a horde of smiling faces and ringing tills, as copy after copy was seized, bought, and marched into line behind dozens of people waiting for an autograph, a handshake, a smile and a chat.

I wrote some inspired words in each book, and was humbled by the rush of affection the public displayed towards me. People pushed to the front saying things like, 'Keep up the marvellous work, Stephen. You're one in a million.'

'We're so proud of you.'

'This copy's flying to Australia, and this one's for a

friend in South America.'

'Will you sign these four, please? They're off to Germany tomorrow!'

One woman stepped forward loaded with eight copies. 'God bless you, my darling,' she said, throwing her arms around my neck, 'Sign these, there's a love!'

Others began to cry as they neared my table. Emotionally overcome by our meeting, they poured out their hearts to me about tragic family losses, and about how much something that I'd said on television or radio, or in the newspapers, had helped them.

'God be with you, Stephen,' said total strangers, who hugged me and clasped my hands tightly. People were so kind that I was deeply moved and overwhelmed, and soon lost count of how many kisses I received on that day. I was presented with babies and children to cuddle, too.

It was a thoroughly emotional event.

The only blot on the proceedings was a small demonstration of narrow-minded Christian pickets who had gathered outside the store; but the bigots were immediately disbanded by the police, and silenced by the public who shouted at them:

'Go home and learn some kindness!'

'Call yourselves Christians? You're a disgrace to your religion!' This particular group of protestors made news the next day in *The Times*, no less. But I felt sad because these Baptists had failed to radiate the Love of the One they claim to follow, someone for whom I have the deepest respect.

My publisher's representative, Wendy, couldn't

take it all in: she was shocked by the foray and even more overwhelmed by the powerful feelings of love and gratitude expressed by the public.

'I've been to book-signings before,' she said, 'but never to one like this.' Taking a deep breath, she composed herself, took some photos and informed the crowds that, 'Stephen's on television tonight, ladies and gentlemen, if you want to see him.'

Channel 4 TV had telephoned. 'Will you appear on the late-night nationally-networked discussion programme, *After Dark*. It'll be a three-hour live debate called *Superpowers: All in the Mind*?'

'Of course,' I said; and before long I'd arrived in London and had been given a slap-up dinner at a top hotel (£10 just to step on the carpets), after which I was chauffeured to the studios.

The late show started about 11 p.m. and sometimes finished at 2 a.m. The programme was cut short only if debates became tiresome, but ours went for the full run. Millions of people watched the discussion, and viewing figures steadily increased. Some of the topics we examined included the USA's latest craze, 'channeling' (spelt the American way), in which sensitives claim to pass on information from Higher Minds in the Beyond to people on the Earth. Some other topics we considered were life after death, psychic work, genuine mediumship, charlatanism and fraud, and we even touched upon delusions of grandeur.

Among the other guests were the inevitable sceptics: on this occasion these were a psychologist, Dr Susan Blackmore, and a conjuror, James Randi, whose screen credit appeared as 'Charlatan', which I found amusing. I delivered my best volley of the match to the psychologist, who continually dismissed the possibility of an afterlife and declared that we should let go of the people we've lost.

**Dr Blackmore:** Perhaps if we grew in moral and spiritual stature we would no longer need the idea of life after death. If I'm just a biological lump of flesh, the best thing we can do is to admit that, and accept that 'the self' is just a construct, just something that the biological system's invented. And if you let go of that, and not cling to the idea that your self is so important –

**Stephen:** Sue, have you ever lost anybody close to you that you really, really loved very much indeed?

**Dr Blackmore:** I'm afraid I haven't: no.

**Stephen:** Well when you have, come back and say that to me again.

As far as I was concerned, that was 'game, set and match,' and I later received many letters praising my remark. But James Randi kept putting forward cases in which he claimed that 'fake' mediums had been debunked and had been proved charlatans. I pointed out that this didn't mean that all mediums were fraudulent, then said, 'Anyway, that's only your opinion.'

'I don't have an opinion!' he rattled back.'

'Then you can't be a human being,' I said.

(Regrettably, this was another favourite remark with viewers.)

When the balanced presenter asked me to deliver

messages 'live' before millions, I received a contact for the charming veteran medium, Ivy Northage, whom I'd never met before. Her late husband relayed specific details about her eightieth birthday celebrations and spoke of their two sons. He also mentioned the words 'Twickers; Twickenham', where she lived. Then he announced that at home, just before leaving for the studios, she'd changed her elegant brooch and her evening-dress, and that she'd made her choice from three gowns and two brooches: these were specific details which, as Ivy pointed out, happened when she was completely alone. No one else could have known them.

When the programme came off-air, a middle-aged cameraman took me aside and said, 'That was wonderful tonight, Stephen. I believe in your gifts; and even though I was behind the lens, I prayed you'd contact my dear mother who died recently. I can't tell you how much I loved her. She was a lovely, wonderful old lady, and I miss her so much.'

'I know what it is to lose a great friend,' I said, shaking his hand in sympathy, and remembering my own mother's agony as she lay dying of cancer which had spread throughout her body.

Thankfully, I was able to offer him a few words of hope and comfort.

He dabbed his eye. 'I'll never forget her you know.'

'No, I know. No matter how long it's been, you never forget,' I said.

After more congratulations, soft drinks, and hand-shakes I was bundled into a chauffeur-driven car which hurtled at 120 miles per hour down empty motorways, back home to Wales. Exhausted by the ordeal I crashed into bed at 5.30 a.m.

Many people wrote to me after that programme to say how dignified they thought I'd been when dealing with the sceptics; all bar one woman who'd penned, 'How you kept your hands off that Randi's throat and didn't throttle him to death, I'll never know. If I'd have been there, I'd have cooked his goose!'

I replied that, 'Mr Randi surely has a right to his opinions, and Love is the message I'm trying to give, not hatred, anger or intolerance. I've tried to live my life according to the Golden Rule: Love everyone as much as you can, and be as harmless as possible. Surely those who seem against us, stand in the greatest need of our love?'

She didn't respond, so I think she got my point.

Travelling back and forth to London became a regular habit and I soon lost count of the media interviews I did, as well as of the occasions when I welcomed to Wales journalists and photographers from magazines like *Woman*, *Chat*, and *Take-A-Break*.

One of the most pleasant London interviews I gave was to the journalist June Southworth, from the *Daily Mail*.

We ended up in a dubious Greek restaurant where she conspicuously prodded at, and apologised for, the strange unidentified food – but we shared such a happy hour together; and what a charming lady she was. 'Oh, Stephen,' she smiled, 'you make it *so* hard to write anything nasty about you!'

'Well, that's a blessing then,' I quipped, as we laughed and made our way out of a taxi and into

Northcliffe House, the *Daily Mail* headquarters. My breath was taken away. It was such an impressive building: so vast, and all made from glass and marble; and there were scenic lifts and waterfalls too. My eyes scanned the tall expensive facades and just kept on going up and up until I felt wobbly at the knees. Everywhere there was bustle and hurried activity, but no one was allowed entry into the building without a computerised pass.

Strangely enough, the editor never published Miss Southworth's favourable interview with me, owing to 'a lack of space'.

(We've heard that one before!)

Another London journalist gave me a similar press-lunch, but this time it was followed by a most unusual photo-shoot:

'Come on, follow me!' she ordered, whisking me into the magnificent British Museum building.

'What on Earth am I doing in here?'

'Just stand over there!'

I obeyed, and she took dozens of photographs of me languishing against giant Egyptian statues, and lining up alongside dried-out mummies and all the other old relics!

Soon the road loomed up in front of me again and I travelled to twenty major cities and gave an 'Evening an Clairvoyance' in each. I also did more television, radio, and press interviews, which all but practically exhausted me and had me on my knees. But valiant to the end, I kept my promise to the spirit world and spread their news of an everlasting life for everyone, touching millions as I travelled the length and breadth of Great Britain.

As soon as those engagements had been fulfilled, another thirty meetings were arranged.

Gradually, the media turned me into a newly-discovered 'celebrity' (since childhood, secretly I'd known this would happen), and now I met many famous people. I arrived at one concert hall just as the famed tenor Luciano Pavarotti was leaving.

Then the box-office staff told my manager, Jeff, 'The comedian Larry Grayson would like to see Stephen O'Brien's event and meet him afterwards. Is that all right?'

'He'd be delighted,' answered Jeff; and I was.

Over the years I'd lost count of the times Larry Grayson had made me laugh in famous British TV shows such as *Shut That Door!* (his own peculiar catchphrase), and BBC TV's *Generation Game*. His gentle humour had endeared him to millions in many countries.

After my evening of clairvoyance, the dressing-room door was knocked and in stepped the silver-haired Larry Grayson. 'Stephen, how lovely to meet you! I really enjoyed the meeting – it was so emotional, a smashing night.'

Michael, a reporter from the local newspaper, formally introduced us and we shook hands.

'I'm very pleased to meet you, Mr Grayson –'

'Oh, call me Larry! I feel I know you so *well*. I'm a fan of yours.'

'And I've watched you on TV for years –'

'Hey, steady on!' he joked, 'I'm not *that* old!' and we all laughed; especially when he told us some side-splitting stories about his comedy characters known as 'Apricot Lil' and 'Slack Alice'. He then produced a copy of my book: 'I can't find out *Whodunnit*,' he laughed, flicking to the back pages. 'Will you sign it for me?'

'Of course.'

We had a marvellous time listening to Larry's hysterically funny stories; he was such a warm and entertaining human being. Whenever he opened residential homes for the elderly, he insisted on staying until he'd personally met every resident. 'He won't go until he's spoken to them all, and made them cry laughing!' said the reporter. 'Oh, and by the way, I was so moved by the meeting tonight. It was amazing, Stephen; and that's praise indeed from someone like me, a newspaper-man.'

I was saved from embarrassment by Larry saying, 'You've got a wonderful gift, Stephen,' and he revealed that a clairvoyant had foretold his rise to fame one year before he became a household name in Britain. 'I've also seen my mother, you know. I was adopted, of course; but after my mother died she appeared to me, standing at the foot of the bed, and told me that she was safe and well. It was very comforting.' He said he'd later told the British entertainer Max Bygraves about it, but Max had tried to explain it all away as pure 'hallucination'.

But Larry had countered, 'You can say what you like, Max, I'm telling you what happened, *and it was true!*'

'One experience is worth a thousand theories,' I commented.

'I couldn't agree more,' he added with conviction. Then he mentioned his friendship with the late broadcaster, writer and humorist, Arthur Marshall.

'Dear old Arthur,' he reminisced, 'I'd ring up and he'd say, "Ah Larry, dear boy – when are you coming down? I'll get a Battenberg cake!"'

After an hour of belly-laughter, Larry gave both Jeff and me his personal address and an invite to 'Pop in and visit whenever you're in the area. And don't forget I want news of all your meetings, 'cos I'm a fan, and *I* shall be *there*!' he exclaimed.

'I first heard you on BBC Radio 2's *Anne Robinson Show,* you know.'

I remember that occasion myself: Anne Robinson was charming. As soon as she knew I was booked she moved the actress June Whitfield to a minor slot and gave the major slot to me.

We chatted away animatedly while records played and Anne declared with her wicked smile, 'Darling, they're lapping it up – loving it! All four million of them are now sitting glued to their sets!' I couldn't help but grin. It's always amazed me to think that millions of people listen to radio shows each day: the studios are such quiet places that it's hard to imagine whole families 'out there' tucking into their salads while I'm answering questions.

I get the same feeling when doing what's called a 'down-the-line' interview, when I'm telephoned at home but linked up 'live' to millions of households across Britain.

It's a spooky thought, but I'm used to it now.

I think I've spoken on most of the country's major radio stations, and the reception was always the same: their switchboards immediately jammed with callers. In my several appearances on Greater London Radio's *Johnnie Walker Show*, poor Johnnie never once got the verb 'telephone' out before all the lights on his desk started flickering madly.

And on the BBC Radio Wales *Level 3 Show* I had a delightful time being interviewed by the renowned author and personality Molly Parkin. I even took part in an amusing comic sketch with the celebrated actors William Franklyn and Nerys Hughes: I was the medium and they were the 'ghostbusters'. We had great laugh.

But on BBC Radio 4's *Loose Ends* programme, my appearance took on a more serious note when I relayed some survival evidence to the presenter, Emma Freud, from her grandmother on the Other Side of life. Emma was touched by the experience. She understood all the facts except two, which she promised she'd check with her family.

Her grandmother had said that the name of 'Johnnie' and 'a rose placed in my hand' (as she lay at rest) were significant details. Emma played the taped sitting to her father, the writer, politician and broadcaster Clement Freud, and was astonished when her grandmother's evidence was verified as 'perfectly correct'.

A rose had indeed been placed in her grandma's hands as she lay in her coffin; and 'Johnnie' was the unusual nickname which the old lady had often called herself.

When the evidence was broadcast to the nation, silence filled the *Loose Ends* studio.

The show's host, Ned Sherrin, referred to it as 'an awesome silence'. And, of course, letters started pouring in all over again, which is understandable. If a medium relays spirit-supplied facts that aren't contained in his sitter's mind, and these are later proved to be correct, he can't be accused of using telepathy, and this often impresses people.

By the time I reached southern Britain in late 1989, exhaustion had set in. My eyes were red; I'd caught a nasty 'flu virus and had suffered from sleepless nights, all of which had drained my energies.

Fortunately, I was staying with one of my friends, Peggy, whose kindness and spiritual healing gifts were well known down South. In fact, a local newspaper had once reported her as being a 'certified' healer – the cause of much amusement because the reporter had meant to write 'certificated'!

'Stephen, you look all-in, love. You've got big blue circles under your eyes. Why don't you lie down and rest? I'll wake you when our lift comes for tonight's meeting.'

'All right,' I said, 'if I can find the strength to get to the bedroom,' and I dragged my feet all the way to the bed, flopped down onto its soft duvet, and immediately crashed into black oblivion.

My next memory was of becoming conscious after a timeless sleep. The air in the bedroom seemed strangely still. I could no longer hear the children's voices, though I knew they were playing outside in the park. An eerie tranquillity had settled all around me, and yet I knew I wasn't alone. Misty figures gathered around the bed and gazed at my drowsy form. I felt the touch of healing hands, smoothing my skin. Coloured spirit-lights hovered in the air while the visitors gently alleviated my aches and pains.

The healers emitted warm feelings of tender compassion for several minutes. My skin glistened with perspiration under the rays radiating from their hands, and the bedroom 'shivered' with vibrant energy. Yet my body felt as heavy as lead and I couldn't move a muscle.

Smarting my eyes into focus, I saw five spirit doctors standing around the bed; three of them were wearing white coats. They were examining me; then I heard a woman speak:

'You need seven days complete bed-rest. You're physically and nervously exhausted,' she warned. 'You must rest immediately.'

On hearing those words, I moved my legs a little and the visitors faded out.

She was right, of course, but I had engagements to fulfil and I *couldn't* rest. My work had to go on. I'd never dream of letting my spirit people or the public down; people like the lovely old lady who showed such courage and devotion at Winchester Guildhall in southern England. I'd just started relaying the messages in the second-half when suddenly a police-woman burst through the doors and shouted:

'A package has been found. It's a bomb-scare. Everyone out, *now*!'

British to the end, stiff-lipped and complaining, the crowd reluctantly obeyed. I stood and watched them go, saying over and again, 'I'm sorry. I'm sorry this has happened.'

Just like a captain on a sinking ship I was the last person about to leave when an old lady shuffled forward to the stage. Extending a bony hand, she clasped my arm, and her eyes were shining. 'I'm not afraid,' she said tremulously. 'I'll stay with you to the end, bomb or no bomb. May I stay with you?'

A lump came into my throat as she squeezed my arm.

'I'm not afraid either, my darling,' I said, deeply moved by such loyalty, 'but the police really do want us to go.' So we gracefully left the hall, side by side, hand in hand.

Once the crowd spotted me outside, standing on an iron fire-escape, they gathered around my feet and circled the steps, and shook my hands and reached up through the bars for me to sign their books. It was like a scene from *Romeo and Juliet*.

'If we don't get back in – it's been wonderful so far, Stephen!' someone shouted.

'God bless you for helping us!'

'Can we buy more books?' a woman called out, and a brave young man ran back into the cordoned-off building and brought out the bookstand. I autographed more than a hundred copies on that night.

After thirty-five minutes, the capacity audience was finally allowed back in.

'And we're not leaving,' I said through the microphone, 'until we've had the meeting that we came for.' There was instant applause.

People cheered, and someone whistled from the gallery when – without hesitation – I picked up the spirit-message which had been earlier interrupted, at the exact point at which I'd left it, and then went on to successfully complete the link.

I'll never forget the audience's love and devotion because it moved me so deeply. Those people really wanted to be there with me.

Another memorable highlight of my recent tours was my appearance at the Wembley Conference

Centre in London, where on 31$^{st}$ March 1990 the Spiritualists' National Union held its Centenary Celebrations.

Some of the most eminent speakers, mediums, and healers in the kingdom were to attend this event; and I was quite surprised to be invited to work alongside my colleague, the world-acclaimed psychic artist Coral Polge.

I also looked forward to meeting some of Britain's leading spiritual thinkers, such as Sir George Trevelyan, founder of the Wrekin Trust, a spiritual charity. Although he was then in his eighties, Sir George delivered an excellent address which gained him a standing ovation.

For posterity, the day-long conference was video-taped by the Union and marketed to the public. I was presented with an inscribed cut-glass paper-weight as a memento of the occasion, and I later received a copy of the video too. Hours before the event began, hundreds of people queued all around the huge Conference Centre, waving their banners and singing, thoroughly thrilled by the prospect of a whole day's mediumship and celebration.

A fevered buzz of excitement ran through the air as over 2,500 people from the United Kingdom and other countries gathered in the amphitheatre stadium. A marked feeling of unity moved through the crowd's bubbling conversations and psychic stories.

After being wired with special radio-mikes, Coral Polge and I walked on-stage and were greeted by loud applause and dazzling bursts of light – not spirit lights, but countless flashlights as shutters popped in all sections of the auditorium.

The Spiritualists had no intention of letting such a special day pass without photographing it. While we were being introduced, several people came down through the crowds to the front of the stage.

'Give us a smile, Stephen!'

'May we take your picture?'

Normally I don't like to be disturbed, but there was no way of stopping so many flashes exploding right, left and centre; so I nodded.

As Coral and I stepped to our places, the audience eagerly awaited her psychic drawings, which were to be projected onto a massive white screen behind us.

### Psychic News

There was almost a tangible atmosphere of expectancy as world-famous psychic artist Coral Polge and Welsh medium Stephen O'Brien took the stage for what proved to be an excellent demonstration and a high-point of the proceedings.

Linking with spirit communicators simultaneously, they reunited one sitter with her great-grandfather, contacted a young boy killed in a road accident, and successfully proved the existence of life after death. As the mediums worked in perfect unison, you could almost see the crowds of spirit visitors excitedly queuing up to make contact with loved ones. With a calm atmosphere enveloping the auditorium, despite the emotional content of the messages, there were many light points during the proceedings.

One woman concluded her message by mentioning the fact that someone had walked off with her brooch after her passing. 'She's waiting for them on the Other Side!' Stephen told a delighted audience.

Another elderly yet comical communicator, who described himself as 'a man of many parts, some of them still working!' was jokingly asked whether he had donated any of his vital organs.

'He just told me they weren't very vital by the time he died!' Coral relayed.

The mediums successfully reunited an RAF pilot, shot down during the Second World War, with a surprised wartime colleague. Silence then fell as the features of a boy began to manifest on the screen...

'I've got a young lad here,' Coral explained, 'who I believe passed on a main road. I have an explosive feeling with him.'

As the features of a bright-eyed youngster filled the screen, complete with a mop of hair 'that has a mind of its own,' a female registered her acceptance from the back of the hall.

'I have the name of Owen; Margaret Owen,' Stephen offered. 'Can you accept that?'

'Yes.'

'He was hit by a vehicle of some kind.'

'He was hit crossing the road at school.'

Gently relaying information, the Welsh sensitive continued:

'He has come back to tell someone not to cry for him. He has not died. I can see a lady still taking flowers.'

'That's Margaret,' the recipient confirmed.

'I have the feeling his mother was not allowed to see the body. He received extensive injuries.'

'That's quite correct.'

Adding the finishing touches to the picture, Coral added, 'He appears to have been rather a forgetful boy, and had a habit of losing his coat rather a lot.'

'That's absolutely right,' the recipient added. 'We still have a blazer of his at home.'

Just about to move on to the next eager communicator, Stephen returned to say:

'Just before I leave you, does the *Chichester Arms* mean anything to you?'

Taking a few seconds to regain her composure, the sitter replied:

'My husband used to investigate and record coats of arms. He was working on the *Chichester Arms* when he died.'

Relaying messages of a consistently high standard, accompanied by Coral's accurate likenesses, the mediums left the stage to unanimous acclaim and deafening applause...

With enthusiastic cheering ringing in my ears, I was suddenly besieged at the front of the stage by crowds of people waving copies of my book, *Visions of Another World*.

It all started when I signed a disabled woman's copy because she couldn't climb the steep stairs to the foyer where I was supposed to give autographs. Before I could breathe, suddenly there were people *everywhere*, and my official minder intervened.

'Stephen will meet you upstairs, ladies and gentlemen, move along now please!' he called, as he whisked me away through a rabbit-warren of corridors and took me to a specially-placed stand. My eyes popped out on stalks when I saw my name in flashing red lights, announcing my arrival.

Then came another shock: endless queues of chattering excited people gathered in droves; and as fast as I signed their books more copies were waved in my direction. I signed for well over two-and-a-quarter hours (and completely missed my tea) and I didn't realise that *Psychic News* had over-heard one of my witty remarks:

> An obvious and deserved success, quietly-spoken Stephen was kept busy for hours after the demonstration as hundreds of people waited in line for an autographed copy of his best-selling book, *Visions of Another World*.
>
> Stephen jokingly concluded, 'I shall have to receive healing for my arm after I've finished this lot!'

By the end of my 1989 tours I was worn out – and £500 pounds in debt, having worked like a Trojan without being paid a solitary penny for all the hard slog and sacrifice. Those people who think I'm a squillionaire with his own country mansion, two white sports cars and a private villa in Spain, couldn't be more wrong: rumours like these have been circulating about me since the early 1970s; and even though I've achieved a degree of 'success', not one of them is true.

My spirit friend once said to me, 'We never promised you it would be easy – but your needs will always be met.'

He has kept his word.

I was in debt to the tune of £500 because my 1989 promoters broke their contract with me when they failed to pay my tour expenses or offer me any appearance fees – after which I immediately broke all contact with them.

So I was back in rainy old Wales with a huge debt

for the back-payment of council rent, and for other bills, hanging over my head.

I'd used up my book royalty fees to pay my tour accommodation bills and expenses; and these, too, were never reimbursed.

I received 'Notice to Seek Possession' of my flat, and the bailiffs were poised to knock on the door, but I battled with the Council and eventually won my case: they agreed I could clear my debt slowly, which I did.

So much for 'fame' and 'fortune' going hand in hand.

With regard to my promoters, I comforted myself that at least they'd promised to donate some of the ticket-sales to nineteen Children's Hospitals across Britain: I'd insisted on this from the outset.

Weeks after the tour finished, I found myself thinking about the wonderful times I'd shared with many thousands of strangers across the country.

Sometimes I'm a sentimental old thing – but the public's love and support had touched me.

All too soon the helter-skelter of work started up again. In addition to newspaper, television, and radio personnel requesting interviews, spiritual organisations from across Britain invited me to work for them, and a constant stream of mail poured through my letterbox.

I was asked to demonstrate my mediumship in the USA, Holland, Canada, Australia, Germany, and other countries, and I was even given the chance of a free private villa in Gibraltar for a week! But I was far too busy to accept any of these offers. Besides, I felt that my place was here in Great Britain.

But I was certainly becoming quite infamous. People started recognising me in the streets, in supermarkets, on buses, and in other public places. I got quite paranoid at the finish and went out wearing dark glasses, only to be stopped by a woman who smiled brightly and exclaimed, 'Oh, hello, Stephen. You're looking grand!'

On another occasion two women in curlers were whispering about me in a huddle at an antiques fair one afternoon. 'No, Doris: it *can't* be him: you're mistaken. It must be a *lookee–likee*!'

As well as besieging me with letters, the public sent gifts to halls and theatres. People also donated much-welcomed postage stamps, which helped me to answer the many correspondents who didn't enclose a stamped-addressed envelope.

I also received a tape of Luciano Pavarotti's arias, and some delicious apple-tea specially bought for me in Turkey!

Even Sooty got fan-mail, and kitty-toys too.

Journalists came from all around the kingdom to attend my meetings, and some astonished me by presenting me with flowers. Everyone was kind.

And the public travelled hundreds, sometimes thousands, of miles to see my work. One woman flew in specially from America; others travelled from one end of Britain to the other, because I wasn't appearing soon enough in their own region. And, bless them, they queued in all weathers, and sent so much love to me and my spirit friends.

A further round of public meetings was booked, and my appearances began to draw bigger crowds. At Cheltenham and Middlesbrough Town Halls in

England, over 1,000 people turned up on the door. Somehow, we managed to squeeze them all in.

At Middlesbrough, I was still on-stage testing the microphones when suddenly the main doors burst open too early – and I'd never seen anything like it in my life! Hordes of people stampeded down the hall to get to the front. First in line was a wizened old man on crutches: he came bombing down the aisle, hitting old ladies out of his way, right, left and centre – but he got his first row seat!

At some venues, many people were turned away for lack of room, which saddened me because I believe that the message of the spirit should be available to everyone who is willing to listen to it. Because of the huge crowds at some meetings, I was even given personal 'body-guards'.

Eventually I lost count of how many thousands of books I autographed. I signed other objects too: one woman produced an umbrella case! (I didn't dare ask where the umbrella had gone.)

Whenever we sold-out of books, Jeff came to the rescue and I signed sticky-labels!

As people pressed forward, I had to wittily ask, 'Book or sticky-label?'

'Sticky-label please, Stephen!' and the whole queue rocked with laughter.

On one sunny evening after the publicity fuss had died down for a week, my guide congratulated me with, 'Millions of souls have been touched… and we cannot place a price on this.'

And he's right, you know – we can't.

Mind you, I did feel strange queuing for groceries in the supermarket after being treated like a sparkling celebrity everywhere else. But it was nice to get back into the swing of everyday-life again. Yet strangers still called out to me across the baked beans counter, 'Hello, Stephen! Saw you on the telly last night. Great stuff!'

After so many years of feeling ill-at-ease in this world, I began to think that people were finally accepting me as one of their own kind – which kept my feet firmly on the ground.

After all, I'm nothing special. I'm just an ordinary man, who sometimes happens to hear voices from another world.

# Part Two
## Journeys into the Spirit World

## The Veil

Draw back the Curtains of Sleep
and pass into the Light,
through a myriad Planes of Living Thought,
Worlds within Worlds,
where Heaven and Hell are States of Mind.

Fly through your waking dreams
into Reality,
where Mind is King.

When the Spirit is free, it drinks in Wisdom,
Power and Life;
and through the Eyes of the Soul
it beholds
The Children of Darkness
and
The Children of the Light

*Stephen O'Brien*

# 19

# The Kingdoms of Hell

## I

It was a moonless windy night, and the hollow sound of heavy raindrops drummed on the flat roof above my bedroom, and then bounced off it.

Curled up tightly under the bedclothes, I hid my face from the storm and entered a troubled sleep: waking, sleeping, rousing, dozing. I was conscious at dawn when I heard an odd buzzing sound, as if a swarm of bees had gathered in the distance. The noise got closer and closer until it seemed to engulf my senses – and then it faded out.

Silence followed, but in the next instant I suddenly left my physical body far behind me on Earth, and found myself standing in the spirit spheres beside my guardian soul, White Owl.

'Come,' he said. 'See where the selfish and greedy live. Behold with me the kingdoms of hell.' And all at once we were walking down the slopes of a misty grey valley. The air was heavy dark-blue and thick.

The smell of damp earth was all around us, and there was no warmth of happiness living in that freezing, bitter place. Even the grasses had bent under the weight of the insipid atmosphere.

Everywhere, utter silence reigned: not a pleasant stillness, but a chilly, cold and unnerving deadness. No birds were singing; no animals basked in the fields.

'Where is everyone?'

'They are near. What you feel is their minds, which are colouring the countryside and darkening it. The souls who live here shed little light.'

Not fully understanding my guide, I remained quiet and followed where he led, feeling safe in his company. We walked towards a distant township. Through the heavy air I just about recognised it as groups of shacks, made from something like tin sheeting; and when we drew closer I saw the dirt that encrusted those derelict, ramshackle hovels. 'Surely no one lives here?' I asked disbelievingly. But White Owl gave no reply.

Along the dirt-track just ahead of us were some broken wooden hutches. I ran to them but was shocked to see that they housed underfed rabbits, kittens, and a few thin hamsters. Loving animals as I do, I instantly went to release the poor creatures, but my hand was stayed.

'No: there is a reason. The people who live yonder show no love – these little creatures are here in the hope that someone may pity them and tend them

They are willing participants; they hope that those who dwell here may learn to show them compassion, and learn to love something other than themselves.

Compassion fans the flame of spiritual growth; and there is always hope.'

My mind jumped in amazement.

As we neared some sheds, a small plump woman dashed out and stood defiantly in her doorway. Her yellow-skinned brow was deeply furrowed, and years of constantly-selfish thoughts had turned down the corners of her mouth.

'Hello,' I said brightly. She only scowled hard through piercing jet-black eyes; and it was such a dreadful look that I immediately sensed her vicious nature, contained in the electro-magnetic energy fields (or aura) that surrounded her. Her auric colours were a deep muddy scarlet, and a murky green and brown.

Suddenly she stepped back, slammed the door in my face, then quickly fastened the door-bolts. The key twisted in the rusty lock and made a sickening sound.

'She is a typical dweller.'

'But why did I feel so cold next to her?'

'*Because all of her thoughts centre on herself*. The iciness betrays a lack of love and compassion in her heart. She believes herself to be very poor, but far beyond those dark hills' – and he pointed them out on the horizon – 'live people who think they are rich; yet you would get a worse welcome there.'

'Outward appearances don't always reveal what's in the heart?' I observed.

'You have said it.'

I understood the lesson but couldn't help wondering how long the woman had lived in that state. My thoughts were instantly read.

'She has been there for forty years, as you measure time.'

I was astounded; then my guide quoted:

'*In my Father's House there are many mansions.*'

'I understand. There's a place for everyone.'

My teacher agreed. 'Countless billions of mental states have produced an equal number of spheres in which to exist. Heaven and Hell are purely states of mind; they are not geographical places.'

'I see.'

'From now on, Stephen, we are invisible to our surroundings.' I suppose I expected a blinding flash of light to accompany his words, but nothing came; so I just accepted that if he said we were now invisible, then we were – yet I could see us both with perfect clarity.

We walked on... and I witnessed some horrific sights on this journey (some of them too upsetting to record). I saw people with cracked and bleeding skin: their extreme states of mental torment had shadowed their spirit bodies and inflicted these 'injuries' on them, and they suffered because they couldn't love themselves. Their appearances had been altered by their subconscious thoughts.

I learned that in the next world the power of Thought manifests its effect more immediately than it does here on Earth.

In those lower-astral realms I saw places that were like nightmare cities: grotesque sequences of ugly images, places in which each self-centred and vengeful soul lived in a twilight world of his own making because he'd extinguished from his Being all compassion for others.

In Eternity, the more love and compassion a soul possesses, the more radiance it projects into its surroundings. The power of Love is manifested as Light. The brightness of the mind-energy increases with each noble act and thought, in the same way as the brightness of an electric fire-element does on Earth, when it's stimulated by electricity.

In those lower planes I saw social misfits: ignorant and abusive souls; murderers who hid themselves away in dark caves and wept for the crimes they'd committed, unable to forgive themselves – even though their victims had long-since forgiven them.

I saw a great deal more, all of which taught me that within everyone there's a Divine Monitor called the Conscience, and this inner voice judges our acts, and records each fragment of our thinking and each moment of our lives. Our memories are responsible for the punishments that we inflict upon ourselves, because their powerful energies continuously exert their influence on our souls: and this is the only 'Judgement Day'.

In the next life our perceptions are heightened and we're confronted by the stark memories of our acts, whether good or bad; and the Voice of Conscience dictates to us the price that we must pay in order to 'right' the 'wrongs' that we've committed.

Inner peace returns to a man's troubled mind only after he's rendered service to those he has wronged.

My teacher and I continued our journey, and came across a wizened old woman sitting on a riverbank. Her ragged shawl was pulled tightly round her thin form and she was weeping mournfully, reproaching herself.

'I killed it! I killed my own child,' she cried out bitterly, pulling her straggling hair until some of it came loose. Freely-flowing tears wet her twisted mouth.

Moved by her plight, I placed my hand on her shoulder, 'Don't cry,' I said.

But there was no reaction.

'She cannot hear, see, or sense our presence,' my friend said.

'May I comfort her?'

'If she wishes it.'

'But she needs help. Why isn't she aware of us?'

'Because she cuts herself off from all aid. She wraps a cloak of anguish so tightly around her mind and spirit that there is nothing anyone can do to help her. She has chosen.'

'Please let me try,' I countered, placing my other hand on her shoulder and whispering a few words of comfort into her ear. But he was right: she was deaf to my influence.

'What *we* want is unimportant,' said my teacher. 'Her own mind has created this prison – she alone is responsible for it. Not even Angels can help this woman unless she desires it. It is similar on Earth, is it not?'

I agreed; and another spiritual lesson hammered itself home.

Then the woman pitifully cried, 'I killed my baby, my precious little child. I'm not fit to live, not fit to breathe.'

'Neither does she know that she has died,' said White Owl; and the whole sad tale made me reel. 'Ordinary guilt and regrets that plague the human mind do not bring the devastating effects upon the spirit that you see in this case. She is mentally and emotionally unbalanced in the extreme.

'Negativity thrives in these spheres. Normal fears and doubts wouldn't place a balanced human being in these planes of thought.'

That, at least, comforted me, for some of my own thoughts are far from spiritual on times.

'I'll pray for her,' I said.

'A noble thought, but I assure you that Unseen Hosts await the moment when she genuinely calls for help.'

'What will happen then?'

'Once the desire is born she will be lifted up into the light, out of this world and into another.'

'Because of one thought?'

'Yes: the power of thought is mighty.'

'Please,' I begged him, 'will you allow me to be seen? Give me a chance to reach this soul.'

A long pause followed, during which I knew he took private counsel with some higher authority, before he said, 'It can be done, but only for a few moments. You are now visible to her.'

I gently moved in front of the poor woman, and spoke quietly. 'I've come to help you. Please don't cry.' But as the words left my lips she cowered to the ground, paralysed with fear, buried her head in her hands and shawl and screamed in terror: 'No! Leave me! Go away! Don't torture me! Punish me no more! Get away! Get away from me!'

Her chilling cries were so unexpected and filled with such dread that they numbed my mind. A frightening shudder coursed through my body and I realised that I was invisible again. The hysterical woman tore at her hair, and wept bitterly, 'Why am I plagued so? Haven't I enough to bear? Send the devil's child from my eyes! Send the spirits away!'

I was stunned.

White Owl touched my arm and led me aside. 'Her fears distort her vision. Her troubled mind colours everything much darker than it really is. She feels threatened, and this clouds everything she sees. The blackness of her mind turned you into a ghostly figure.'

'I feel ashamed of myself,' I said, lowering my head, 'of causing her more suffering.'

'She is to blame; you offered service.'

'But who am I to relieve such misery?'

'One of God's Children, motivated by compassion. But she is not ready: you cannot help any soul, in any world, until it is ready. Only then will it respond, my friend.

'This woman is tortured by her own conscience. Not long ago on Earth she brutally murdered her baby. In a psychotic rage, a frenzied fit of madness, she cruelly dismembered it. Afterwards, she took her own life. Now she is haunted by her cruelty. Her mind projects endless horrific scenes before her gaze. She sees her child's terrified expression, its gaping eyes, and feels again her own unbridled rage.

'She is the only one who can find her peace again, no other.'

'How?'

'She must learn to understand, and then to forgive herself. From this new beginning she can go forward until she finds rest. Her future will involve service to others and, eventually, reconciliation with her child. People cannot escape the consequences of their acts: eventually they must all be faced.'

I was lost for words.

We departed slowly into the dark grey mists that divide some spheres of Eternity from each other; but as we went I glanced over my shoulder at the weeping form and murmured to myself, 'May God help you to resolve your troubles, and may you find your peace.'

My mind was so pained that I hardly noticed our changing surroundings, and I was taken by surprise when I realised that the light around us had completely gone...

## II

As I clasped my blue spirit robes tightly round me, they changed into a dull grey colour and perfectly blended in with the gloomy environment which now surrounded us. The chilling air was as sharp as a needle; in this place there was no love-light.

Still shocked by what I'd seen on my journey so far, I lowered my eyes – only to find that my guide and I were 'hovering' over a wide, marshy mudbank.

When we 'landed', our feet sank into the mire right up to our ankles. Then I spied some huge iron gates a little way off. Intrigued, I wanted to go nearer.

My companion instantly read my thoughts and we moved forward.

'There are tyrants here,' he said as we came upon the gates, unseen and unheard by the people I could see within.

Beyond the barriers a feeling of pernicious vengeance hung in the air: it was a spiteful arrogance and a cold selfish cruelty. No words could adequately describe those coarse vibrations of thought; but they were so awful that they chilled my heart.

At either side of the imposing gates stood a massive brown-skinned guard, on duty: each man wore only a loincloth, and carried a whip of leather thongs in one hand and a long razor-sharp spear in the other. Both were frightening, to say the least. Although the gates were locked, I longed to know what secrets lay within. 'Can we pass through?' But White Owl didn't answer. Turning to ask him again, I froze to the spot and gasped. He'd gone.

Childish panic flooded my mind. I'd been abandoned in this dismal place and feared that the guards could now see me, and I wanted to run like the wind in the opposite direction. But I controlled my instincts and calmed myself, until composure returned. Then I realised that this was another spiritual lesson – and one that I must face alone.

Taking a deep breath I bravely moved through the locked gates, thankful that I was still invisible, but trembling nevertheless.

Behind me the resounding crack of whips split the twilight, and in front of me I heard the soul-strangling cries of people in great distress. Curious, I peered through the freezing air and was horrified to see that a great pit had been dug, and cowering on the ground inside it was a group of emaciated men and women, sparsely clothed in torn and weathered rags. They were pathetic souls who were terrified of their captors' anger. A few more venomous guards circled these 'prisoners' and taunted their prey by shouting obscenities at them and jabbing at them with sharp spears.

Then into my hearing, from out of nowhere, came the thoughts, 'Cruel minds seek power over the weak. This is their sport: frightened victims are locked in thought-cages of their own making, and are held there by their own negative fear, which is born deep within them.

'Escape is easy: first they must banish fear, and then, through positive thoughts, exercise their desire to seek another environment; this would raise them out of oppression – if they believed it were possible.'

'Who can help them?'

'Only they themselves,' answered the deep voice. 'It is their own thoughts that trap them. Many invisibles are waiting for just one soul to discover the key to freedom. Look and learn.' And I did. And sadly, my guide was right: these wretched souls *wanted* to be in that pit. As unbelievable and perverted as it might seem, these 'prisoners' revelled in their subjection, just as some people do on Earth when they bask in their illnesses and refuse to let them go, fearing that if they did they'd lose the world's attention.

'Couldn't we end this masquerade?'

'Why?' asked my teacher's mind-voice. 'These guards follow their perverted desires, and those people have found their places. By their thoughts, both parties maintain their positions. Who are we to interfere?'

'But shouldn't someone try?'

'Bright Souls are filled with compassion but they

fully understand that each individual has the right to govern his own life. If Angels ended this cruelty by force, they would be no better than those people who are perpetrating it. It is by our example that we teach.' Then his voice faded away.

I felt frustrated, and somehow my angry thoughts instantly made me visible to the guards, who quickly seized my arms in a vice-like grip. Sudden terror paralysed me and instantly 'locked' my thoughts into the same cage-of-suffering as that of the other souls – then struggling I was dragged towards the pit.

All at once, sheer dread forced me to assert my willpower. Shutting my eyes tightly I demanded my freedom by thinking myself far away from that malevolent place – and in a flash of a second I shot upwards like a fork of greased-lightning, and flew from that repulsive world. But as I hurtled through pitch-black space, past stars and planets, I knew I was being followed – someone was close behind me.

Plagued by confusion, my visions collapsed into a blur, and all at once my eyes gaped wide open back in my bedroom – and I jumped out of bed. My heart was beating against my ribs and the sheets were drenched with perspiration. I leaned against the door to catch my breath.

Looking around me, I sensed my pursuer's threatening presence. He'd followed me back, but he couldn't touch me now: we were worlds apart, and I was safe inside my body again. I was home.

And outside on the windowsill, a small bird was singing his dawnsong as if nothing unusual had happened.

# III

...I became conscious in a small, claustrophobic, and untidy flat above a grocer's shop. Everything was dirty, and the smell of rotting food and human waste was vile.

White Owl extended his arm and silently pointed into a corner of the drab bed-sit where I could see a crumpled form, twisting and writhing in the bed: it was a woman of great years. She was lean and pale, had short-cropped greasy grey hair, and a tight thin mouth. She seemed in pain. Her eyes were mere slits in her yellowy skin; and in her troubled sleep, she groaned and wrung her long hands.

I sensed that her heart was giving out, and she was about to die. I watched as she took her last breath – then she gave up her spirit, which vacated its old shell in urgency. Instantly she scrambled to her spirit feet and started rummaging around the room, trying to lift papers and objects, and bits of shredded matting and stained teacups.

'Searching for money,' said my friend.

'But of what good is that to her?'

'None whatsoever. She thinks she has woken up from her usual sleep. She does not realise that she has died.'

'The poor soul died alone,' I lamented.

'No: we were here.'

She scratched and pulled at objects, trying to find her banknotes, getting more and more flustered by the minute because her bony fingers kept passing through the furniture.

Then suddenly she vanished.

'Come! We must follow!' said White Owl, clasping my hand – and immediately we were walking through a neglected and overgrown graveyard. The night was pitch-black, and the grasses and weeds were lit by intermittent deep-blue light only when the clouds scurried past a huge moon.

'She is yonder.' And he pointed at a gravestone where the bedraggled old woman was kneeling and scrabbling at the earth. She was moaning and weeping.

'This is the tombstone of her husband. She is childless.'

'But where is he now?'

'Far away. Death for him was a grateful release from bondage.'

'Then why is she here?'

'To recapture her past. She is lonely, frightened, and afraid; and now: unsure whether she sleeps or has died. We must wait in case realisation comes.'

But as soon as he'd said this, she disappeared again. For quite some time we followed her, and she called on people who owed her money, and berated them; but none of them reacted to her shouting, which caused her great distress. She hurled wicked abuse at one young man who was living in a derelict apartment that she owned, and accused him of not paying any rent. But he clearly didn't live in the flat – it was too filthy, damp and unclean. It was obvious that he only sheltered there at night because he was homeless. But like all her other tenants he didn't register her belligerent ravings, and she became more and more angry.

Soon after leaving him, she ceased hurrying and

became quieter and a little more thoughtful.

'Now she mourns, for she knows she has died.'

Suddenly the scenes changed again, and her greedy thoughts instantly transported her back to her own dreary bed-sit.

She was now kneeling by the dishevelled bed, weeping profusely and not even noticing that her own 'dead' body lay in it. White Owl quietly bid me to remain at one end of the room, and he stepped forward. He raised an outstretched hand, and in a twinkling of an eye his body glimmered golden-white. He was now visible, and she looked up – then immediately cowered down in fear.

He spoke to her gently:

'Woman, why do you weep?'

'I think I've died. Or... is this a dream?'

'No; you have indeed crossed into the land from whence you originally came.'

She seemed confused and disorientated. 'But I felt nothing, no pain.'

'God is kind.'

Suddenly she reared up and spat at him, 'God!' – and anger flashed across her face. 'Don't talk of God to me! What did God ever do for *me* in my old age? I'm lame and weak and have no friends or lovers.'

And gently he said, 'In order to be loved, one must first love others.'

'The only man who ever loved me is dead...' She stopped bellowing, realising that she'd now joined him – then sudden panic gripped her throat. 'But where is he? Why hasn't he come for me, if there's a life after death?'

White Owl stood motionless, his kind eyes shining

while full realisation dawned in the woman's mind. Having then read her thoughts, he said sensitively, 'In your heart of hearts, you know that he did not love you, and that your feelings for him were born of possession. Your soul knows that death for him was a happy release.'

Despite the sympathy in his voice she immediately howled and wailed and buried her head in the dirty bedsheets, because she knew that he was right.

He stepped a little nearer to her. 'Why not follow me out of this place? I will befriend you in your hour of need.'

'Go away!' she hissed, and then yelled angrily, 'Get out of my house – leave me alone! All you want is to rob me of my things. Just like that good-for-nothing tenant in my flat. Get away! You're nothing but a bad dream.' She tried to push him aside but her hands went through his legs, which made her scream, and she ran from the room.

'Where has she gone?' I asked.

'To a field outside, where she buried jewellery and semi-precious stones several years ago. She now wants to retrieve them. Those who cry for their heart's desire, which they have lost, will presently seek to find it again.' My guide was philosophical but his manner was kind-hearted. 'This woman is Earthbound. It is her lust for material things that binds her to these well-frequented surroundings; and she will not come away until she loses these desires, then wishes for a better life – one of giving, and not always of taking.'

'*Where your treasure is, there will your heart be also,*' I quoted.

'Just so. There are many millions like this soul in my world, trapped by their greed and thoughts, "haunting" or frequenting places and possessions all over the Earth-plane. They do not wish to progress, even though this path is open to them. Many will not even accept that they have made the transition.

'That poor soul believes herself to be old and lonely, and unloved. She has "trapped" herself on Earth, where she will remain until she changes her thought-patterns; she will not find happiness until she does. No one can grant contentment to another soul. Everything has to be earned.'

'I perfectly understand.'

## IV

One moment I was resting in the armchair by a blazing fire, and the next instant I'd projected out into the Realms of Spirit, where my courage instantly curdled when I realised I was flying high up in the air above a thrashing midnight sea. Hovering over the ocean, my friend and I marvelled at the wild waters as they smashed against the distant cliffs and sent huge spurts of foam screeching into the cold night sky.

It was a dark and dismal night at sea. No soul would be safe on the ocean in such a hazardous thunderstorm. Angry clouds had killed the moon, and fork-lightning seared down from heaven and ended in a watery grave.

Travelling incredibly fast now, we were flying way out over the unwelcoming deep and heading around a bend of dangerous coastline: it was like being in a terrifying nightmare. 'Tonight you will see another aspect of hell,' said my friend. Above and beyond the roaring storm his tranquil voice floated through my mind, 'Tonight we shall visit two people.'

Before I could question him, all at once we came upon a distant point of light that twinkled through the darkness. It was an old lighthouse, and we were speeding towards it at such a rate that I felt sure we'd smash into it – but instead of crashing into the stones, we passed right through them in a flash of a second, as White Owl said, 'We are here.' And we found ourselves standing in the small living-quarters of the lighthouse-keeper.

It was such an eerie place. One solitary candle flickered in the shadows; clothes were scattered hither and thither; and old crates packed with empty beer bottles took pride of place on every available surface. The whole room had an atmosphere of lived-in homeliness, except that the air felt strange: not cold, but bitter. A numbing bitterness permeated the room – that's the only way I can describe it. And a reek of stale beer filled the air.

White Owl silently outstretched his arm and pointed at a miserable figure heaped over a nearby desk. The lighthouse-keeper was obviously drunk; an array of broken bottles and glasses on the floor clearly said so. I wondered if he was hurt, for he lay there groaning as if in some terrible great pain. I thought of stepping nearer but was checked with, 'He is not damaged, but his pain is very real. Can you not sense from the depths of his mind what ails him so?'

And when looked, I did discover some startling

facts. 'He's cut through with bitterness and regret,' I said, 'having given up his life ashore for this hermit existence. But... I can't see why.' And I tried harder to psychically glean the reasons from the photo-sphere of images and thoughts that were swirling within the man's mind and auric fields.

My teacher broke in. 'He was once a successful politician who made his living from a world of corruption, into which he easily slid. He smiled for the nation but lied to himself. He projected a public image of stability and honesty, but lived a secret life of emotional torment and deceit.

'Now he lives here, far from the glare of publicity, rejected and filled with savage remorse. Here is a man who is thoroughly ashamed of what he has done. He cannot forget his past, or forgive it; and his conscience now pays the price. See how his mem-ories torment him so?'

Then I understood why the whirling images in his mind had upset me, and I felt sorry for the man slumped over the table. I discerned that he was 'haunted' by one particular memory of a time when he'd accepted illegal bribes, which had led to the death of an innocent girl.

'I can now reveal we are not in the world of spirit, but on the Earth,' said my friend. 'This man is alive in your world, and we are only visiting him.'

These remarks stunned me.

The next instant I felt the touch of my guide's hand and we were outside again, once more flying high in the midst of the thunderstorm, slicing through the wind and driving rain.

Where were we going now? What would be our

second destination? Would it be on the Earth, or in the next world? The power of speech left me during this fantastic flight, since all my concentration went into gripping my friend's hand to stop myself from falling into the angry sea. Sheets of blinding rain surrounded us and obscured everything in sight, wrapping us in a fast-moving shroud.

Then he spoke within my mind as we zoomed forward, 'For this next visit, you will need great strength and objectivity.' He sounded extremely serious. What on earth did he mean?

I glanced across and just about made out his earnest face through the deluge: his brow was dark and troubled, which betrayed a harrowing lesson to come…

## V

All around us, bright lightning forked from sky to sea, and our speed seemed so great that even if we'd passed through a blazing thunderbolt I don't think we'd have been hurt. But White Owl smiled – I'd completely forgotten we were in our spirit bodies and that no harm could befall us.

Beneath us, waves smashed wildly against one another as the rolling swells thundered and rose and then fell back into the murky waters. The coal-black seas tossed and foamed like a horde of savages bent on murder. Everywhere as far as the eye could see there was frenzied chaos: crashing and thundering, lightning and storm. Rainclouds collided and burst; the seething ocean boiled, and deafening gale-force winds obliterated every noise, bar one.

Somewhere up ahead I picked out the faint and struggling sound of a motor, chumming in the waters. A vessel? Surely not: not on such a dark and fearsome night. No one could be so foolish as to be out in this maelstrom. But someone must have been there. Straining to listen, I heard the valiant motor splutter and choke, then it made a strangling noise, and suddenly died. And once more, only the howling winds and rains could be heard.

'See there!' said White Owl, his finger piercing the gloom. 'See, the boat!'

I focused my eyes and amidst the storm-tossed waves I saw a brave little fishing-boat: its swaying deck was deserted, and lit only by spasmodic moon-light and a tiny lantern that flickered in the cabin. Surely there was no one aboard? Any crew would be risking certain death.

I prayed to God that the boat was empty.

As each moment passed we got nearer, and still the vessel heaved and fell under the mighty power of the sea. Like an insignificant cork, it was flung into the air and received again by a gaping, watery mouth; its cabin roof had been half-ripped apart by the gales, and its rigging now whiplashed against a broken mast. How helpless and fragile it looked, pitted against the elements.

My teacher's grip tightened. 'We are here.' And we immediately passed through the boat's side, and floated over to some up-turned charts and crockery that were lying in the corner of the cabin. Half of our spirit-forms were inside the boat, and half of them were outside its timber walls; and even though violent waves pitched the vessel's contents from side to side, our bodies were both unmoved. Untouched and silent, we witnessed a heart-breaking sight.

A bearded man of middle years, obviously the captain, was desperately fighting to reach the battered ship's radio; but each time he touched its controls, the ocean threw him against the timbers, again and again. Summoning all of his strength he frantically tried to transmit an emergency call, but failed.

'The radio is dead,' said White Owl, 'and the boat sinks fast. The crew is already gone.' I saw the black flooding waters seeping through a hole in the bow and my hope for the doomed captain failed. His efforts would be useless: the sea was too strong and he was too weak; and my mind prepared itself for the inevitable. In a final determined bid for his life, the terrified man grasped hold of the radio once more:

'*Mayday*! *Mayday*! In the name of God, *someone*, anyone, please help me! *Mayday*! *Mayday*!' But the tipping boat hurled him against the opposite wall. Desperately he scrambled to his feet, struggling to keep his head above the rising waters, and dragged himself over to the gaping hole in the bow, and tried with all his might to stem the rushing flow by pushing his heavy coat into it. But it was no use: the tides wouldn't yield – they rushed in faster, quicker than before. Mentally, I heard my teacher say, 'Only in times of deep crisis does the soul truly find itself, and its God.'

Pitifully, the doomed fisherman fell to his knees and cried and sobbed, and in a half-dazed state between life and death he touched his spirit and found his Maker; and he began to pray in snatches, but some of the words wouldn't come.

'The Lord's my shepherd, I'll not want... Our Father in Heaven... forgive us our trespasses... Dear God, I'm dying... I'm dying... but not like this... Please help me. My wife and children... my little ones. Take care of my children, and my Elizabeth... Please help... help me, my God, I'm dying...' – and the cries from his heart shrunk away into his shivering form, wracked with tears.

Then my tears joined his, and White owl averted his gaze in helplessness.

When the last moments came they were mercifully swift for the brave fisherman, who fought to snatch the final fragments of oxygen trapped in an air-pocket in the cabin's roof. And the little boat whirled round and round in the deep currents, and was filled with hungry black water as it turned up on its end, then sank quickly beneath the foam without a trace...

His last cries will always remain brightly lit within my mind. As long as I live I shall never forget his gaping eyes. A man had drowned before my gaze and there was nothing I could have done to save him; nothing.

But his face: that fearful expression – I covered my eyes in dismay.

In a matter of minutes the ruthless sea had claimed everything in sight, and the ocean had shown no mercy. Not a splinter of the boat was left anywhere, not even a trace of spilled oil marked the brave man's grave.

We 'stood' in silence, my guide and I, hovering over

the tempestuous sea, thinking and praying.

Then White Owl said: 'Behold a form of hell.'

And the North Wind howled and whined.

'...But now comes the Light.'

Instantly, a bright yellow light flashed across the water: like a mighty burnished flame it shot up high into the heavens; and out of the merciless sea there rose a glowing form: a Bright Angel of Light. He had no wings: there was just a man's body wrapped in a vast aura of loving radiance, surrounded by golden rays – and safe in his arms he bore the spirit of the 'dead' captain, unconscious and sleeping like a babe.

And as I watched in wonderment, the Angel sailed smoothly upwards into the troubled skies, and both he and the peaceful captain faded out from sight into the furious night.

'Behold a form of heaven,' I heard again.

And just for a moment, the storm didn't matter because a deep sense of peace touched my soul.

'Thank God his prayer was answered,' I sighed gratefully.

'But his life was done, and nothing could have changed that. We were powerless to prevent the transition because his time had come. In this sense, we too have visited hell tonight.'

'Let us leave this place,' I begged in sorrow.

And 'So be it' were the last sounds I heard, for – my eyes quickly opened, with tears still brimming in them. I was back in my armchair on Mother Earth, sitting before the dying embers of my living-room fire.

# 20

# The Kingdoms of Heaven

## I

In the dimness of my bedroom I watched as the grey ceiling slowly became transparent and faded away to reveal a deep black velvet sky, speckled with diamond stars. It was such an exquisite vision that it made me want to fly up into the depths of space. Then a man's bare arm appeared over my head: as it hovered in the dark room, a thrill of expectation swept through me.

'Take my hand, and come with me,' said the gentle voice. Eagerly I gripped White Owl's strong hand; and, as we touched, all sensations of the Earth liquefied – and my awareness of another world strengthened.

Shooting upwards towards the stars, we seemed to be travelling faster than light. We flew through space, then into blackness, then into banks of thick grey clouds: the borderland mists that divide some spheres of Heaven from the Earth. Suddenly the blinding fogbanks vanished, and my whole being trembled with joy as we shot out over the greenest fields I'd ever seen.

The rolling hills of lush green grass seemed to possess consciousness, and the turquoise heavens above us were filled with radiant energy: a healing force, which I sensed was ever available to anyone who wished to draw upon it.

'We are here,' he said. 'Behold the children.'

Under majestic giant trees, a short distance from us, a small group of beautiful children were playing and singing joyfully in a circle of fun and laughter. We slowed down; and as our feet touched the land, they seemed to be 'kissed' by it.

The magnificent young spirits in front of us, who revelled in their freedom, captivated me.

Then my teacher spoke. 'See how carefree they are? If only all who walked the Earth could bask in the moment and take no thought for tomorrow, as these little ones do.'

'*Could* we?'

'Of course you could. People allow the pressures and stresses they have made for themselves to disturb their inner balance and break down their inner peace. Worry dwells within them, and fear corrodes happiness, and eats away at joy. If men learned to live in the Ever-Present Now, they would be much happier beings.'

'But it isn't that easy,' I commented.

'Nothing is. The Peace of the Spirit is a treasured prize that must be earned; it is not a gift.'

'But these children don't have the difficulties that beset us on Earth.'

'True, but they know how to cope with problems.' His lips moved into a wise smile and his brown eyes glistened. 'These children are creatures of the moment. They take no thought for the morrow, for they know that tomorrow never comes. But when obstacles *do* come – and we have many here that you do not have on the Earth – they deal with them without allowing the poisonous black thoughts of worry to destroy their spiritual balance and harmony. Do you see?'

'Yes,' I replied softly, my eyes delighting in the youngsters' games: they were throwing a bright red ball around the circle, and laughing because a clumsy boy had dropped it. 'I do understand. But on Earth we must forward-plan, and that's why we become stressed.'

My guide spoke wisely:

'Man makes the art of living so complex and unnatural. Simple needs, and a life close to Nature, would bring him complete harmony of body, mind and spirit – and the treasured prize of peace.'

There was a sincere longing in his quiet voice. 'Watch now,' he said, and he called to a five-year-old black boy. The boy came scurrying over to him and they embraced like life-long friends.

White Owl told him, 'I have some news for you, Thomas. Your mother on Earth has been praying for you again, and she worries about your sister in university.'

The little chap frowned.

'Oh, not again!' he whined. 'When will she ever learn? She still doesn't know about God's love, and that we're all safe – even when we're away from her.'

And with that, Thomas threw his arms around White Owl's neck, kissed him, then wriggled free and dashed off to join his playmates under the cool trees.

'There is much more to see,' said my guide. And in an instant we were flying high over sparkling crystal seas that glittered in the sunlight.

We moved through the skies so fast – with our stomachs facing the ocean and our heads toward the horizon – that my breath was taken clean away. 'Thank God we're high up!' I cried.

'Do you still fear the water?'

'You know I nearly drowned when I was a boy.' The very sight of the waves beneath us sent my head reeling. There was water everywhere, as far as the eye could see, and not a foot of solid earth in sight.

'Look down,' insisted White Owl. 'See the rolling tides, how they smash and break!' But I couldn't. Although we were three hundred feet or so above the raging blue, each passing second pulled us nearer to what looked like a watery grave. 'Look down!' he called again; so, reluctantly, I did.

Immediately, childish fear swept through me like a ghost from the past. And I vividly recalled the day when I nearly drowned: the frantic gulping for air, my body sinking helplessly, my feet struggling for something to stand on... and the terrible black fear that pulled me under the water again and again.

The memory of those spinning terrors now seemed to pull us downwards, closer to the restless sea, closer to oblivion. I clasped my guide's hand with all my might – but still we descended: down and down, nearer to the thundering waves.

Even though I knew that in the spirit world no one

could possibly drown – we could have walked under the sea and even breathed it in harmlessly, if we'd wanted to – I still couldn't overcome my fearful memory.

'I'm falling. We're falling!' I cried.

'Then think positively.'

'I can't.'

'Remove the fear.'

'I can't!'

'*Think* – and we shall rise.'

'We're going to crash into the sea!'

'*Only if you will it.*'

Feeling a sudden surge of encouragement from my friend, I pitched a last chance to save us. With all my might I willed us to soar upwards, away from the deep. On opening my eyes I just caught sight of the waves as we skimmed their crests at incredible speed and shot up into the sky like two jets making for the sun.

'Well done!'

I was filled with sheer relief. 'Never say die!' I laughed out loud.

'Lesson learned!' smiled my friend, as we zoomed out towards the horizon – and then there was nothing but blackness.

## II

...The next thing I knew, I was standing beside my teacher in a golden cornfield. Releasing my hand, he said, 'The power of the mind is mighty. The mind is the Ruler, and not the servant; and you control it. Dark, negative thoughts are actualised unless they are removed and replaced by bright positive ones. Come, I will show you.'

When he touched my skin the cornfields instantly vanished and we stood in a leafy woodland clearing, surrounded by trees and singing birds. Before us, amongst the tall rushes and flowering plants, was a red brick wall as high as a house. I gazed up at its twenty-foot surface.

'If you believe you can do something,' said my friend, 'then you can do it. Come.' And he led me thirty paces away from the wall. 'Now, jump over it.'

My face must have said it all, but nevertheless I managed to squeeze out, 'You must be joking. I'd never make it – not until the desert freezes over and the camels come skating home!'

'But you will – if you *believe* you can.'

'And that's the trouble,' I said.

'Remember: Thought is King, and it can accomplish anything. Now,' he smiled, 'jump over the wall.' Then he stood like a patient father awaiting his child's first stumbling steps. I guess his trust must have moved me because I persuaded myself to try. Sheepishly, I stepped back a few more paces, believing I'd need a good run at it. 'Preparations are unnecessary,' he said.

Taking no notice I bent my body forwards, scuffed the brown earth with my feet, and pelted full stretch towards the big wall. I quickly gained momentum and felt that I'd succeed. But as I sprang upward, sudden doubt killed my confidence and my black thoughts flung me hard against the bricks, ten feet from the ground.

I felt the shuddering impact of bones on stone as I

twisted and fell to the earth, stunned and shaken. But there was no pain, and no cuts or bruises.

'You doubted,' he said, as I clambered awkwardly to my feet and dusted myself down – but no dirt had clung to my blue spirit robes, and there wasn't even a scratch on my bare feet. 'Fear robbed you of the power to win, and therein lies the lesson: think positively *always*. Man should never allow fear into his mind, for it destroys his equilibrium and ruins his efforts; not only here, but also on the Earth – even more so there.'

I nodded, knowing that he was right.

'Now watch,' he said, and he drew upon his positive willpower, floated up into the air, and soared over the bricks without so much as a raised eyebrow.

An amazing moment later he walked right through the 'solid' wall and stood beside me again, grinning from ear to ear. 'If a man has faith, he can move mountains,' he smiled. 'Now you try.'

Well, what could I say? Now that believed myself equal to the task, I mimicked him and rose into the air like Peter Pan and sailed regally over the wall. Then I poked my head through the misty red bricks, and together my guide and I rocked the trees with laughter.

When White Owl placed his arm about my shoulders, I felt as if I were shrinking, dwindling downwards. The whole scene blurred and collapsed like a tent when the centre-post is whipped away – and I felt as if a black blanket had been thrown over my head. And I remembered nothing more until I woke up the next morning.

## III

Back in the 1980s, at the time when I was estranged from my father and had little money and even less food, I was feeling quite sorry for myself. The walls and floors of my flat were cold and bare, and no coins chinked in my pocket. It was Christmas Eve. Outside, the gloomy streets were whitened by torrents of crystal snowflakes: millions of crystals drifted from Heaven down to the Earth and formed glittering banks of ice. The inside of my bare flat was just as cold as the night was outside; so I took to my bed early, feeling more than a little downhearted. Snuggling under my warm duvet, I closed my eyes, and floated away into Eternity.

I was meandering down a pleasant country lane in the Beyond. The day was hot and dry, and the trees and flowering hedgerows seemed happy to sense my presence as I strolled by: I 'knew' they were bidding me 'Welcome.'

In the verdant fields I could hear the droning of a swarm of bees, and high up in the oak trees songbirds were singing. As the radiant heat beat down upon my bare back, I sensed that my spirit body was absorbing energy from it.

The countryside colours were vibrant and full of life – so much brighter and more intense than any we have on Earth. The fields beyond the dusty path seemed to beckon me, so I ran through their grasses and flowers, then sped down a sloping hillock, trailing my hands through long red poppies as I went.

The plants *enjoyed* my touch; I felt their pleasure coursing up my bare arms: these flowers had consciousness and they possessed feelings.

Stopping in the shade of some cool beech trees I took deep health-giving breaths and filled my lungs with vitality. Some unusual wild flowers were growing on a bank nearby, and I approached them in wonder, never having seen their like before.

Their stems were about two feet long, and their translucent petals resembled wafer-thin rainbow dragonfly wings. When the petals caught the light and nodded their heads in the breeze, they shone with moving colours. From the heart of the flowers, bright orange stamens exuded a sweet scent unlike any I'd smelt before. And when the flowers were caressed by quiet winds they made a musical sound, a pleasant tinkling noise, as if dozens of delicate silver bells were being rung all at once, with each bell chiming at a different pitch. How I wanted to pick one! Such a flower would have looked splendid in my flat on Earth.

Tempted by their beauty I reached out – but stopped when a mind-voice said, 'Much better to let the flowers grow.' I agreed, and instead stroked them and sensed their gratitude, then I moved off down the unmade path. I didn't know where those words had come from.

Perhaps the flowers themselves had spoken.

Then the whole scene changed dramatically and I found myself inside a pleasant airy building: it was some kind of hospital.

I was standing in a waiting-area outside a corridor which led to some children's wards, and I could hear the youngsters playing within, laughing and running around with their nurses.

On my right I saw a crumpled artificial Christmas tree and sparkly decorations stacked in boxes; and next to these were several unwrapped presents, piled up on old tables. Among the gifts there was a large fortress – a fairy-tale castle with turrets – and I smiled at the pleasure this would bring to some lucky spirit lad.

Although the children sounded happy I knew that they'd suffered at the hands of cruel parents and guardians, and then they'd 'died'.

They'd either been abused or been rejected: it was easy for me to register this because my spirit body possesses a highly-developed intuitive 'sixth' sense.

These children were resting – holidaying, while being cared for by nursing staff who wanted to heal their broken trust and show them that adults are capable of giving unconditional love.

Just to the left of the swing doors I noticed a tall cupboard. Being naturally inquisitive (some would say a born nosey-parker) I opened it, and inside there were three strikingly-fine feathers: both two-and-a-half feet long, looking like a cross between ostrich and peacock feathers.

I ran my fingers through the delicate blue-and-green fronds, speckled with yellow, and thought they'd look nice on the bare walls of my flat back home.

Could I take one? After all, weren't these beauties created to be enjoyed? The children already had dozens of Christmas gifts, so I convinced myself that these feathers wouldn't be missed. I reached out and took one from the shelf – I was only going to 'borrow' it – then all at once I felt a piercing hard stare stabbing me in the back. I swung round, and in the doorway stood a formidable plump Matron, in full outfit. She was leaning against the door jamb, scowling with displeasure, her hands folded tight across her chest and her head tilted to one side. Words were unnecessary; her expression said it all: 'So you're *pinching* it, are you?'

Dreadful guilt flooded me. I'd been caught in the act and wanted to escape as fast as I could: and this thought catapulted me backwards – like a rag-doll on a piece of stretched elastic – right out of the hospital, and deposited me in an ungracious heap on a riverbank in the country.

*Thud*!

Ruffled and shaken, I stood up by a bubbling mountain stream and thought about those brilliant feathers. Although I wouldn't get them, at least the children would have a lovely Christmas. Then from behind me a gentle hand touched my shoulder: it was White Owl, standing resplendent in the clear sunlight, his deep-tanned skin glistening and his eyes bright with smiles. It was obvious that he'd been watching me all along.

Lifting up a clenched hand and opening it, he revealed a shining object resting in his palm: it was a delicately-engraved silver box. The hinged lid swung open to reveal a thick roll of well-thumbed banknotes, secured by elastic bands. 'Treasures,' he said; and he snapped the lid shut and flung the box headlong into the fast-moving river. It sank beneath the waters and bounced up and down, clinking over the sharp rocks as it disappeared quickly downstream. Then he touched his chest and spoke again, 'Earthly treasures are transient, but the soul is eternal. What a man builds into his soul and spirit, remains. The treasures of the heart and mind: only these matter.'

And I knew that he was right.

'Yes,' I responded, as a sheet of black muslin fell before my eyes, obliterating the landscape.

For a moment I was confused, but when I looked again – I was lying back in my bed on Earth, and just awakening in the middle of the snowy night.

## IV

I'd only slumped onto the big sofa for a moment's rest when quite out of the blue a spirit voice whispered, 'See your new vocation.' I turned over and tried to forget it. But I must have left my body because I became aware of standing in the middle of a pleasant schoolroom in the Beyond. Nearby, there were a dozen or so small chairs placed in front of a large blackboard. 'I am with you no more,' said my guide, and his presence withdrew.

Suddenly, the doors burst open and in ran eight young children, laughing and shouting for all they were worth. They clambered over me, pulled me to the ground, yanked at my hair and playfully slapped me on my back and legs. Brimming with joy they called out things like, 'Hooray! He's back!' and, 'It's been too long, Uncle Stephen!'

And in a flash of recognition I remembered who these six-year-olds were: I'd sat patiently with them while they'd been 'dying' on Earth; I'd watched over them and tended them in my 'sleep-life' until they'd passed over into Eternity. That had been one of my old jobs: to care for dying children, and help them to make the crossing from a world filled with darkness, into a land filled with light and love.

These were some of those beautiful children who'd passed over so tragically: one had died after being beaten by her parents; another had been a battered baby.

Another child had passed in a coma in hospital, after her mother had viciously struck her: this was little Louise, a bright and intelligent girl. I remembered sitting at her bedside and waiting to greet her when she became conscious in Spirit. 'Let me die,' she pleaded, in a semi-dazed state. 'I don't want to go back. It hurts too much. I want to die; please say I can be here for ever.'

'In a little while,' I reassured her, 'just be patient, Louise, and the Angel will come for you soon.' I leaned forward and stroked her hot forehead.

'...And I'll never have to go back?'

'No, you'll be safe with us. There'll be no more pain, and you'll never have to go back.'

The young child threw her arms about me. 'Uncle Stephen, pray for me. Please ask God to let me die soon... I want the Angel to come and take me... Nobody loves me on Earth.'

Humbled by her plea, I couldn't stop my voice filling with emotion.

'I'll pray for you,' I said, cuddling her tiny form. 'It won't be much longer now, then you'll be free of your nasty pain, and safe with God, for ever.' Louise couldn't wait for death to claim her, for the moment when an Angel of Light, a Bright Soul, would stand quietly at her bedside to welcome Home her grateful spirit. 'Soon now,' I whispered, 'very soon.'

And she settled back into the bed and quietened down after this.

If only those people who fear death could have heard this child's cries, her plaintive requests to be allowed to forsake the Earth and move into the Kingdom of Heaven, they would view death as a blessing instead of a curse.

Here now, in the schoolroom, were all my little friends. But more surprises lay in store. As well as the greetings I'd already received, there was to be another visitor: I knew this. I felt that someone was approaching, but I didn't know who it was. Perhaps a Shining One was coming to show me how best to teach my new charges? I just had to wait. But my heart began to pound, as if some greater part of me already knew the visitor's name and had become excited at thought of our meeting. Then suddenly the door swung wide open:

'Stephen.'

'Mam!' I cried, as I ran across the room and fell into the arms of my beloved mother. An aura of love wrapped us in a cloak of glowing light. It was so wonderful to see her again, this woman who'd been the very centre of our family on Earth, but who'd suffered the torments of cancer and had died a painful death.

'Welcome to your new work,' she said in familiar warm tones, as she held me at arm's length and smiled. 'I see the children have already greeted you.'

And a loud cry of delight rose from the little ones, who surrounded us and pulled at my robes and laughed, as my mother embraced me again, then gazed into my eyes.

The atmosphere was filled with happiness, and in the midst of it all I heard my mother's comforting voice saying, 'This is the Kingdom of Heaven.'

She smiled; and the children laughed as this wonderful moment faded far, far away into nothingness... and I remembered no more. The visit was over, but it would never be forgotten.

## V

As I became conscious, White Owl and I were moving together towards a vast building made of marble, or some similar material. The huge dome-shaped roof of the magnificent edifice was held aloft by several tall pillars, which looked as if they might have been transported direct from ancient Athens.

The marble-like columns were shot through with living blues and greens, and violets and pinks, creating a wonderful, striking effect.

Despite the brilliant heat of the sun, when my feet touched the smooth steps I felt the delicious coolness of the stone. The towering building was immense, about as high as an Egyptian pyramid; and as we passed under the open archways, which led us to its centre, soft breezes enfolded us.

'This is one of the many Halls of Healing,' my teacher said. 'Here the spirit can be refreshed and can replenish its vital energies; here it can relax and find a greater sense of its own worthiness, and gain a deeper understanding of its own Being.

'Here one can discover a fuller realisation of the unity that binds all living things together, and the all-pervading power of the Creative Mind that is known as the Great Spirit.'

Wrapped in velvet peace, we moved through the cavernous hallway and were greeted by the most wonderful sights and sounds. People were gathered all around the circular marble walls. Some souls were lying on brightly-coloured couches, others were sitting on the floor with their backs against the walls; but all of them were totally at ease, and they emitted auric feelings of inner contentment and harmonious peace. High above us, in the vast circular dome, beautiful music was playing; although it wasn't an orchestrated piece, its blend of wonderful sounds delighted the listeners' ears.

Good music is one of the great loves of my life: but not even the great masters could have created such a symphony of magical, healing harmonies as I heard under that pulsing, translucent dome.

Imagine, if you can, a million different silver bells and chimes all tinkling in concord, and some in discord, heard as if from a mile or so away.

The gentle rhythmic pulsing continually created light within the dome – moving rainbow-light: count-less colours mixed and blended as they gently swirled in the atmosphere above us.

Then the coloured mists undulated and began to descend slowly, almost as if they possessed a grace and dignity of their own. The souls in the Hall up-turned their faces and 'breathed in' the lights and energies, and their bodies sparkled and glowed with pure radiance as they 'bathed' in the rays. Standing or kneeling, the people allowed the glistening lights to cascade over them, through them, and around them, as if they were showering naked under some huge celestial waterfall.

The souls absorbed the energies, delighting in their caress, and responded by feeling refreshed and renewed.

'These healing lights are Thought made manifest,' said my friend, 'as indeed everything is. These thoughts are made up of gathered energy which is projected by the Bright Ones whose self-appointed task is to bless all troubled minds with healing and peace. Those who are being healed are grateful; you see?'

And I could actually sense their gratitude permeating the air. In Eternity we can't hide our feelings as easily as we can here on Earth.

While we watched and breathed in the healing rays, two attendants arrived carrying a sleeping woman, whom they placed in the centre of a photosphere of vibrant light. She was a new arrival, someone who had recently 'died'. The two male healers gently set down her unconscious form on a bright yellow couch, then knelt at either side of her.

White Owl spoke. 'Do you see how troubled she is?' And it wasn't difficult to sense her distress, for she carried the memories of her deep emotional disturbances prominently in her aura. 'She worries needlessly about her young family, about her life and her money, and about much more. She is one of those souls who, if they have nothing to worry about, will create something to fret over. That is her mental state. And although she has now "died", this habit persists because death cannot change what she has programmed into her own mind – only she can do that.'

I became aware that her toil-worn face and twisted form were reflections of her over-anxious thoughts. Then something quite extraordinary happened: while gazing at her I suddenly perceived her inner-most mind. Instantly I knew that she'd left two small babies and a husband back on Earth, and that since her passing she'd become aware that he'd deserted the children and placed them in an Institution.

Her thoughts betrayed that she couldn't come to terms with her husband's insensitivity, or with her own death, and that this combination of circum-stances was responsible for her present state.

Aware of my thoughts, my teacher said, 'Correct. She is also very bitter towards the Deity, believing that God has been unkind to her family. But now, Stephen, be still awhile; and watch and learn.'

Gradually, two Bright Souls in shining raiments 'materialised' within the rainbow-lights encircling her. One placed a hand on her brow, and the other man touched her feet, and they began transmitting healing energies to her. These two advanced beings had developed their power of compassion to the point where it could be seen and felt with deep intensity; and I knew that this energy could heal. Surging psychic lights came from the Angels, embraced the sick woman, and conveyed spiritual strength to her form. And quite by some miracle, right before my eyes, a completely different person seemed to 'appear' in her place. So great was the transformation that the twisted bitter woman had now gone and had been replaced by a peaceful sleeping soul. She was still a worried spirit, but her countenance now shone with a child-like tranquillity. She looked as if some great burden or pain had finally been lifted from her mind.

One moment later, the couch, the woman, and the Healing Ministers blurred, then vaporised from sight, which is not an uncommon happening in the spirit world.

'She has gone to a place of rest, where full recovery will be made. When she wakes she will be helped by someone to re-adjust to her new environment, and she will discover that her prayers for her babies have all been heard.'

'What's happened to the children?'

'They have been adopted by a good family.'

'But won't she fret over this?'

'At first. But every night she can nurse them in her arms like any other loving mother. While her babies are physically asleep their spirit forms can rock gently at her breast.'

I was still concerned. 'But will she approve of their new lives?'

'No, for she is a possessive soul; and she displays these characteristics as black-reddish colours in certain sections of her aura. But as time unfolds she will learn to be more content. The new family will provide her children with more than she could have offered them.'

'You mean materially?'

'No: I mean opportunities for spiritual growth.'

'Are they poor then?'

'Yes, but this will provide exactly the right challenges that her children will need to achieve their soul-growth. A pathway of roses and constant sunshine will not test and try the spirit, or help the soul to expand its beauty and touch its deeper levels. A care-free life may be deemed by some to be "pleasurable", but little of any lasting value would spring from it to aid the developing Mind. Their lives will not be easy.'

'But you said they'd be taken care of.'

'Spiritually, yes. Challenges which are faced and overcome will enrich the soul's experience. How can you appreciate the suffering of others if you yourself have never endured the agonies of heart and mind? How can a soul serve those who stand in need of care and education if it has never struggled to free itself from mental and emotional darkness?

'From Darkness we travel towards Light – and when we arrive we will appreciate it all the more. Only when the cup of human experience has been drained can the soul say with conviction, "I have learned." Her children knew this long before they chose their mother and their new family.'

And there we had to leave the matter, for I felt as if the land was about to be whisked away again, but I was wrong – what I'd sensed was our imminent departure. In fact, we walked slowly out of the Healing Temple and into the bright sunshine, and we strolled for quite some way along a country road, in silence. Rich green fields and bobbing flowers surrounded us on all sides; and about a mile later (at least, it felt as far as that) we stood before our next destination.

# VI

Sauntering into what appeared to be a small country house that was set in its own extensive grounds, we moved through the open French-windows and entered a room that was pleasantly arranged like a hospital ward.

But there was no one fussing around, and there was also a marked absence of chemical smells, instruments, and medical charts. There were six beds arranged in this light and airy drawing-room, and in them six people slept – and one of these was the worried woman we'd met earlier at the Healing Temple.

'This is a Home of Rest,' said White Owl.

'Are these people sleeping or are they in comas?'

'They are unconscious. In deep sleep, they rest.'

'But the spirit body functions in perfect health,' I asserted.

'Yes, but those who pass after long periods of stress or strength-sapping illness sometimes feel they need recuperation, and the best way to gain this is to rest.'

'Who are these people?'

'Just new arrivals.'

And as we walked through the room I sensed my guide's powerful healing energies automatically transmitting themselves to the sleepers. 'This man died quickly in a car accident,' he pointed out. 'And this woman had a brain haemorrhage after many months of suffering from cancer. That young girl was killed by being pulled into machinery; and these twin boys were gassed to death in a home tragedy. The troubled woman, you already know.'

'How can you know these things so accurately?'

'By reading their minds: this clarity comes with practice and experience. In this world nothing is hidden, all is known, provided you have the eyes to see it.' And I knew that what he meant was 'the awareness to register it.' He continued, 'Just beyond this room there is a special area. Come with me.' And the very next instant we were standing in an adjoining ward.

'And who are these people?' I queried, gazing at more sleeping forms.

'These are the stubborn ones.'

'What do you mean?'

'Take a long look at their minds. Can you see their reasons for sleeping like this?'

'No,' I said, after quickly scrutinising their auras as best I could.

'None of them needs rest. Do you agree?'

'Yes,' I said, looking at their minds again.

'But they do not wish to wake.'

For a moment I was nonplussed. 'You mean they *choose* to sleep?'

'Yes. They know that they have died, but they wholeheartedly believe that they must rest until some distant Resurrection Day arrives.'

'So their beliefs are closing their eyes?'

'What are beliefs but Thoughts? Those who think that a man's beliefs do not matter have not yet learned that beliefs colour Thought, and that Thought leads to *action*. What one believes either binds the human spirit or frees it. Beliefs are important and should be founded upon Truths. These souls are sleeping because of their religious training, because of their Thoughts. They have chosen.'

Strangely enough I wasn't then surprised, for I'd already made the acquaintance of many on Earth who'd feigned to be intelligent and wide awake, yet they'd actually been 'mentally unconscious'.

My guide was aware of my memories:

'The Mind shapes *everything*,' he said, 'in whatever world we inhabit. What we *think* – we *are*. Now let us proceed.'

And we left the sleepers, knowing that they would rise only when they wanted to. But I couldn't help thinking of how easily we can ruin the quality of our lives.

In the next room there was a man I instantly recognised: my recently-deceased grandfather.

Grancha Price, as he was known, was sitting upright in a comfortable bed and looking perfectly well, but he seemed quite tired. I approached his bedside. 'Hello, Grancha!' I said, embracing him.

'Stephen! How lovely to see you! You're only visiting us, I hope?' he asked, and his brows knitted together.

'Of course! I'm not dead yet!'

'No, but *I* am!' he laughed. 'And it doesn't hurt a bit!'

'Were you surprised to find yourself still living, Grancha?'

'Well, not really. I never said anything before, but I used to get the "odd experience" myself, now and again. But I couldn't tell anyone, could I? They'd think I was mad.' A broad grin lit up his face. 'Been very far?' the old man asked.

'Everywhere, Grancha. But not alone.' And I glanced across at White Owl, who then exchanged eye-winks with my grandfather.

'Yes, I know your pal very well. Don't look so surprised. One of the first to meet me when I died, he was. Oh, that cancer! The pain was shooting right through me – and they weren't feeding me right either. They kept giving me soup, but what I wanted was a three-course meal.'

'But that would have fed the disease.'

'Aye, I know that *now*, but I was desperate for a bit of dinner and the beggars wouldn't give it to me.' We all smiled. Then he became thoughtful for a moment and, lowering his voice, said, 'It was the cigarettes that killed me, you know.'

'Yes, I know. But even on your death-bed you had a little smoke,' I recalled.

My grandad nodded in agreement. He was plainly quite exhausted. 'Well, we're all human, I suppose,' he said. 'But if I had my time over again... (*and he yawned*)... I'd leave the ciggies well alone, my boy. They ruined my chest, they did. Great big patches of cancer stopped me breathing.

'Tell me... (*and he yawned again*)... did Mary-Ann get the money?'

I assured him that the coal-dust which they'd found in his lungs had meant that my grandmother did receive some compensation, which pleased him.

'It's only fair, see. I worked all my life down that pit. Those mines were no joke, I can tell you.' Then a flicker of sadness moved across his eyes as he remembered my grandmother's grief. 'Although she comes to see me when she's asleep, she can't recall it when she wakes up in the morning. That happens to many people, they say.'

And his face was troubled. He loved my grandmother dearly, and she'd been broken-hearted since his passing.

'Never mind, Grancha,' I said, squeezing his shoulder, 'one day you'll be together again, just like the old days.'

'Ah, the old days…' he said. (*then he yawned once more*) 'Marvellous times they were… They've all gone now, those people. Aye, boy… all gone now…' And the old man drifted gently into a wistful sleep. He looked so angelic, leaning against his pillows; so I kissed his forehead and left him to rest quietly.

As I reached the doorway I heard him murmur, 'Tell them all I'm alive… won't you…?'

Then he was sound asleep, like a baby in its cradle. White Owl and I walked out into the flowering gardens.

# VII

Outside the Rest Home there was no time to discuss my grandfather's new life, for my guide spoke in sudden urgency.

'Something is very wrong,' he said; and one second later a flash of red light exploded above his head. 'Someone calls. We must be quick!'

He'd received a spirit message and he took my hand and we began travelling, soaring upwards faster than a lightning-bolt.

I couldn't make out any definite shapes as everything streaked past us: all I knew was that we were now travelling through the mists – those fog-banked clouds that divide some parts of Heaven from the Earth. We accelerated so fast that I could barely think straight. Then a millisecond later we began to lose speed, as if a powerful magnet impeded our progress. I felt as if we were dropping down through the atmosphere like two heavy stones sinking to an ocean bed; this sensation was caused by the slowing-down effect that Earth's magnetic fields exert on all spirit bodies.

Emerging from the fog, I saw nothing but waste-land before us; but here and there amid the greyness, people had erected makeshift tents, which were scattered across the dry landscape.

Everywhere, I saw lines of homeless natives: some were as weak as kittens, crouched on blankets, but most of them lay on the dusty brown earth, help-lessly close to death. These people were so thin and hungry, so emaciated, that they looked barely alive. We'd arrived in Cambodia, a country that had become a war-torn land of famine, death, drought, neglect, and want, in the last quarter of the twentieth-century.

We found ourselves standing next to an ailing mother and her dying baby, who had been separated from a nearby group. It was obvious that the little one was only minutes away from its passing: I sensed this and also that the mother was beside herself with fear and grief. The psychic, auric light around the child's lungs appeared as a dark muddy brown shadow, shot through with black streaks.

Death was near.

My guide spoke. 'This child must live,' he said.

'But wouldn't it be better if she came to Spirit?'

'No, she must live. She has important work to do in these parts of the Earth. The girl must not yet cross over to us.'

Puzzled by the conviction in his voice, I watched as he moved away from me and spoke quietly with two spirit people standing close by. I took a step towards the mother and child, who were huddled together on the dry ground, and tried to send to the woman a feeling of comfort, a feeling that help had now arrived and that she shouldn't worry too much, and that she should try to calm down.

Because my guide stood only a few paces away, I overheard his conversation with the two spirit healers. 'What is wrong?' he asked the first man.

'The baby has a fever, contracted from polluted water. We've tried everything, but can't break its hold on her life. We need your assistance. Her body has almost released her spirit, and this prompted our call.'

'Then join with me now, and we'll do what we must,' he replied; and they gathered around the mother and babe.

I stepped back and watched as the three men stood tall, fell silent, closed their compassionate eyes, and then linked their minds. Next, from out of nowhere, there came a swirling white mist – a glowing, 'living' light. It circled the three healers, and then the mother and her child; and as it did so, it brightened and condensed. It was pure energy: an immaculate healing light that was composed of the very essence of God's Life-Force.

Spellbound and feeling a little dizzy while this treatment took place, I watched in astonishment as the glistening energy-rays gathered around the baby's lungs and chest, encompassing her tiny frame in their radiance, penetrating her flesh, and illuminating her spirit body.

The baby's aura glowed like burnished copper, shot through with blue-and-white electric sparks. Her lungs seemed to breathe more easily then, as if they'd been psychically strengthened.

The God-Force had re-energised them; and under the influence of this power I began to sway gently.

Soon it was over.

The shimmering mists melted away into thin air but left a battery of radiant energy within the sick child. The healing was complete.

The exhausted mother, who had also been helped, seemed quite tired now, but more free of worry; and she began to fall into a regenerating sleep.

The three healers opened their eyes and smiled in satisfaction: their work had been accomplished, and it had been a success.

White Owl addressed the second man. 'All is well. The fever breaks, and she remains on Earth. Thank you.'

The three men shook hands, and when my guide moved over to me I felt I had to ask him, 'What special work does this child have before her?'

'I cannot say; but her starved pathetic body houses a great and noble spirit. When she reaches maturity she will be most influential in this war-torn country.

'She will have a great love for her people, and her life is destined to touch many others. Her gifts of organisation and her deep respect for humanity will affect many lives here. And your presence has helped us to conquer her illness.'

'I helped?'

'Your powers were drawn upon. Did you not sense them leaving you?' And I confessed that I had. Then I turned and saw the dying and the sick all around me in that terrible mournful field, and I wondered if they were all equally tended with such loving care.

'Yes,' spoke my teacher. 'Not one is neglected. No genuine cry for help from Earth is ever overlooked. That is our promise to all God's Children who are still clothed in the flesh.'

For a short while longer we walked among the needy and the dying. Unsensed by the many nurses who worked with the poor, we helped wherever we could by administering healing light to all those in need.

Near one group of desperately sick children, who were being cared for by an American nurse, I stopped and gave whatever energy-rays I could muster, concentrating so hard that I had to support my swaying frame by holding on to some nearby tent cloth. Puzzled as to why I could feel the fabric in my grasp, instead of feeling my hands pass right through it, I suddenly awoke – clutching the pillow under my sleepy head.

It was early morning, and I was back on Earth.

# 21

# An Angel's Promise

Six good friends and I were sitting in a peaceful room, in an evening meditation class where we gathered each week to recoup our strength, and to make contact with the Other Side. Little did I know what would happen on that night.

Just when I began to relax, the mists rolled aside and I was suddenly caught up in the spirit.

But where was I?

And who was making that bustling sound in front of me?

When my spirit vision focused and sharpened, I found myself floating in the air, suspended vertically above what looked like an Eastern market-place. There was a gathering of about five hundred people beneath me, all pushing forward to get close to a raised platform at the front of the square where, in the brilliant sunlight, a man stood facing the crowd. Now no more than a few feet from him, I found myself gazing down upon his form. Undoubtedly, he possessed great wisdom, for I sensed he was known as a Teacher of Righteousness. Although he was just a slender youth, he had an unquestionably ancient soul. There was something startling about his striking presence: of middle height, and clothed in a long white seamless shift, he gazed at the crowd with penetrating brown eyes that were solemn, yet bold and full of fiery bright compassion. His slightly-bearded slim face radiated a deep sense of concern for those whose minds were reaching out to hear him, for those whose bodies were pushing forward to be near him.

The Power of the Spirit was strong in this man.

Then, in that odd way in which spirit vision operates, suddenly my sight was 'telescoped', and I was gazing directly at his profile – close up.

Searching his eyes, I began to wonder: was this the man that the world had come to know as 'The Nazarene'? Could it be Him? But what did *He* look like? No portraits of Him exist. And if this *was* the Prophet, what was I doing here in a Past Time? Or was I visiting a Present Time in the spirit world? Or could I actually be witnessing this past event *right now* – as a part of Earth's ancient history? Maybe this was merely a set of images of what had once taken place in antiquity.

But everything was so *real* to me: the smell of the peasant crowd, the heat of the brilliant day, the sounds of the animals braying, the voices of the caged birds squawking for their freedom. It was all quite confusing.

Then, in a twinkling of an eye, the man ceased speaking, turned and stared right up into my face. Even though I knew I was invisible to the rest of the people, he had found me. 'Behold!' I heard his thought-voice say – and instantly the market-place vanished, and I could see only a dark wooden table, old and well-worn, and upon it lay a yellowed-with-age scroll made of wax-like parchment. A pair of hands began to slowly unfold the scroll, and I saw revealed at the bottom of it, the words:

*Your Map of Life.*

As the parchment unfurled a little more, drawings of boulders and obstacles on a winding pathway were revealed, and against them someone had written:

*Challenges.*

And further along the many bends in the road, I could see more words:

*Happiness and Sorrow.*

Then the man's thought-voice spoke again. 'Your path is long-since written, but it will be revealed to you only one step at a time. Just take each step as it comes. Everything is progressing as it should.'

This message brought instant relief to my anxious mind.

Then the parchment misted over and the vision disappeared, and I was once again gazing into the arresting eyes of the Teacher who was standing in the market-place. But the strangest thing was that although moments had passed while I'd received my personal message, it seemed to me as if I'd never moved from his face, and that no time had been lost at all. Just then, I heard someone speaking in the distance back on Earth: it was a pale insignificant voice compared to the powerful orator who kept the multitudes enthralled.

All at once I was aware of hurtling down through

nothingness, and I couldn't contain my feelings. My restless spirit cried out loudly to him, 'I don't want to go: I don't want to leave you!'

Yet the travelling continued and I was pulled nearer and nearer to Mother Earth, until my flight was surprisingly arrested by some unseen power, which now held me fast in its invisible grasp.

All around me was the deepness of space, infinite in its blackness, but pierced by brilliant starpoints of light. And again the compassionate voice spoke within me:

'See there, beneath you!' And when I looked down I discerned the planet Earth – the Great Mother who houses and protects us. Silently her blue-and-milky-white orb revolved on its hidden axis, in mystery and wonder. And the Teacher said, 'Many sleep peacefully there tonight because of what has so far been achieved. But our tasks are not yet over. There is still much more to do, and few to do it.

'We are engaged in constant conflict against the Powers of Darkness: selfishness, greed, hatred, anger, jealousy, vested interests, the possessive god of materialism, and the lust for power over the masses.

'*Your* part in the Brotherhood of Light continues. But never despair: keep your spirits high, and know that the Power of Love and the Might of God is with you. Go forward then, and open the Mind of Man to his Origin, Purpose and Destiny. Touch his soul with compassion, and bring with you into the Light of Love as many as you can.'

'Yes,' I responded, thunderstruck by the sheer beauty of his words, and by the awesome sight of the

Great Mother pulsing beneath me.

'The road is long, my son, but never spiritually lonely. We will not forsake you. We will never desert those who serve. We will guide and bless you for ever, and ever...' he said.

Then the greyness of the planet again pulled me towards it at an alarming rate, and the Earth drew ever nearer as my spirit groaned within me to retain the visions now slipping from my grasp:

'But I want to stay longer,' I cried. 'I don't want to leave you!'

And as soft as a bird's wings rising in graceful flight, the gentle Angel Voice sounded its Eternal Promise deep within my heart, my mind, my soul:

*'Lo, we are with you*
*Always —*
*Even unto the end of the World...'*

If you enjoyed this psychic book,
then you will enjoy reading Stephen O'Brien's
other best-selling titles,
and also listening to his acclaimed
spiritual and psychic teachings
on audio-cassettes.


Books are available through all good
Bookstores and Libraries everywhere;
and signed Cassettes and Books are available
from the Voices Mail Order Service,
or via the Internet from
the Voices Online Shop™
at: www.stephenobrien.co.uk


Full details, and a contact address for
Stephen, appear on the following pages.

**'VISIONS OF ANOTHER WORLD'**
The Autobiography of Medium,
by Stephen O'Brien.

### *Every Journey has a Beginning...*

Phantom hands hammering on a door
in the dead of night:
THE SPIRIT WORLD WAS CALLING...
and Stephen O'Brien had to accept the remarkable powers
that brought him *Visions of Another World*.

Then the tragic early death of his mother broke his
life in two; but miraculously she appeared to him
from beyond the grave
and her love changed the course of his life:
he became a Medium and a Visionary.
He promised the soul of a long-dead American Indian
that he would serve the Spirit World,
and countless thousands packed out venues
to hear him relay messages of Hope,
Light and Survival
from their loved ones on the Other Side of Life.
Hundreds of thousands of the so-called 'dead' have now
communicated through Stephen O'Brien's amazing gifts:
including war heroes,
accident and murder victims,
innocent children who died too young, animals,
and even the world-famous actress, Judy Garland.

Now you can read Stephen's compelling life-story.

'Big powers in other-worldly communication
and healing' *Irish News*

A Voices Paperback (384 pages; illustrated)
ISBN: 0-953-6620-3-9

## 'ANGELS BY MY SIDE'
The Psychic Life of a Medium,
by Stephen O'Brien.

*'We are not alone in this Universe...'*

Stephen O'Brien's extraordinary spiritual and psychic
gifts have comforted millions of people and have
silenced sceptics around the world.
In *Angels By My Side* Stephen reveals through his
acclaimed powers:

◆ Timeless Wisdom from the 'Silent Sentinels'
and Angel Beings who watch over us.

◆ Fascinating glimpses into Mankind's Future.

◆ The secret Psychic Powers of Light and Colour that
enhance Well-being and Self-healing.

◆ A compelling view of 'The One Living God'.

◆ What kind of life awaits us all after death,
and the secrets of the Next World.

◆ Irrefutable evidence of survival.

He also shares with his countless readers
more of his amazing Out-of-the-Body excursions
into the Spirit World itself.

A Voices Paperback (384 pages; illustrated)
ISBN: 0-953-6620-0-4

**'IN TOUCH WITH ETERNITY'**
Contact with Another World,
by Stephen O'Brien.

> *'As the hazy shape materialised
> there was revealed to us an Angel of Light,
> a beautiful woman with golden hair,
> whose eyes were deep blue-green like
> unfathomed ocean waters.
> "Peace," she said...'*

Make incredible journeys into the World of the Spirit
with Stephen O'Brien's remarkable
True-Life Psychic Experiences:

Go behind the scenes at Séances and discover how
Guardian Angels strive to contact us through the
Psychic Power that we unknowingly provide.
Read stunning Survival Evidence of human and animal
souls after death, including children's messages to their
parents and a communication from
Dr Martin Luther King.

♦ Unveil the truth about Reincarnation, Telepathy,
  Life Before Life, Out-of-the-Body Experiences,
  Soul Powers, and how to Heal with Psychic Sound.
♦ Encounter *'The Shining Ones'* deep within the Spiritual
  Spheres of Light, and learn of their concern for
  the human family and for our planet.
♦ Meet the Nature Spirits, and some amazing Animals
  that can communicate with us.

A Host of Fascinating Spiritual Experiences from
Britain's Renowned Visionary, Medium and Healer.

A Voices Paperback (352 pages; illustrated)
ISBN: 0-953-6620-2-0

**'A GIFT OF GOLDEN LIGHT'**
The Psychic Journeys of a Medium,
by Stephen O'Brien.

The Press described this remarkable book as
'un-put-downable'.

Follow Stephen as he recalls his exciting 20-year psychic
apprenticeship and strives to perfect the extraordinary
paranormal skills which have brought happiness, comfort
and hope to millions of people.
With warmth and candour he:

♦ Shares his thrilling encounters with apparitions,
   hauntings, spiritual healing and telepathic powers.
♦ Reveals the mystical Gift of Golden Light which
   illuminates everyone's spiritual journey through life.
♦ Presents a compelling array of survival evidence,
   proving the immortality of human and animal souls.

'The epitome of mediumistic excellence' –
*Psychic News*

*Available from our worldwide Mail Order
service, or you may order these titles through
good book stores and libraries everywhere,
or Online through Internet outlets. Signed copies are
available from the Voices Online Shop at:*
**www.stephenobrien.co.uk**

*Keep in touch with our Mail Order Department
for news of new titles and other products
originated by Stephen.*

A Voices Paperback (384 pages; illustrated)
ISBN: 0-953-6620-1-2

## The Spoken Word:
### *Six Acclaimed Recordings by the Same Author.*

These high quality digitally-recorded stereo audio
cassettes, running-time 60 minutes each, contain a wealth
of information and education that all seekers, healers,
mediums and psychic readers should know.

Stephen O'Brien's gentle voice can speak in your home
or in your private development class, teaching and
explaining each subject in easy-to-understand terms.

Develop your Mediumship & Psychic Powers:
*A step-by-step guide to the unfoldment and
safe practice of your psychic & mediumistic skills.*

Heal Yourself:
*Gain peace of mind & freedom from stress.
The way to spiritual, physical, emotional and mental
self-healing and well-being; includes meditations.*

4 Meditations:
*Obtain peace & tranquillity; health & strength;
guidance & inspiration; sensitivity & awareness.*

Develop your Healing Powers:
*Everyone's guide to success as a healer:
'We all have the power to heal.'*

4 Visualisations:
*Relax your body; calm your mind;
quieten your spirit; refresh your soul.*

Life After Death:
*What awaits the soul after its transition.
Life in the world of spirit is revealed.*

Available by Mail Order or from
the Voices Online Shop at: www.stephenobrien.co.uk

*More titles may be released.
For details of our world-wide
Mail Order Catalogue Service, see page 384.*

For further information on all aspects of the
life and work of visionary, spiritual healer,
medium and poet, Stephen O'Brien,
including how to obtain by Mail Order
his best-selling books, educational cassettes,
spiritual healing crystals, and a full range of
other quality products (or to contact him directly)
please write, enclosing a large SAE, to:

VOICES MANAGEMENT
(Dept VB2)
PO Box 8
SWANSEA
SA1 1BL
UK

Or search the Internet for 'Stephen O'Brien'.
Visit our Online Shop where you may order signed
copies of all of the Stephen O'Brien products at:
www.stephenobrien.co.uk

Voices Management regrets it cannot reply
without a large stamped self-addressed envelope
and correspondents are respectfully advised
not to mail irreplaceable items to the author,
for neither Voices nor Mr O'Brien
can accept responsibility for the loss or damage
of any unsolicited manuscripts, poems,
sentimental objects, photographs, or cassettes etc.,
which are posted by the public.

Your letters are always welcome,
but please keep them brief and to the point –
and be patient when awaiting your replies,
for Stephen receives vast quantities of mail
from around the world.

Thank you.